THE GOD DEBATES

JOHN R. SHOOK

THE GOD DEBATES

A 21st Century Guide for Atheists and Believers (and Everyone in Between)

WILEY-BLACKWELL

A John Wiley & Sons, Ltd., Publication

This edition first published 2010

Blackwell Publishing was acquired by John Wiley & Sons in February 2007. Blackwell's publishing program has been merged with Wiley's global Scientific, Technical, and Medical business to form Wiley-Blackwell.

Registered Office
John Wiley & Sons Ltd, The Atrium, Southern Gate, Chichester, West Sussex, PO19 8SQ, United Kingdom

Editorial Offices
350 Main Street, Malden, MA 02148-5020, USA
9600 Garsington Road, Oxford, OX4 2DQ, UK

The Atrium, Southern Gate, Chichester, West Sussex, PO19 8SQ, UK

For details of our global editorial offices, for customer services, and for information about how to apply for permission to reuse the copyright material in this book please see our website at www.wiley.com/wiley-blackwell.

Library of Congress Cataloging-in-Publication Data

Shook, John R.
The God debates : a 21st century guide for atheists and believers (and everyone in between) / John R. Shook.
p. cm.
Includes bibliographical references and index.
ISBN 978-1-4443-3641-2 (hardback : alk. paper) – ISBN 978-1-4443-3642-9 (pbk. : alk. paper) 1. God–Proof. 2. God (Christianity) 3. Christianity and atheism. 4. Faith and reason–Christianity. I. Title.
BT103.S447 2010
239–dc22

2010016219

A catalogue record for this book is available from the British Library.

Set in 10.5/13pt Minion by Thomson Digital, Noida, India.
Printed in Singapore by Ho Printing Singapore Pte Ltd

02 2011

Dedicated to my mother
whose bookshelves made me a philosopher,
where I found the life of the mind
and vowed to someday add noble thoughts

Contents

Preface

As a philosopher and a professor, and as a participant in god debates, I hope to enrich our understanding of religion and the human world. Philosophies and religions offer their learning, but I wonder how well we are learning from each other. Debating a question, like any conversation, is an opportunity for intellectual growth. Arguments and debates have winners and losers, yet judging a match only raises more debate. That's the point – the real winners are those who think about the questions, reflect on proposed answers, and come up with new questions. The winners are the learners, not those sure that they already know.

In the god debates there are many proposals about what a god may be like, and what a god is supposed to be doing. New speculations about this or that god are not foreign to religions. No religion today is precisely what it was 500 years ago, or even 100 years ago. Thinking, debating, and learning enrich religion as much as anything. Doubting and questioning, and the fresh insights aroused, are the signs of intelligence at work. Believers dismayed by religious questioning overlook nourishment for their religion's vitality.

Many kinds of gods are considered in this book, revolving around the theistic god of the Judeo-Christian traditions. Where the specific God of the Bible is discussed the upper-case 'God' is used, and in all other cases the lower-case 'god' is used. No disrespect is intended by using 'god', quite the opposite – the diversity of conceptions of god ought to get due attention and respect. There simply is nothing that everyone means by 'god' any more. The conformity imposed by medieval thinking upon Western civilization has mostly dissolved, and the West has greeted the East. To avoid presumptive agreement with any single concept of god, our conversations shouldn't be about some upper-case 'God' as if that term means the same for everyone.

Vibrant dialogue about religion in the twenty-first century now includes both believers of many religions and nonbelievers too. Nor can we overlook, as the subtitle of this book indicates, how there are plenty of people feeling "in between." It is easy, too easy, to sharply divide people into believers and nonbelievers. There are so many different notions of divinity available for consideration, and new ideas about god, religion, and spirituality emerge constantly. A broad spectrum of belief has brightened a complex religious landscape, now looking so different from the static black and white portrait of bygone days. What we do with all this new, light, fresh perspective and beautiful color is our responsibility.

This book is designed to prepare readers of any religious belief or no belief for participation in religious dialogue. The god question, like other perennial questions about truth, beauty, or justice, is a grand conversation. The god debates, if conducted respectfully and intelligently, can only continue to enrich and preserve what is best about civilization. If the god question instead halts thinking and stops the conversation, we lose our humanity. So let the god debates go on.

My own journey in this conversation has been assisted by fellow debaters and questioners at my lectures who are too numerous to individually thank. Colleagues at the Center for Inquiry have been especially helpful, although this book presents my own views and does not necessarily reflect those of the Center for Inquiry.

Debating Religion

Religion promises a rewarding relationship with the supreme reality. Religions offer views about what supreme reality is like, how best to relate to it, and why believers benefit from that relationship. Nonbelievers don't deny that reality is impressive, but they doubt that any religion knows best about reality or how to relate to it. Nonbelievers instead use some nonreligious worldview, some account of reality and humanity's relationship with it, that lacks any role for a god. It can seem that believers and nonbelievers, divided by such a wide chasm, would have little to talk about. But appearances can be deceiving.

Religions are also divided, yet believers meet to share and compare their religions. Ecumenical dialogue among Christian denominations is a frequent and familiar pleasure for participants. Dialogue between different religions has also grown. An Ayatollah, an Archbishop, a Pope, or a Dalai Lama are world travelers for cooperation on secular or spiritual matters, urging political reforms and joining peace councils. Less frequently, but no less importantly, theological issues can be the topic. Disagreeing over dogma sounds less promising, but dogma needn't stand in the way of learning. Believers sharing their personal experiences and idealistic hopes can find common ground hidden behind doctrinal walls. Theological arguments for completely different gods may have common features, pointing the way towards shared perspectives.

If religions benefit from comparison and discussion, why can't the nonreligious join the ecumenical conversation? Surely "belief in god" cannot be a prerequisite for getting a seat at the table. What god would a participant in the room have to accept first? Religions as different as Christianity and Buddhism, each dubious that the other's god could possibly exist, would be hypocritical for closing the door to a nonbeliever's doubt that either god exists. There are enough doubters in the world to justify full participation, too. China, Russia, and much of Europe are largely skeptical about a supernatural deity. Even in America, the fastest-growing segment, now almost 20 percent of the adult population, is composed of the "Nones." The Nones typically say they have no particular religion, although many of the Nones still regard themselves as religious or spiritual, even if they don't identify with any denomination or church (see Fuller 2001, Kosmin and Keysar 2008).

The Nones are evidently rethinking god. Supernaturalism isn't the only kind of religion to consider, as well. There are non-traditional Christians, and those influenced by other religious traditions, who suspect that god and nature overlap, interpenetrate, or combine in some way. Many people find religious inspiration and connection through divine or spiritual aspects of nature. Pantheisms and spiritual naturalisms (see Levine 1994 and Stone 2009) are serious worldviews, meriting discussion in the concluding chapter after supernaturalism has been debated. If religions' reasonings are on the agenda for open discussion, why shouldn't outside evaluations of arguments for god carry some weight too? If religions expect their theologies to be persuasive, trying them out on non-traditional minds and nonbelieving skeptics could hardly be a waste of time.

Respectful and rational dialogue among believers and nonbelievers, and everyone in between, holds great promise. This book is most helpful for the curious reader eager to join the conversation, who only needs a clear guide through the debating points and counter-points. But perhaps you looked into this book expecting something even more exciting?

1.1 Religion under Scrutiny

Arguments over religion are getting louder, while respectful dialogue gets drowned out. Debating the existence of god is only one part of a much wider field, the field of religious criticism. Criticism for the sake of criticism has taken center stage. Nowadays, noisy attacks on faith, religion, and believers get the popular attention. Strident rejection of everything religious attracts the spotlight. Atheism is not new, but the publicity is. Academic debates over god's existence on college campuses draw crowds, but who else is paying careful attention? Unfortunately, debating god has gotten dragged down into the mud of religious criticism, where we can't see the difference between a respectful debate and a dirt-throwing fight. Some religious critics maintain a composed posture, but they aren't imitated enough any more.

The attacks of religious criticism have been around a long time, about as long as religion itself. The complaints are pretty much the same: religious leaders caught as hypocrites; religious people behaving immorally; religious scripture endorsing unethical deeds; religions promoting hatred, conflict, and wars; religions promoting injustice and discrimination; and the like. People often abandon religion because of such issues (read the stories contained in Blackford and Schüklenk 2009). These disappointed apostates probably outnumber those who reject religion on intellectual grounds (ask two preachers, now atheists, Barker 2008 and Loftus 2008, or a Bishop, the nontheist Spong 1998). We are a practical species, after all. From naturalism's perspective, there are ways to explain why people invent and use ideological mythologies for about any purpose, good and evil, people can imagine. The allegations of religion's harms have been catalogued (see Russell 1957, Harris 2004, Hitchens 2007). Science's investigations have been summoned. Perhaps religion is the result of biological and/or cultural evolution (see Firth 1996, Rue 2005, Schloss and Murray 2009, Wade 2009), although evolution can pass on vices as well as virtues (Teehan 2010). Religion's psychological dimensions are also receiving fresh attention (Paloutzian and Park 2005, Newberg and Walden 2009). Perhaps religion consists of viral "memes" contagiously infecting many human minds (see Dawkins 2006, Dennett 2006). While all these examinations of religion are revealing fascinating facts about human beings and their belief systems, god's existence remains a separate question.

Any sophisticated religion, such as Christianity, is intelligently designed for dealing with religious criticism. The faithful can respond that genuine religion is mostly beneficial and ethical. For them, religion is the only fund of joy, hope, and wisdom in the world while atheism is a cruel deprivation of all of this life's meaning and the next life's bliss (Zacharias 2008, Harrison 2008, Hart 2009). Atheism is associated with a foolishly optimistic worldview expecting reason and science to make life better for people (though believers appreciate mathematics and medicine too). People who lack much hope for this life and really want an afterlife have great incentive to be religious, and they construct social institutions to reinforce collective belief. Some wonder whether humans still need religion, though. Religions may fear that lack of religious belief causes moral and social deterioration, yet today's most advanced, healthy, and peaceful countries are among the least religious in the world (Paul 2009). Believers can reply that most people around the world are still content to believe in a god. Religion has no trouble explaining why there are atheists – there will always be wicked deviants in any society. Atheists are either innocently ignorant so they need to read scripture (Balabat 2008), or they are willfully stubborn so they need to accept grace (Pasquini 2000).

Atheists get blamed for secularization, yet secularization was well underway in the West long before enough atheists accumulated to add support to the separation of church and state. Secularization is not the same as atheism. Secularization has to do with religion's control over the outer world, not over the inner mind. Secularization is the gradual replacement of religious control over major political and social institutions. Political secularization prevents governments from favoring religion and it also protects religions from government interference. Social secularization finds most civil organizations, such as for-profit businesses and non-profit colleges and hospitals, no longer controlled by any religious denomination. America is a good example of a country in which secularism is the norm while most people sustain their faiths. Some of religion's defenders fear secularization, as if peoples' faith in god could depend on religion controlling the world. Curiously, we also hear religion's defenders proudly displaying demographic trends showing how faith is remarkably resilient around the world. If faith is doing so well, perhaps secularization should not be such a terror. Apparently, billions of people can freely enjoy their private faith in god while letting governments do their public jobs (indeed, that was the aim of secularism). Political and social secularization continues, affecting the world as much as faith's propagation (Berger 1999, Bruce 2002, Joas and Wiegandt 2009, Micklethwait and Wooldridge 2009), and both believers and nonbelievers should grasp the global consequences (see the analyses of Berlinerblau 2005, Taylor 2007, Zuckerman 2009). Religions tend to view any competition as another religion, so secularism gets accused of quasi-religious indoctrination and totalitarianism (London 2009). Religions proudly chart the number of their adherents, as if the real god would have the most faithful. Demographics and social statistics measure intriguing trends to track, but they don't track god.

Nothing about religion's capacity to satisfy personal, social, or political needs can determine whether or not a god exists.

Religious criticism in general is directed at believers, not god, and we humans do deserve harsh judgment. Some religion can be used for evil, while nonbelievers can be evil too. Still, religion cannot show that god exists by complaining that nonbelievers tend to be more evil or just want to evade god's condemnation of sin. Pointing to Hitler, Stalin, or Mao as consequences of nonbelief cannot prove the existence of god. Besides, Hitler was religious, hated atheism, and most Nazis were Christians (Steigmann-Gall 2003), while atheist Stalin and atheist Mao eradicated millions for totalitarian power, not for atheism (and Italy's Mussolini, like France's Napoleon, was Catholic). Some perspective over centuries is needed: the deaths from African colonial wars and slave trade, the genocide of American Indians, and the Napoleanic Wars (all conducted by millions of Christians) together approximate the twentieth-century numbers attributed to two atheists. The sheer numbers of twentieth-century dead are appallingly large, but that mostly reflects more murderous weaponry and bigger populations to kill. Not even secularization could be associated with such killing. Democratically secular countries are the least likely to engage in wars or destroy their own populations (Rummell 1998). Nor can religion complain that science is responsible for a world more immoral or warlike. Powers have always used science and technology for murderous ends. Christian kings used the finest weaponry of their times to kill as many as they could, and a Christian president was the first to drop nuclear weapons on civilian populations. National and international struggles tend to overpower religion or even co-opt religion's involvement (see the American Confederacy, Northern Ireland, or the Middle East). The god debates are not about politics or war, however. Religion, like everything else involving humans, can be a benefit and a harm. Some of the faithful can even agree that religions are culpable for their transgressions, by God's own standards, so it is better to follow God directly instead of tracking a religion's beliefs (Carse 2008, Lesperance 2009). There is no way to establish whether god exists by criticizing the conduct of believers or nonbelievers.

Other kinds of religious criticism similarly lack relevance to the god debates. For example, it has been fashionable for skeptics to claim that religious belief is just nonsense, because it cannot be verified and fails to make any claims about reality. This is an odd claim, exposing an ignorance of theology. For centuries, theologians have led the way towards interpreting scripture in ways other than taking it literally or factually, and understanding god in ways other than attributing mere existence or reality. Interpreting religious claims for their analogical, metaphorical, poetic, aesthetic, or mystical meanings has been a full-time enterprise for Christian theologians ever since they tried to read Old Testament passages as forecasts about Jesus. Perhaps valuable meanings for religious belief are inspirational and transformational. Indeed, nonbelievers can easily agree that religious claims should not be narrowly understood as merely literal descriptions of god and god's work. Curiously, many contemporary theologians complain that atheism overlooks religion's metaphorical, poetic, inspirational, and ritualistic functions. Atheism recognizes these functions all too well, since atheism has always claimed that religious language could not be expressing factual truths about god, so religious language must have quite different functions. Curious too how some liberal theologians dismiss atheism by warning that mere existence is no attribute of a god, even while they reassure believers in the pews that god really exists. If people didn't think that there is a god, such distracting misuses of language could be avoided (and people would not be bothered by atheism). We need some straight talk about god. Rather than get distracted by discussing all the things that religious language can do besides talk about god, the god debates are only about the existence of god.

Another common criticism of religion starts from its love of mystery. Religion does not avoid mystery, to be sure, but does that make religion irrational? Acknowledging mystery doesn't really help anyone in the god debates. Popular religious literature appeals to mystery to defend belief in god. Christians are told that god is so transcendent from this world that people would not discover god through evidence or science, and that the human mind could not consider such a transcendent god as anything but a deep mystery. This strategy is self-defeating; how can the lack of information (the mystery) help create more information (about a god)? This "argument from deep mystery" proposes that, since deep mystery exists, it is reasonable to believe in god. The conclusion doesn't follow, though. God may be quite mysterious, but if god is completely mysterious for humans, then a person's belief has nothing to aim at, nothing to believe in, even if this person really wants to believe. All the same, nonbelievers can't deny the reality of mystery – mystery about what lies beyond current knowledge, and what may lie beyond all future knowledge. Precisely because everyone admits the deep mystery, no one can claim to know what lies out there without contradicting themselves. Deep mystery by itself only produces a skeptical stand-off between believers and nonbelievers. We shall simply have to see where the evidence and argument leads us.

Distinguishing itself from the wider (and wilder) field of religious criticism, the god debates should stay focused on its own task. Religions, like everything human, need criticism. What is special about the god debates is its tighter attention to the most important question: is supreme reality a god, or not? Having an answer to that question cuts to the core of what religion is, and what it should be. The god debates are worthy of our most serious and careful intellectual efforts. Our timing couldn't be better. Western civilization is in the throes of birthing a new post-Enlightenment worldview. We are sensing the breakdown, the opportunity, and the cost of failure. The religious and naturalistic worldviews now competing for influence in the West must not ignore each other. And Eastern wisdom traditions deserve serious engagement too. Some worldviews are more prepared than others for engaging in dialogue and debate. The final chapter identifies their respective advantages and limitations, and suggests where alliances might prove fruitful. The world is waiting.

1.2 Debating Dogma

For the reader willing to turn away from the spectacle of religious criticism, the god debates beckon. Still, there might be a good reason why more energy goes into attacking and defending the conduct of religions. Respectful dialogue sounds good, but what might debating god's existence really accomplish? Looking to the past, we may despair of hope for any reasonable progress. The world's major religions have had centuries and millennia to carefully formulate their doctrines and arguments. All the same, these theological stances need to be reexamined and perhaps redesigned. Indeed, recent theology, especially Christian theology, has now far surpassed those traditional arguments formulated during a different age. Believers have noticed this as much as nonbelievers, and everyone needs a better education in religion.

Traditional theologies can seem antiquated and alien, cramped by microscopic obsessions over messianic prophets and angelic visitations and virgin births and miraculous healings and blissful trances and karmic avatars. Such fixations on earthly dramas were impressive indeed to Bronze Age wonderment but they bewilder the modern mind's computations. The universe is just so much bigger and wilder to our telescopic view. It's not just nonbelievers who view theologies like tourists view Stonehenge – wondering that anyone would go to such trouble to build it – but ordinary religious laypeople don't grasp much theology, either. A Catholic may admire Aquinas' theology like she admires a Gothic cathedral, but she intuitively sees how she doesn't live in that civilization any more. Nowadays, a charismatic faith healer or wild-eyed herald of the apocalypse only manages to initiate small cults, to the embarrassment of mainstream religious believers and nonbelievers alike.

If real opportunity for constructive thinking and debate over religion and theology is still available, we must assess the current situation carefully. What are the prospects for religious debate at present, in the twenty-first century? Debating about religion usually doesn't feel like it's worth the effort. The prevalent attitude among nonbelievers seems to be that faith just can't be reasoned with anyway. Regrettably, little serious debate occurs between people of different faiths, too. Most religious people won't endure argumentative challenge for very long, even if conducted in the most polite tones. It's probably not their fault; few laypeople are as informed or trained as their religious leaders in the reasoned defense of doctrines. There is no need to suppose that religious people are less intelligent, more easily confused, or overly sensitive. It would be easier to respectfully debate with lots of people about their religion if they were better educated about their creeds. The same thing goes for nonbelievers who want to discuss religion. You don't have to be a believer yourself to have enough of an understanding of a religion to engage in debate. Before criticizing religion, a nonbeliever should be aware of ways that Christians can theologically explain and defend their beliefs.

Should respectful debating about religion be deemed impossible just because of the current situation, for both believers and nonbelievers, in religious education? That would be hasty and unfortunate judgment. We should instead expect, as many religious intellectuals have hoped, that debating would inspire deeper knowledge of one's religious beliefs. After all, religions are hardly strangers to debate. Many religious texts contain examples of debating. For example, accounts of debates between Jesus and Jewish rabbis can be instructive for Christians, while Krishna's arguments to Arjuna in the Bhagavad Gita teach Hindus. Questioning and debating has helped shape many religions (Berger and Zijderveld 2009). Most major religions today explain their beliefs in sophisticated ways, designed to widely persuade and withstand scrutiny. Such sophistication resulted from internal doubts, disagreements, and debates among religious leaders, scholars, and laypeople. Examples abound. Confucianism originated in philosophical meditations. Much of modern Hinduism and Buddhism developed in the context of intellectual argumentation as rigorous as any in the Western philosophical tradition. Both Judaism and Islam have produced some of the world's finest religious literature and heights of philosophical thought. It is impossible to understand the Catholic Church if its 1700-year record of theological systematizing, and council debating and voting by bishops, is overlooked. The fragmentation of modern Protestantism into thousands of denominations and churches is, from a certain perspective, nothing but a long tale of disputation in the pews over ever-finer points of scripture interpretation, theological doctrine, and church practice. Religion's intellectual progress, like any kind of learning, always begins from doubt. Fanaticism, not doubt, is the greater danger for religion.

It might be supposed that underlying all this debating are fundamental dogmas, a special set of beliefs, that never get modified or questioned. Actually, questions about which dogmas are most fundamental, and what practical implications such dogmas have, are the questions most theologically interpreted and thoroughly debated during a religion's historical evolution. Christianity is no exception. Christian theology was powerfully developed through systematic "apologetics," in which Church Fathers organized reasoned justifications for core doctrines in order to facilitate conversations and conversions among the better-educated in the culturally Greek and Latin world. Apologetics remained a central activity for Christian theologians, whose competing systems of religious thought have frequently rivaled their secular philosophical counterparts.

Is anything and everything about a religion really up for questioning? What about god's existence? Surely that can't be up for debate among the faithful. Well, which god are we talking about? A Christian is quickly tempted to reply, "You know, *the* God, the god that all we believers accept." However, a religion's believers will not all share the identical conception of that god. Let's use Christianity as a paradigm case. There are numerous rival conceptions of the Christian God available to believers. Is God only as described in the New Testament, or does the Old Testament add essential details about God? Are there three separate divinities (God, Jesus, and the Holy Spirit), or does God consist of three persons in one (the Trinitarian theory), or does God have a unique and unchanging nature? If Jesus is eternally divine, does that mean that a god really died on the cross, or was only a human being sacrificed for other humans' sins? Are all of God's and Jesus' commandments throughout the Bible legitimate and binding rules, or are only some of them truly God's will for us now? Is this God still supplying new revelations to special people down to this day, or does the Bible record the final Word of God? Did God create the world in one great act and then rest for ever, or does God continually remake and adjust the world with fresh miracles? Does God precisely plan out everything that happens in the world, or does human free will control some of the world's destiny? Is this God loving and merciful towards all, or is wrathful punishment this God's priority? Does eternal punishment really await the damned, or does God want everyone to eventually get into heaven? Does God answer prayers from only Christians, or does God listen to non-Christians too? Might Hitler be in heaven (if he repented right before death) while Anne Frank is in hell (for being Jewish)? These sorts of questions about God's character and motivation can proliferate quickly. Even complicated ways of reconciling some of these opposed notions have been vigorously debated.

Furthermore, other religions have raised these issues and taken attitudes towards Christianity. The debating advice in this book wasn't written just for nonbelievers and Christians. The reasons that Christians give for their beliefs have long had global interest, and the god debates have generated defenses of god in general (such as Armstrong 2009) and of Christianity in particular (such as McDowell 2006 and D'Souza 2007) which are quite readable for laypeople of any belief or no belief. The twenty-first century now presents an almost unprecedented opportunity to meet and compare religious doctrines on a planetary scale. Tough questions from the nonreligious, who emerged in the last fifty years as a small minority of the world's population, are also posed by the peoples of many other faiths, who together comprise the large majority. Non-Christians may be inquisitive about Christianity's supernaturalism and spirit–body duality, or about its theistic god of limitless power and knowledge. Christianity's peculiar dependency on alleged miracles involving Jesus may strike some non-Christians as somewhat familiar (if their own religion is also based on miracles by divine visitors to Earth), or as strangely exotic. The Christian manner of erecting a moral and social code upon carefully selected Bible verses, and endlessly arguing over which verses matter most, also arouses curiosity.

Christianity is ready for this higher level of dialogue on the global stage. Christianity from its early origins has been an evangelical movement reaching out to convert all who would listen, regardless of their prior religious or intellectual views. Cultural mutation has been Christianity's strength powering its growth. Over two millennia, Christianity has borrowed and incorporated tools of persuasion from the civilizations around it, including aspects of Judaism and other older religions, along with adapted parts of Greek and Islamic logic and philosophy. If Christianity is well prepared for debating a newly evolved skepticism, it is only because its doctrinal framework is intelligently designed, for arguing with both internal heretics and external rivals. Many internal heretics (preferring the role of "reformer") founded their own varieties of Christianity, and in turn were obligated to explain their new doctrines. Christianity now presents to the world a paradigm of interfaith dialogue. Its numerous denominational species, from Greek Orthodoxy to Pentecostal Fundamentalism, are all highly adapted in the competitive campaign for followers.

Continuing their spread around the world, Christian denominations are taking advantage of new technologies of mechanical travel and electronic communication invented in the twentieth century. Priests and missionaries no longer follow the dusty roads opened by the silk trade or the sea routes charted by mercantile shipping. And it is no longer merely the church intelligentsia who shoulder the entire burden of sharing the message and advancing their own denomination. A better-educated class of churchgoers emerged during the past 200 years, knowledgeable about much more than just the scripted creeds, and getting familiarized with theological reasonings explaining them. The internet then released this intellectual energy from the pews and broadcast it around the world. There are far more personal websites about religion than church-run websites. Ecumenical discussion and debate, led by laypeople as well as by ecclesiastics, is a fascinating worldwide web phenomenon. Other religions are available for exploration and discussion on the internet too. There are fewer and fewer good excuses for remaining ignorant about one's religion.

There aren't many excuses for believers to avoid the god debates, either. If a Christian would be ready for answering questions from people of other faiths, why not people of no faith as well? The basic questions, about the Christian god, Jesus, the Bible, etc., all remain the same. Answering them should proceed no differently, whether replying to a Muslim, a Hindu, a Buddhist, a Taoist, or a nonbeliever. Learning from debating god with nonbelievers should be much like learning about a different religion. Sharing in faith is hardly a requirement for learning. Actually, close sharing could be an impediment to learning. You don't learn much from someone who already agrees with you. Too often ecumenical dialogue presumes the strange notion that only people having large overlapping areas of faith can benefit. By this rule, any two denominational cousins within Protestantism, like Presbyterianism and Congregationalism, would have more to learn from each other than two different religions, such as Christianity and Buddhism. But that doesn't make any good sense. The most interesting and important aspects of your own religion are probably those arousing great curiosity in a person from a very different religion. Learning is principally about acquiring good answers for yourself – and the more questions you are asked, the more answers you must supply. The opportunities to learn from discussing religion with an nonbeliever range from learning how to explain the basic beliefs of Christianity all the way to learning where Christian justifications for its doctrines can most effectively answer skeptical questions.

Dialogue about religion with atheology should not be viewed as a distasteful encounter or a tiresome chore. It is not for everyone, to be sure. On the other side, many nonbelievers avoid debating with Christians, too. Debating has a reputation for being confrontational and unpleasant. People involved in debates are usually more interested in "winning" than learning. Even the label of "debate" carries the expectation that everyone already has their mind made up. If debating is only about winning, and confessing to learning something is an automatic "loss," then total close-mindedness seems necessary. Not surprisingly, then, we think of debating as a stiff competition between inflexible positions. If that is all debating could be, then no one could be blamed for avoiding it. We should all avoid dogmatism, and seek educated knowledge.

1.3 Theology and Atheology

The god debates involves theology, and theology can be intimidating for believers and nonbelievers alike. To become knowledgeable about religion, theology is unavoidable. When religion elevates its intellectual level, it develops a theology. In our god debates, we will cover much of philosophy of religion and philosophical theology, focusing on Christianity and, by implication, related theistic religions of Judaism and Islam. Christianity calls the supreme reality by the name of 'God' and urges faithful beliefs about this god. Christianity is a supernaturalistic religion, holding that its god shares no essential properties or powers with the physical world of nature and this god does not overlap in any important way with nature. Christianity is a theistic religion, as its god is taken to the only god, the almighty god, and a personal god who cares for creation and humans. Christianity is a theological religion, as its core doctrines have been shaped by theological efforts to explain and defend its supernatural and theistic worldview.

What is theology? Thoughtful religious people who try to reasonably explain god and relationships with god are doing theology. The term "theology" comes from a Greek combination of words: *theos* means god, and *logos* means reason. Theism is a worldview that includes a god, and theology tries to explain that theistic worldview. The Greek language can also add the prefix 'a' at the start of a word to form another word for its contrary. Many English words were borrowed from these Greek combinations, such as apathy (a-pathos, or "not caring") and atheism (a-theos or "not godly"). Just as "atheism" is the contrary of "theism," theology has a contrary in "atheology." Atheology is the intellectual effort to explain why a worldview should not include any god. Where theology offers reasons to believe in a god, atheology criticizes those reasons and skeptically denies god's existence.

Since Christian theology the focus of our god debates in this book, the kind of atheology involved would be accurately labeled as "Christian atheology," but we'll only use "atheology." In a discussion of many religions, different atheologies would have to be specified. There are as many atheologies as theologies, one for each religion. Hindu atheology is quite different from Christian atheology, for example.

Atheology is narrowly focused on questioning the existence of anything divine or supernatural, but it not primarily about atheism. Atheology is for almost everyone, not just atheists, because most religious believers deny other religions' gods. Atheists do atheology in debating about gods, but many religious people are good at atheology, too – atheology skeptically targeting someone else's god. When a Christian forms a reasoned justification for rejecting Islam or Hinduism, for example, Islamic atheology or Hindu atheology are undertaken. Christian intellectuals who specialize in explaining and debating why Christianity is the more reasonable religion are quite good at atheology. In fact, most of the people doing atheology are religious believers, not atheists. An atheist would simply be someone who accepts the view of "complete" atheology that all atheologies about all religions are reasonable, and so the atheist is skeptical towards all religions and gods. But all thoughtful religious believers are partial atheologists: they can appeal to some reasons why they don't believe in other gods. The atheist just believes in one less god than the theist.

In succeeding chapters we will explore arguments in both theology and atheology. They are complex enough that they deserve the labels of "philosophical theology" and "philosophical atheology" respectively. Philosophical theology consists of the search for the best reasoned justifications for a religion; the converse of philosophical theology would therefore be philosophical atheology: the search for the best reasoned justifications for skeptically rejecting religious claims about gods. There are two basic types of philosophical atheology. "Negative" philosophical atheology skeptically reacts to the positive theological arguments supporting religious claims about god. By showing how such arguments fail, the reasonable default position is to be skeptical towards god. "Positive" philosophical atheology constructs its own positive arguments based on reason and available knowledge which try to show that specific gods (such as Christianity's theistic god) do not exist, or that they are highly improbable. Because this book is primarily concerned with theological arguments and skeptical responses to them, negative philosophical atheology is more thoroughly discussed. Occasionally, as opportunity arises, some of the important positive philosophical atheology arguments are presented as well.

Because philosophical atheology appeals to what we do know about ourselves and nature, and it considers naturalism as a fair rival to supernaturalism for skeptical comparison, philosophical atheology takes nature seriously. Philosophical atheology is not equivalent to science or naturalism, however. Naturalism is a general understanding of reality and humanity's place within reality. Naturalism can be briefly defined as the philosophical conclusion that the only reality is what is discovered by our intelligence using the tools of experience, reason, and science. Naturalism is about as old as the few religions which still survive to challenge it. The so-called "Axial Age" from around 800 to 300 BCE saw a sudden explosion of religious and philosophical creativity in Europe, the Middle East, India, and China. Greek philosophy and science was invented; Judaism became monotheistic; Zoroasterianism enveloped the Persian empire; Hinduism was transformed by the Vedanta theology in the Upanishads; Buddhism arose to challenge Hinduism; Taoism was systematized in the Tao Te Ching; and Confucianism was founded.

What caused this sudden eruption of sophisticated thought? There are two main explanations, and these hypotheses are compatible with each other. First, all four of the main centers of civilization – Europe, the Middle East, India, and China – were suffering from political fragmentation and civil wars. Much of the moral and political philosophy from the Axial Age arose in efforts to deal with these severe political crises. Second, all four of these civilization centers learned about the amazing discoveries of

Babylonian astronomers made during the period of around 1600 to 900 BCE. The Babylonian astronomers were the first to accurately record and calculate the regular motions of the heavenly bodies. Suddenly a brand new idea detonated in the imagination: the universe is ruled by law. This idea brought immense changes to every aspect of civilization, from Greece to China. Religions had to adapt and absorb this amazing idea of universal and perfect law. In the Middle East, gods laid down natural laws. In India, the gods upheld righteous dharma. In China, the way of the Tao controls everything. In Greece, natural science was born. Although naturalism is most often associated with its Western philosophical and scientific tradition, other naturalisms began during the Axial Age as well. Taoism has often been understood as a naturalistic philosophy, since the ultimate power of the Tao is still part of nature. Several important varieties of Buddhism have no beliefs about the afterlife or anything supernatural. The Carvaka school of Hindu philosophy, notable for its defiant materialism and atheism, also dates from this Axial Age. For over 2600 years, religions in the major centers of civilization have been matched by a powerful alternative that looks to nature alone.

Modern naturalism is primarily indebted to the boldness of Greek rationalism and science. The origins of science come from such theorizing about what nature is made of and how nature works. In this new scientific way of thinking, more complex things are to be explained in terms of simpler things, and fairly unpredictable events are to be explained in terms of more predictable regularities. A religious mode of thinking proceeds in the opposite manner: simpler things are to be explained by more complex things, and regular patterns are explainable by unpredictable events. For example, a religion may say that human beings (simpler) were created by a god (more complex), or that the pattern of the four seasons (fairly regular) was instituted by a divine act (not predictable), or that a moral rule (strictly valid) was ordered by a god's command (which could have been otherwise). Religious thinking attempts to apply ways we understand each other in our attempts to understand nature around us. Religions are basically about complex and unpredictable events happening at special times to privileged peoples. Such anthropocentric (humanity-centered) reasoning actually is highly unreasonable when applied to the world, since it privileges the human perspective all out of proper proportion to nature. Instead of privileging one perspective, natural science tries to offer explanations that can work from anywhere. Simple things and predictable regularities, valid anywhere in the universe, are precisely what science seeks.

Finding their all-too-human gods unsatisfying, many Greek intellectuals put their confidence in scientific thinking. Greek philosophers, starting with Thales and the Ionian school around 600 BCE, offered speculations about the origin and constitution of the world that left little or no role for gods or spirits. Perhaps everything is made of one of the four basic elements known to the Greeks. One philosopher suggested water, another fire; another proposed that underlying the elements is a more fundamental, formless energy that can become anything. Democritus (*c.*400 BCE) declared his radically materialistic view that only tiny atoms and gaps of empty space really exist. Aristotle (*c.*350 BCE) catalogued a wide variety of these speculations, and added his own reasoned theories. Skepticism about the gods was more openly discussed. By 100 BCE, sophisticated schools of Greek philosophy argued their merits, and in turn they taught Western civilization, including its Christian component, how to reason. Today's naturalism takes advantage of the vast amount of scientific knowledge we now possess. But the naturalistic spirit is far older than experimental science, and traces its birth back to the very origins of reason itself.

While philosophical atheology relies on reason, it is not equivalent to naturalism and it does not presuppose naturalism. Philosophical atheology does require the use of ordinary common sense and logical reasoning, but it does not presume that naturalism is superior to supernaturalism. As we shall see in later chapters, some kinds of theology try to justify religion on grounds other than human reason and knowledge, so they would dispute the ability of philosophical atheology to fairly judge supernaturalism. However, philosophical atheology is not a rival religion or worldview or philosophy, so it really isn't a competitor to supernaturalism, but only a neutral critic. All the same, a highly successful philosophical atheology, capable of justifying skepticism about the supernatural, tends to send the skeptic in the direction of naturalism as an alternative worldview. Furthermore, we shouldn't forget how many people feel "in between" supernaturalism and naturalism and aren't sure whether labels such as "agnosticism" or "atheism" are good fits for them.

Nonbelievers who reject traditional theistic Christianity have many options for positive worldviews. Besides other nontheistic religions, there are many kinds of pantheisms, spiritualisms, and mysticisms, along with varieties of humanism and naturalism. Forming a positive worldview is hard enough; selecting a label for oneself from a limited menu is even harder. Demographers polling people in America and around the world consistently find that few nonbelievers prefer the label of "atheist" for labeling their own position (Zuckerman 2007). This reluctance probably has more to do with the perceived meaning of atheism rather than the actual views of nonbelievers. Besides its strongly negative connotations, attached to the label by believers' scorn or fear towards atheism, the term "atheism" became associated with dogmatism. Nonbelievers, quite understandably, do not want to be perceived as evil or dangerous, or stubbornly dogmatic. It is ironic how believers could accuse atheists of dogmatism, when the word "dogmatic" was a preferred label for true religious believers since the early days of the Christian Church. The meaning reversal that happened to "dogmatic" in turn caused "atheism" to shift meaning. In earlier centuries, an atheist was simply a skeptical nonbeliever, characterized by an inability to be dogmatic about religion (Thrower 2000, Hecht 2004). This lack of dogmatism was precisely what distinguished the wayward atheist who strayed into ignorance about religious matters. Unable to be persuaded by sacred scripture, religious creed, or theological reasoning, atheists expressed their unbelief and uncertainty. That's how you could tell a religious believer from a nonbeliever back then: the religious person pronounced their confident knowledge about religious matters, while the atheist could only admit hesitant ignorance. Nowadays, however, the atheist is often accused of dogmatism.

The rise of the label "agnostic" is connected with the strange fate of the term "atheism." In the 1860s Thomas Henry Huxley recommended "agnosticism" – the contrary of "gnostic," a Greek term for knowledge. An agnostic recommends admitting our lack of knowledge about any ultimate reality, such as a "supreme being" or whatever caused the universe. Huxley offered agnosticism as a reasonable stance towards not just any religion's overconfident dogmas but also about any philosophy's overreaching conclusions as well. Skeptical towards both theology and metaphysics, Huxley and many other rationalists adopted "agnosticism" as a convenient general category for their conservative philosophical stance. The agnostic is not a complete philosophical skeptic who claims to know nothing. The agnostic's standard of knowledge is just our ordinary reliable (not perfect or infallible) knowledge of the natural world around us. While presently unable to know anything about ultimate reality using these empirical tools of intelligence, the agnostic, like everyone else, is able to know plenty of other things about the natural world, where ordinary human investigations yield practical and reliable results.

Since agnosticism's conservative approach to belief is also the basis for atheism, confusion between atheism and agnosticism immediately ensued, and has not stopped since. What exactly is the relationship between agnosticism and atheism? An agnostic, like an atheist, does not accept supernaturalism, specifically, because no supernatural belief has yet passed the reasonable standard of empirical knowledge, and so a confession of ignorance is the only conclusion. Despite the obvious overlap between agnosticism and atheism, the impact of agnosticism in the 1800s and early 1900s had the rhetorical effect of clearing a middle ground between religious belief and atheism. This adjustment in turn affected the meaning of "atheism." If the agnostic cannot know that supernaturalism is right, and if the atheist isn't an agnostic, then the atheist must therefore be someone claiming to know something about the supernatural. What might an atheist claim to know? The common meaning of 'atheism' began to shift towards "disbelief in god" and "the denial that god exists" so that many people began taking atheism to mean "it can be known that nothing supernatural exists." The agnostic, on the other hand, could still be religious through other means besides the intellect (such as faith), so that there could be agnostic theists as well as agnostic atheists (see Flint 1903).

It is not easy to track dictionary definitions of "atheism" over the centuries, since this subject, so distasteful to Christians, rarely received its own entry. By the time the term began regularly appearing in dictionaries, around the turn of the twentieth century, the distinction between two kinds of atheism was already noticed. The eleventh edition of the *Encyclopaedia Britannica* (1911) was the earliest edition of that reference work to include atheism. It distinguishes between dogmatic atheism and skeptical atheism. Dogmatic atheism "denies the existence of god positively" while skeptical atheism "distrusts the capacity of the human mind to discover the existence of god." The entry goes on to add that skeptical atheism hardly differs from agnosticism. But skeptical atheism kept fading from view, lost in the glare of its new cousins, agnosticism and dogmatic atheism. Dogmatic atheism is now widely taken to be the only kind of atheism, especially in the recent form of a "new atheism." This new meaning for atheism has achieved common parlance, dictionary affirmation, and philosophical usage. Instead of being an ignorant skeptic about the divine, an atheist is now supposed to be just another overreaching gnostic possessing confident knowledge about ultimate reality. Agnosticism has now re-emerged into popular view as a nonbelief option to atheism's dogmas and religion's faith.

The distinction between agnosticism and atheism has been additionally confused because a fourth competitor to gnosticism reemerged in the 1800s, in the form of "fideistic theism" or "fideism" for short. Disdain for intellectual paths to god was hardly new for Christianity (mysticism was always an option, and Protestant Martin Luther denounced abstract theological argumentation, for example). Drawing on the Latin root word for "faithful" or "loyal," fideistic theologians recommend faithful belief in god despite the absence of any conclusive empirical or logical demonstration. Religious belief is not fideism, nor is fideism defined by contradicting reason. Fideism is similar to agnosticism in this crucial respect: they both agree that the supernatural cannot be defended by reason and cannot be known. As a theological stance, fideism is a strange partner to traditional theology, since the original aim of theology was to rationally defend belief in god. Perhaps fideism is more of an abandonment of theology's reasoned defenses of theism, calling for a return to straightforward religious conviction, pure religious emotions, and sincere witnessing. Fideistic theology has had plenty of help. Philosophical fideisms inspired by Immanuel Kant, Søren Kierkegaard, Friedrich Schleiermacher, William James, Ludwig Wittgenstein, and others sought new harmonies between reason and faith; still more thinkers sought faith's liberation from reason entirely.

Forms of fideism multiplied throughout the nineteenth and twentieth centuries and competed for attention from Christians (see Penelhum 1983, Phillips 1986). Modern fideism discovered additional allies as it questioned reason's supremacy. In the first half of the twentieth century, fideism received support from the social sciences such as anthropology and sociology, which treat religions as practices of communities. If religion is essentially about what your community traditionally preaches or practices, then nonbelievers could not share any reasonable common basis for criticizing faith. In the second half of the twentieth century, some kinds of fideism partly merged with various postmodernist views urging suspicion towards the pretensions of reason and science. If reason and science either fail to yield any knowledge, or only manages to yield incomplete and partial knowledge, then the grounds for dismissing religion shift dramatically or even vanish. Could fideism deliver knowledge of god where reason could not? Or perhaps fideism better opens a path to god that is not properly a kind of knowledge at all? Fideism tended to provide Christians divergent methods of seeking god, but it gave many Christians encouragement despite traditional theology's troubles.

Fideism also encouraged Christians to define atheism as the claim to know that nothing supernatural exists. After all, if such knowledge is impossible, atheism is disproved, and the resulting admission of agnosticism is simultaneously a potential vindication for fideism. Fideists recommending agnosticism are not contradicting themselves; the confession that the intellect cannot reach god helpfully justifies reliance on faith instead. Agnosticism also proved useful against atheism. Debates between believers and disbelievers began to take the form of "If you can't prove my god doesn't exist, then you have no basis for criticizing my faith." The only way for the nonbeliever to back out of this fideistic trap is to appeal to the original skeptical principle behind atheism: where one cannot know anything, one should not believe. The fideist adopts the contrary principle: where one cannot know, one should faithfully believe, at least where Christianity is concerned. The accusation by the skeptical atheist that fideism is precisely the abandonment of reason is simply met by the fideist's reply that believing without reason's assent is the essence of religious belief. Christians sometimes echo Martin Luther's declaration of "Faith alone!" A Christian, recalling Jesus' emphasis on believing in him, and taking belief in the words of the Bible as bedrock, is quite capable of setting aside intellectual theologies in favor of dogmatic faith.

In a way, the reemergence of fideistic theology presents an opportunity for skeptical atheism to constructively rejoin the god debates. When the skeptical atheist complains that human reasoning cannot reach any god, the fideist replies that its god cannot be reached by unaided reason. If the skeptical atheist urges doubt towards all gods, the fideist replies that such doubt is inevitable so religion uses faith to reach the Christian god where reason fails. It turns out that fideism and skeptical atheism share much in common: they agree that there is insufficient reason to believe in god, and that a Christian's belief in a god is ultimately sustained by faithful conviction. An atheist believes in less than a Christian, to be sure. Yet, if the fideist insists that believing in god cannot be justified by evidence or reason, the skeptical atheist entirely agrees. Even though the competition between skeptical atheism and fideism in the god debates has been getting fiercer, it becomes harder to see what they are disagreeing about.

The skeptical atheist – the original and genuine atheist – faces an odd sort of competition even from other atheists. Some people who have no belief in god cast their doubt towards science's pretensions and naturalism in order to defend an uncertain agnosticism (Berlinski 2009, Corlett 2010). Other nonbelievers want to retain faith and spiritualism while they discard god (Comte-Sponville 2009, Schaeffer 2009, Antinoff 2010). Distinctions between 'positive' and 'negative' atheism, and between 'strong' and 'weak' atheism, have appeared in the literature (for example Martin 2007). However, definitions of these types of atheism vary across atheists, and too often such definitions are designed more to deal with confusions with agnosticism, or to avoid any need to justify disbelief, than to describe how actual nonbelievers think about god. Fortunately, a clear and simple definition of atheism is already available: an atheist is someone who does not believe in any gods. It must be immediately added that an atheist does not have any faith in a god, either, just in case we could imagine someone lacking belief but having faith. Whatever it may take for a person to take god's existence seriously, an atheist does not have it. The essence of atheism is lack of a belief that god exists.

To repeat, an atheist is someone who does not believe in any gods. But you wouldn't know this just by asking people. It sounds like four views have gotten stubbornly entrenched. One view says that atheists are those denying the specific theistic god of Judaism/Christianity/Islam; another says that atheists are those who deny that any god exists; still another says that atheists claim to know that no god exists; while a fourth view says that atheists simply lack belief that god exists. They are also arguing over how many atheists there are, and whether atheism can avoid all burden of proof in the god debates. This chaos is affecting agnosticism, which is now looking like a useless category; skeptical atheism encompasses agnosticism entirely. Agnostics used to know where they didn't know where to stand, but now they don't even not know what it is that they are not supposed to believe or to not believe. Agnostics can't define themselves, but they do like to define atheism as excessive confidence that no god exists, just like religion's defenders.

There are understandable causes for disagreement over a precise meaning for "atheism." Lexicographers point to the Greek *a-theos* for the origin of the term. However, atheists can select among interpretations of prefix and term: what about "anti" *theos* (denial of the gods), or maybe "non" *theos* (not believing in gods), or "anti" theism (denial of a specifically theistic god). Translations can't decide this issue. Demographers often describe an atheist as someone who will reply to a pollster, "Atheism? Yes, that's me. I think that God does not exist." But few people make that selection, especially in America, where only 2–3 percent seem willing to apply that understanding of atheism to themselves. Self-identity atheism can make an atheist feel lonely. By contrast, lacking the belief that a theistic god exists may broadly cover at least one-fifth of the world's population (by including nature-worshippers, pagans, pantheists, spiritualists, agnostics, people unacquainted with the notion of a god, infants, comatose people, etc.). Atheists seeking guarantees that all default burden of justification rests on religious believers also admire this broadest category of absence of belief. However, the notion that broad atheism needs no justification is wrong, since mere ignorance is unjustifiable (that's why we value education).

These confusions over atheism can be straightened with a couple more distinctions. An atheist is someone who does not believe in any gods, that much is still clear. Lack of belief in something will ordinarily have two causes: inattention and skepticism. That's why two main varieties of atheism are constantly promoted. It is crucial to grasp that "not believing that god exists" is different from "believing that god does not exist." Both positions are genuine kinds of atheism, and may be conveniently labeled as "apatheism" and "skeptical" atheism. Apatheism combines "apathy" and "theism" to label people inattentive about god and religious matters; apatheists lack belief in a god because they are not paying attention to religion and don't care enough to think about god. Skeptical atheism is doubtful disbelief towards god and religious matters; skeptics lack belief in god because they have considered religion and believe that god probably does not exist. "Strong" atheism is the extreme end of skeptical atheism where some people confidently assert that no god exists.

Apatheism by itself offers no rational justifications for itself – an apatheist doesn't know or care enough to bother. A genuine case of an apatheist is a person who would not rationally justify such lack of belief, since she either has no concept of god to think about, or she has no interest in thinking about what little she has heard about gods. The notion that an apatheist believes that god does not exist or that an apatheist is skeptical towards god can't make much sense. The typical apatheist simply does not have that affirming belief or active doubt. In response to the question, "Do you believe that god does not exist?" an apatheist is likely to instead reply in this fashion: "What are you talking about?" or "A notion of a god seems meaningless to me," or "I have no idea," or "I have no belief about that." It is more correct to simply say that the apatheist does not have the belief that a god exists, rather than supposing that the apatheist believes that god does not exist. Apatheists are the wrong people to ask for justifying lack of belief. Justifying apatheism must come from some other atheist position. That's the job of an educated skepticism. This skeptical atheism is doubt towards all gods on the grounds that available information and sound reasoning shows how it is improbable that any god exists. The skeptical wing of atheism composes the "disbelievers" portion of the larger whole of "nonbelievers."

Religion's defenders often show a preference for defining atheism as the strongest claim to know that no god exists. If atheists cannot justify such an extravagant claim (and they can't – see the next section), perhaps belief in god then appears reasonable? This tactic fails, since it uses the wrong definition of atheism and conveniently forgets how religious believers do claim extravagant knowledge of a supreme infinite being. It is religion that credits an extraordinary capacity for knowledge to humans, not atheism. Those who propose the existence of something always have the burden of justification. This is especially valid where religion is involved: extraordinary claims require extraordinary evidence. Theology well realizes that skeptical atheism is the bigger problem than apathy; theology accordingly demands that skepticism justify itself. It is too late for the skeptic to announce apatheism or agnosticism (which is just a flavor of skepticism anyway) in order to dodge this demand. Such dodging is unnecessary. Skeptical atheism has an educated position and a task of responding to theology with atheology in the god debates.

Successful atheology would diminish the likelihood that supernaturalism is true. Since skeptics believe that nature exists (a sane and commonsense belief shared even by supernaturalists), their doubt towards supernaturalism leaves naturalism as their default worldview. Positive philosophical atheology goes the farthest to defend and apply natural scientific explanations, so it blends into the effort to provide philosophical naturalism with its firmest foundations. Strong atheists are typically those who are persuaded by both negative and positive philosophical atheology, and hence they take naturalism to be the only reasonable worldview.

1.4 Could Atheism Prove God Doesn't Exist?

Some readers may wonder about faster shortcuts in the god debates, some ways of proving whether god exists once and for all. Strong atheism might supply such a shortcut – are there any proofs that god cannot possibly exist? There are some strong atheists who feel confident about such proofs.

For example, some atheists are so impressed by the argument from the existence of evil that they conclude that this argument proves that god cannot be omnipotent, omniscient, and benevolent. There are many ways for Christian theology to reply to this argument, and we will cover the ensuing debate in a later chapter. But suppose, just for a minute, that there is a perfectly valid argument for that negative conclusion. Well, what could that argument exactly prove? Only one thing: that one specific kind of god cannot exist – a god having omnipotence, omniscience, and benevolence. Two lessons are learned here. First, the atheist is reminded that there might be other kinds of gods. Second, the theologian is reminded that it is possible, in theory, to prove that some specific gods do not exist.

There are two basic ways to design nonexistence proofs. The "dialectical nonexistence proof" argues that two or more characteristics of a specific god are logically incompatible. A definition of something having logically incompatible characteristics can only be the definition of a necessarily nonexistent entity. Successful dialectical nonexistence proofs can show that specific kinds of gods cannot exist. For example, many Christians believe both that god is perfect and that god can suffer along with us. Maybe these two characteristics are contradictory. Figuring out how a perfect being can suffer requires conceptual refinements to god to avoid the negative verdict of a dialectical nonexistence proof. And even if these refinements go badly and one characteristic of god must go, theology can revise its conception of god. Avoiding dialectical nonexistence proofs is, from a flexible theology's point of view, just another way for humanity to learn more about god.

The other kind of proof confronts a specific kind of god with the actual existence of something else, where it is necessarily impossible that both can exist together. This "evidential nonexistence proof" attempts to demonstrate that some specific god cannot exist, if something else (the "disprover") actually does exist. Of course, this sort of proof works only if there is conclusive evidence of the actual existence of the disprover. Theologians can simply deny the existence of the disprover. Consider the example from the previous paragraph. What sort of evil could disprove the existence of god? Christian theology has available means to insulate god and god's plan for the universe from any and all possible evidence. By this tactic, what appears to be evil really isn't; what certainly seems evil (such as the Holocaust) still has god's approval as good, for all we know. A debate over god and evil then sidetracks into a debate over the extent of our knowledge of god. Here's another example. If theology admits that natural evolution shows how god did not create humans, theology can propose that god did design the natural laws responsible for humanity's origins, so evolution cannot prove that no god exists. Science has always kept theology busily defensive, constructing a more and more sophisticated god.

Positive philosophical atheology can offer demonstrations that specific and inflexible gods do not exist (see Martin and Monnier 2003, Everitt 2004, Stenger 2007, Schlagel 2009). Positive philosophical atheology has plenty of material to work with. Logic, obvious evidence, and scientific knowledge can rule out a wide variety of gods, and render highly improbable many more kinds of gods (see Martin and Monnier 2006). Still, the number of potentially conceivable gods (some have already been thought of, but most have not) far outruns the number of disprovable gods. The human imagination will, in all likelihood, forever stay ahead of reason's logic or science's facts. There are simply too many creative ways to intelligently design fair compromises between science and religion (see Clayton 2000, Frank 2009, Drees 2010), so long as science remains humble and religion stays flexible. An excessively strong atheist claim of proof that no god can possibly exist only overstates any actual success, ignores imaginative theology, and encourages religious believers to assume that all atheists (and naturalists) claim to know that no god exists.

Worse, permitting the god debates to collapse into pondering proofs that no god exists only perpetuates a runaway "atheism vs. theology arms race" which no one can win. Theology has the task of defending religion against atheism, so arguing against disproofs of god can then take priority over positively arguing for god. Laypeople cheer on theologians protecting god from refutation, but defensive theology only makes the conception of god more complicated, and changes the target of skepticism. That forces atheists to design ever more intricate arguments against that god too, and when these arguments fall short of proving that this god can't exist, believers rejoice at the atheists' dismay and congratulate themselves for their faith in a more complicated god. Over time, theology can construct a conception of god so sophisticated that the average believer can't understand it any more, leaving god quite mysterious. Theology needn't worry about mystery, of course; believers can hardly fault god for being somewhat mysterious. However, the runaway theological race against atheism has gone too far. Mystery itself now seems like a theologian's best defense, resulting in blind fideism. It is just too easy to proclaim a mysterious god, deride dogmatic atheism's inability to prove that such a mysteriously unknowable god cannot exist, and conclude that the faithful should not be criticized (a procedure exemplified by Hedges 2008).

If a sufficiently mysterious god's existence is safe from disproof, has theology achieved a final victory, or has the very idea of god become practically incoherent or meaningless? Perhaps theology should pull back from that brink. For its part, atheism should not get fixated on proving god's nonexistence. Skeptical atheism's use of atheology is sufficient for effective debate with theology. Atheists are not foolish for their humble naturalism and they aren't exposing any logical weakness if they refrain from 100 percent certainty that nothing supernatural exists.

1.5 Could Religion Disprove Atheism?

Nonbelievers persuaded by strong atheism will be naturalists, in the broad sense of taking environing nature to be the reality. There's no shortcut to proving naturalism by disproving god, as we have seen. Might there be a shortcut for believers? In theory, supernaturalists could try to speedily defeat naturalism by showing that nature does not exist, but this tactic is rarely tried. The obvious reason for such reluctance is that any definition of the "supernatural" depends on already possessing a conception of, and belief in, the "natural." Otherwise how could the supernatural be contrasted against anything else, and how could the supernatural be given credit for creating the natural world?

The less obvious reason why supernatural religions are not skeptical towards nature is because those other religions (such as varieties of Hinduism and Buddhism) which do argue that nature is not real still try to explain the illusion, by giving ultimate spiritual reality the credit for generating the illusion of nature. By treating nature as a by-product of spiritual reality, these religions actually bring nature and spirit into close relationships, tending to result in theologies that look more like pantheisms. Instead of sharply dividing spirit from nature, many of these Eastern theologies tend to integrate them. Genuine supernaturalisms instead depend on sharp dichotomies between the spiritual and the natural. A supernatural religion, at the very least, must explain how it distinguishes the supernatural from the natural. This can be done efficiently by defining the supernatural in terms contrary to the properties of nature. For example, if the natural only has physical properties, obeys natural laws, exists within space/time, and so forth, then the supernatural can be defined as having no physical properties, need not obey natural laws, is not constrained by space/time, etc.

We should admit that at least nature exists. One shortcut refutation of naturalism wants to set a higher standard for naturalism. This "argument from imperfect naturalism" goes like this:

1. Naturalism is the worldview which says that science explains everything.
2. Science does not explain everything.
3. Naturalism is false. (From 1 and 2)
4. If naturalism is false, supernaturalism is true.
   Therefore,

Conclusion. Supernaturalism is true.

The second premise is correct, but the first premise uses a poor definition of naturalism. Naturalism has never been properly defined in such a simplistic and refutable way. Some naturalists prefer something like "science would eventually explain everything" but such confidence does not even represent the majority of naturalists. Naturalism is more complicated than that. Without starting a second book about naturalism in this section, it suffices to say that naturalism accepts the environing world as understood by careful observation, reasoning, and scientific inquiry, and rejects anything too mysterious or too immune from investigation. Naturalism, like science, doesn't have all the answers, nor does it expect to have all the answers. Naturalism does prioritize rational intelligence, however. Might naturalism's strength actually be a weakness in the god debates?

Perhaps reliance on intelligence could be naturalism's weakness against religion. A second shortcut argument for supernaturalism, an "argument from prejudiced naturalism," accuses the strong atheist of an intellectual prejudice against religion:

5. There are a variety of means (using evidence, argument, intuition, etc.) to advance the reasonableness of Christianity.
6. Any skepticism towards the reasonableness of Christianity must be grounded on premises that already favor scientific method and naturalism's worldview instead.
7. It is unreasonable to appeal to biases favoring science and naturalism to complain about Christianity's claim to reasonableness.
   Therefore,

Conclusion. Christianity is reasonable regardless of naturalism's skepticism.

This shortcut argument won't work either. Christianity might still be unreasonable, regardless of any perceived bias in skeptical complaints against it. For example, much skepticism towards Christianity is not based on science or naturalism, but just logical common sense. An atheist can refuse to believe stories about gods or miracles, for example, simply because those stories display the sorts of omissions, inconsistencies, and exaggerations that characterize mythical legends.

Neither skeptical theism nor naturalism claims to perfectly know all reality. What follows? It cannot logically follow that someone else must know, like a supernaturalist. Yet there is enormous tactical and rhetorical benefit to be gained by surviving skeptical criticism, appreciated by theologians worried about fewer people coming to church.

A popular literature defending Christianity against atheism is hitting the bookstore shelves. The core message to Christians often amounts to "Just keep the faith, and be assured your faith is not unreasonable." Instead of trying to explain theological justifications for dogmas to lay Christians, these books defensively react to atheism's criticisms. Does an atheist say that Christians commit too much violence? Well, most evil-doers couldn't have been real Christians anyway, and as for the rest, the Bible nowhere says that people are perfect. Does an atheist say that Jesus didn't rise from the dead? Well, Gospel testimony might not rise to the courtroom expectation for crime-scene evidence, but why should everyone adopt such a high scientific standard? Does an atheist say that the universe looks like it only accidentally produced life? Well, science can't rule out a god's intervention in the course of evolution. Does an atheist say that mystical experiences are hallucinations? Well, since so many people have had them, who's to say that they aren't caused by contact with god? Does an atheist complain about too much evil in the world? Well, an all-powerful creator's plan would make it hard for us limited creatures to figure it all out. Does an atheist show that a purely rational argument disproves some particular god? Well, the real god of Christianity actually has somewhat different qualities that are immune from rational criticism.

A third shortcut argument for religion replies to criticisms of religion's practical and intellectual defenses by pointing out that things really aren't so bad. Why abandon the faith when such criticisms miss their mark?

8. The criticism that religion suffers practical failures only targets some regrettable by-products of religion, not the core teachings or benefits of the Christian faith.
9. The criticism that religion is not verified by science only repeats the point that science cannot comprehend the supernatural, so Christian faith is unaffected by science.
10. The criticism that religion cannot be approved by pure reason only rules out some odd gods, not the actual god of Christian faith.
11. Even if each argument for god can't show that god exists, they can be added together to increase the reasonableness of believing in god, so Christian faith can't be unreasonable.
12. Neither practical reason, scientific reason, nor pure reason can rule out Christian faith as completely unreasonable.
    Therefore,

Conclusion. Faith in Christianity is not unreasonable.

This conclusion shouldn't really surprise anyone. A faith too reasonable wouldn't exactly be faith. If a Christian's conception of god is imaginatively flexible enough, it can stay ahead of reason.

What do all three of these shortcut arguments for god have in common? Notice how they all depend on making claims about what can't be known, rather than teaching believers about what religion can know. Theology can do better than that. Only stalemate results from shortcut tactics by either side. There is no theological shortcut to dismissing atheism, just as there is no atheological shortcut to dismissing god. Only a careful examination of all the specific theology–atheology debates can reveal where any advantage may lie. Chapter 2 distinguishes five types of Christian theologies, and subsequent chapters examine the arguments of the god debates.

Five Types of Theologies

This chapter sketches the five major types of Christian theology now involved in the god debates. They are discussed in everyday conversation, popular books about religion, and theological treatises. These five types of theologies have similar counterparts in other theistic religions, and some are developed by non-theistic religions too. They don't capture all of the arguments that have ever been offered for a god, but they are the five major ways of doing Christian theology.

Those who would debate Christianity must note how theological defenses of the supernatural have taken many complex forms throughout the history of Christianity down to the present day. Consistent with this book's focus on the contemporary situation, it updates the medieval categorization of arguments for god. That categorization was arranged while Christianity was dealing with Greek science and philosophy. Since the 1700s, modern theology has creatively struggled with the Enlightenment, the "higher criticism" of scripture, discoveries of modern science, and existentialist and postmodernist theories.

2.1 Categorizing Theologies

Look into philosophy of religion textbooks and you will likely see something like the outdated medieval scheme. The textbooks need to be updated. The traditional ontological, cosmological, teleological, and revelation arguments may still sound familiar even you get their names confused. If god is that being than which nothing greater can be conceived, then this god is great enough to actually exist (an ontological argument). If the natural world must have a beginning, and every beginning must have a prior cause, then something supernatural caused nature's origin (a cosmological argument). If something, such as an organism, is so impressively complicated that only an intelligent designer could be responsible, and we rule out earthly makers, then a god made it (a teleological argument). If an extraordinary experience reveals a god to a person, then this person is justified in believing that god exists (a revelation argument). The medievals had other arguments for god as well, but few have rivaled the influence of these four arguments.

Much has happened since medieval times. These traditional arguments for god have taken diverse new forms, and several new arguments have been added to the theologian's toolbox. They all require fresh reorganization so they can be clearly understood and debated by everyone in a twenty-first-century conversation. The god debates cannot remain tied to misleading technical labels from eight centuries ago. Medieval theology had to deal with Platonic notions of perfect knowledge, Aristotelian conceptions of substance and essence, and Ptolemaic pictures of a cramped universe of concentric circles. The twenty-first-century god debates cannot keep debating only the ancients using just the medievals.

Modern science and philosophy have dramatically changed the targets of theology. The philosophies of Descartes and Kant demand radical revisions to any attempt at an ontological argument. The cosmological argument over a "first cause" has fragmented into issues involving the big bang and quantum mechanics, pondering such things as whether science could endorse a "cause" prior to the start of all space-time-energy. The "teleological argument" has taken several new forms, dealing with science's discoveries in biology ("intelligent design" vs. Darwinian evolution), or in astronomy (does an "anthropic principle" demand an evolving universe that must produce us), or in cosmology (do the basic laws of nature seem artificially "fine-tuned"). Appeals to revelations are hardly the simple affirmations of testimony any more; testimony in biblical scripture can't be treated just like testimonials from believers today, and neither can it be lumped together with the experiences so prized by "born-again" Christians. The successive revolutions of biblical hermeneutics for interpreting scripture, psycho-sociological theories of groupthink and mass hysteria, and cultural anthropology's account of tradition's capacity to shape experience have all dramatically altered conceptions of revelation. New theological arguments, as powerful and persuasive as the traditional arguments, are now dominating the god debates, such as the mind–body problem of explaining consciousness, arguments from morality that suggest a divine source of moral truth, and arguments from reason that suggest a divine guarantee of all truth. Cognitive sciences are investigating why human brains and minds naturally bend towards religious experiences and worldviews. The immense diversity of religious experience and belief is also preoccupying theologians, as global contact and comparison of religions has flourished in this communication age.

Theology need not remain disorganized, even while its arguments mutate and multiply. There is a general pattern to the tasks of Christian theology: explain scripture, rival science, explain creation, secure religious knowledge, explore religious experience. A novel categorization for theological arguments could follow such a pattern. Christian theology began where Christianity began: the life of Jesus and the stories about his deeds and death, preserved in scripture and taught as apologetics. This is a revelational source of Christianity, inspiring what can be labeled as "Theology From The Scripture." Christianity encountered rival worldviews, so its theology expanded to ensure that the natural world and human beings are understood as a divine creations, giving rise to a "Theology From The World." Unlike most of the older religions it encountered, Christianity located its god entirely outside the created world as well, requiring an account of creation by a supernatural god in a "Theology Beyond The World." Theology then had challenges from the modern sciences and philosophies claiming equal or better knowledge than religion. Theologies reserving a special mode of knowledge for the faithful can be gathered under the label of "Theology In The Know," while other theologies preferring religious experience over reason for divine access can be collected together by "Theology Into The Myst."

Here is a simplified outline of the proposed reorganization:

New category	Old categories
Theology From The Scripture	scriptural revelation; apologetics
Theology From The World	teleological arguments from the design of natural things; arguments from morality; experiential revelation; ontological arguments from human concepts of god
Theology Beyond The World	cosmological arguments; teleological arguments from basic laws of nature
Theology In The Know	Reformed epistemology; foundationalism
Theology Into The Myst	scriptural interpretation; relativism; existentialism; mysticism

The five new types of theologies could have technical names; we only need placeholders. The real argumentative work is done by the many theological arguments themselves. For this book's educational aims (and for brief chapter titles), simple and easily recalled labels will do the trick. Let's take a closer look at the five types of theologies and the arguments they encompass.

Christianity, like many religions, is based on sacred scriptures describing the activities of divine beings and their interactions with humanity. "Theology From The Scripture" attempts to reasonably deal with the complexities and problems arising from such a diverse collection of biblical books, so that ordinary people can understand Christianity's basic views. Greek philosophy proved useful for the next task of Christian theology, which was to defend Christianity against objections raised by intellectuals already adhering to one or another philosophical school, or to a rival religion, of that era. Christianity was primarily trying to penetrate into neighboring regions around the Mediterranean where Hellenic modes of thought dominated both secular and religious thought. Many early Christian theologians accordingly defended their dogmas about such matters as a monotheistic creator, Jesus' divinity, and the Second Coming by adapting Greek tools such as the logical argument, a Stoic vision of the cosmos, and Platonic arguments for immortality.

Christianity's encounters with the paradigm sciences of that era meant that much medieval theology offered itself as a supplementary science, a "Theology From The World" for a supportive mode of knowledge regarding divine matters. Science and theology were not regarded as entirely divergent matters for a long time, but the rise of modern experimental science in the seventeenth century began to challenge theology's ability to offer useful knowledge. The fall-back position was always the philosophical/theological synthesis of Aquinas, and his thirteenth-century versions of Aristotle's arguments for a god creator stood fast for many Christians for six centuries. Offering explanations for the existence and design of the universe, humanity, and morality, theology could go where science seemingly could not. At the edge of scientific knowledge, essential questions about the origin of the universe and the meaning of life still required questions which only religion could answer.

After Darwinian evolution and biochemistry began replacing religious accounts of humanity's origins, the Enlightenment compromise still held steady at the start of the twentieth century. Science seeks explanations of everything in the natural world, while religion explains everything else: the origin and design of the whole universe, and the moral duty and final destiny of the human soul. A "Theology Beyond The World" set the terms of the modern naturalism vs. supernaturalism debate and metaphysical dualisms seemed entrenched. However, enthusiastic admirers of science then tore down the Enlightenment wall between science and religion. A new naturalism arose in the twentieth century with a comprehensive aim and appetite not seen since ancient Greek materialism. According to this new naturalism, science should eliminate the soul (and its traits, like free will and consciousness) with naturalistic accounts of human intelligence and moral conduct. As for theological arguments over the universe's origin, modern naturalism raised counter-arguments proposing the eternality of nature and the huge role of chance at cosmic scales. Furthermore, the sciences of archeology, history, linguistics, and textual analysis challenged the Bible's authority over "what really happened."

Theology had to deal with a post-Enlightenment breakdown of carefully constructed compromises. Alarmed by naturalism's scientific rationality, and its power to replace scripture with its own account of reality, fresh theological thinking ensued. Only selected prominent features of modern theology can be discussed in this book (but see Ford and Muers 2005). A new apologetics, here labeled as "Theology In The Know," sought firm religious conviction having its own knowledge foundations. Revelation, whether from reading scripture or receiving grace from god, was dramatically empowered to guarantee irrefutable certainty and foundational status for everything else a Christian needs to know. Depending on revelation was hardly new to Christianity, but reformulating religious knowledge to rival other modern views of knowledge became a top priority. Other theologians abandoned the effort to clearly conceive and know god, instead focusing on experiences of faith in all their diversity. These theological options can be collectively labeled as a "Theology Into The Myst" of mystical experience and mythical inspiration. Again, relying on mystical experience was not a Christian novelty, yet exploring the rich variety of religious experiences available to Christians seemed to these theologians more important to faith's vitality than guaranteeing knowable certainties.

These five main types of Christian theologies – Theology From The Scripture, Theology From The World, Theology Beyond The World, Theology In The Know, and Theology Into The Myst – have distinct aims and arguments. Let's take a closer look at each type for comparison.

2.2 Theology From The Scripture

According to this kind of theology, the Christian religion should be preached and taught in as coherent and reasonable fashion as possible, to maximize its credibility. Christianity is the sort of religion that has traditionally believed in supernatural powers and miraculous interventions into nature. Christians read the Bible for stories recounting the activities of divine beings, such as God, angels, and Jesus. Other religions similarly dependent on scriptural accounts of the divine use their own distinctive theologies from scripture. Many of the skeptical views on Christianity's Theology From The Scripture apply equally to other scripture-based religions (see for example the Koranic criticism in Warraq 2002).

As a religion reliant on traditional narratives in scripture, Christianity first developed a theology of apologetics, attempting to formulate a consistent and reasonable way of explaining what the Bible says and what it does not say. Apologetics should not be confused with fundamentalism. Apologetics is not necessarily simplified by assuming that every passage in the Bible is literally true, since questions always arise, such as seeming contradictions (the gospels disagree on events during Jesus' crucifixion, for example) or opposed commands from the same God (Old Testament moral rules vs. New Testament moral rules). Christian apologetics from its earliest stages wasn't restrained by strict literalism, since the gospels themselves use the inspirational power of imagery, metaphor, and parable. They recount parables by Jesus and call him "the Lamb" and "the King of Kings" to convey their intended meaning. To depict Jesus as the fulfillment of Old Testament prophecy, early Christians did not treat prophecies literally, destroying their value, but rather as symbolic pointers requiring interpretation in light of later events. Early Church theologians went further in this direction, borrowing the Greek notions of drama, allegory, and analogy in order to weave together the New Testament accounts and then to construct an overarching narrative that includes the Old Testament. Another preliminary task of scriptural theology is to get clear about Christian dogmas, before figuring out how to rationally defend them. For example, was Jesus the Son of God, or was he the Son of Man, or both? How can a divine being be a son to a father? And was Jesus partially human too? These sorts of questions kept early Church leaders thinking for centuries, drawing on additional Greek ideas, and requiring councils and schisms and revised creeds (Pelikan 1995). Such vast effort at scriptural theology, this "Theology From The Scripture," was crucial for the spread of Christianity across educated classes around the Mediterranean world, and essential for recruiting and training the Church's own leadership.

Claims about the deeds of Jesus are naturally crucial for Christianity. For example, scriptural theologians claim that the synoptic gospels' accounts of Jesus's death, resurrection, and reappearance to surprised apostles are based on eyewitness reports. But judging from the available texts themselves, and from what else we know about Roman executions and Jewish custom, is it likely that first-hand eyewitness reports are straightforwardly and truthfully reported in these gospels? How can testimony from the Bible be best judged? Scientific history has verified a surprisingly large amount of information about peoples, places, and events mentioned in the Bible. Having little incentive to entirely fabricate such background facts, the Bible's scripturalists set the scene for the religious dramas that held their primary concern. We may expect much of the mundane landscape depicted by the Old and New Testaments to have a reliability proportional to its age, as prehistoric legend passes into recorded history of the times. It is the stories about supernatural and miraculous events which stand out for closer scrutiny.

Theologians can appeal to Christian historians who find the hypothesis that Jesus rose from the dead to be far more probable that some alternative hypotheses, such as the possibilities that there was no burial, that no one knew where he was buried, or that the body was stolen. Indeed, there is no lack of New Testament scholars, populating religion departments of many Catholic and Protestant universities and dozens of denominational colleges and seminaries, who make careers out of publishing "confirmations" of gospel stories. However, there is a major difference between Christian historians and historians of Christianity. Scholars who set aside religious faith and use only proven evidence, strict reasoning, and scientific method are almost uniformly unable to conclude that anything like eyewitness reports about miraculous events could be accurately attested in the gospels. The community of academic historians in history departments, holding themselves to higher methodological standards, has not accepted miracle stories as historical facts for over a century.

Nevertheless, some Christian historians intent on "verifying" apologetic claims continue to engage in what can only be called "pseudo-history." Unlike genuine history, which applies a scholarly methodology that demands reasonable evidence and testing of theories, pseudo-history places excessive confidence in the veracity of special historical claims and exempts them from critical scrutiny. This problem can arise with any historical topic, not just religion. The academic field of history must stay vigilant against the temptation to presume historical "truths" from any era. Embarrassing pseudo-histories about legendary kings and empires, and even about real historical people from Julius Caesar to George Washington, were eventually exposed and corrected by unbiased research.

Early Christian theology couldn't use the tools of scientific history, of course, but they weren't needed back then. Christianity competed well with numerous rival religions flourishing in the late Roman Empire. However, more tests awaited. Several robust worldviews, based on Greek philosophical sciences, had no place for either a jealous monotheistic god or a divine Son delivering salvation. Could Christian theology become as scientific?

2.3 Theology From The World

According to Theology From The World, religion has similarities with science and can share much of scientific method. For this theology, supernatural hypotheses *should* compete with naturalistic hypotheses in rationally explaining the features and events of the natural world. If hypotheses about the supernatural are better able to explain some things going on within nature, belief in the supernatural would be reasonable.

This theological strategy seemed plausible during medieval times. As a "natural theology" it even permitted many scientists of that age to feel like they were helping to revealing god's design of nature. This sort of theology has much tougher competition in our times. Modern science and its naturalistic hypotheses have proven far more successful. Naturalistic explanations have been plausibly established for so many features of nature, from the origins of galaxies, stars, and planets to the evolution of life, intelligence, and human culture. Even if the supernatural is no longer needed to explain the origin of the earth, or the evolution of life, there still are many things that science has not yet fully explained. Science hardly denies or ignores mysteries – indeed, scientists are driven to explore nature by their fascination with mysteries. The trend is undeniable: science will entirely displace natural theology. Gone are the days when theologians could use theology to advance science; only scientific method advances science.

Theology From The World still lingers on the hope that some natural mysteries remain mysteries to science. So long as science remains unable to explain them, supernaturalism can appear to be the only explanation. For example, suppose only supernaturalism can account for the mind, by postulating a non-physical spirit. On this issue, we presently observe a standoff. Supernaturalism isn't a full explanation for consciousness or mind, since it doesn't explain how a non-physical spirit could relate to the brain or interact with the body. Naturalism, for its part, can only hope that scientific progress will someday explain the mind–brain relationship. Science's knowledge of the brain's functioning is impressive, but it can't yet say how the brain generates consciousness and thought. Theology is tempted to claim that science's admission of ignorance shows that naturalism is inadequate and that consciousness must be supernatural. If Theology From The World only amounts to arguing that the absence of a naturalistic explanation automatically grants credibility to supernaturalism, this type of theology may be reaching a dead end. Theology chasing mysteries is resorting to a "god of the gaps" strategy – for every gap in scientific knowledge about nature, insert god.

In addition to the god of the gaps strategy pointing out what science doesn't know, theologians have another strategy, a "god in the surprises" strategy, pointing to new scientific knowledge. Science is good at coming up with surprises, since the scientific method always seeks new evidence. The "god of the surprises" strategy tries to make naturalism appear inconsistent with cutting-edge science, as if religion does a better job of keeping up with science than naturalism. The trick behind this diverting illusion is to first display to the audience a shabby naturalism, crude and outdated, and then to draw attention to some surprising scientific discovery. News from biology: life has self-organizing abilities! Naturalism wasn't expecting that, what with its outdated notion that life was just the aggregate sum of its mechanical chemical reactions. For life to have such amazing powers, something supernatural must be involved somewhere. News from physics: quantum entanglement is spooky! That's a nasty shock for naturalism's premise that every physical particle always has its own intrinsic properties. For particles to have such deep connections, while so widely separated from each other, something supernatural must be at work. Cutting-edge science can be co-opted by this strategy into humbling naturalism and supporting supernaturalism.

Some scientists are helping theology to align science with religion, suggesting that the divine fits nicely with the mysteries of life, consciousness, quantum mechanics, or cosmology. This genre of spiritualism meets metaphysics has been around since Isaac Newton discovered gravity. For example, thin scientific credentials paired with stout paranormal beliefs in psychic phenomena produce books like *The G.O.D. Experiments: How Science Is Discovering God in Everything* (Schwartz and Simon 2006). Books by reputable scientists, such as *The God Theory: Universes, Zero-point Fields, and What's Behind It All* (Haisch 2006), also give the false impression that supernaturalism is helped by current science. Scientists who aren't really trying to defend religion can seemingly endorse religion along with science. Book titles like *The God Effect: Quantum Entanglement, Science's Strangest Phenomenon* (Clegg 2006) and *Reinventing the Sacred: A New View of Science, Reason, and Religion* (Kauffman 2008) comfort many who seek signs that science can support spirituality or supernaturalism. Perhaps publishers rather than authors are composing book titles to pander to the mass market, but it's no accident that theologians are cheered. The "god in the surprises" strategy can make supernaturalism appear to be more reasonable than naturalism precisely where surprising science discovers that nature is stranger than had been supposed. Is naturalism, the worldview of science, so easily refuted by novel scientific discoveries? If naturalism must mean whatever science affirmed fifty years ago, then supernaturalism may look promising by comparison. But that's far from what naturalism really is. Of course, naturalism revises and updates itself right along with science. It's not easy work, but naturalistic scientists and philosophers stay busy updating the naturalistic account of reality to keep pace with science's confirmed discoveries.

Mystery-collecting and surprise-gathering theology isn't anything like traditional natural theology. Perhaps Theology From The World has little to offer any more beyond just religious "pseudo-science." Pseudo-sciences about psychic abilities, ghosts, astrology, and the like covet the prestige of science but ignore the rigors of science. Like other pseudo-sciences, appearing scientific by "investigating" and "explaining" the facts without troubling over sound scientific method, religious pseudo-science can't contribute to human knowledge. Unfortunately, religious pseudo-science will probably be around as long as there remain mysteries and surprises in the natural universe. It's just too tempting for a theologian to argue that any tough mystery or stunning surprise leaves naturalism unable to defend itself. All the same, naturalism's inadequacies can't prove supernaturalism. Supernaturalism would have to prove that some things in the world can never be scientifically explained, and that is an impossible task. Can any theology know where to firmly set the limitations of science to deal with the world? However, the limits of science may not be in the world, but beyond the world.

2.4 Theology Beyond The World

According to Theology Beyond The World, supernatural hypotheses should not try to compete with naturalistic hypotheses for explaining things within the universe. Science can have that natural realm to itself. Even if the supernatural is no longer needed to explain anything within nature, there still remains dark mystery where science's knowledge stops at the very edge of known nature itself. Out beyond nature, theology may have the permanent advantage, since, no matter how far science goes, there will always be more questions and more darkness.

According to this kind of theology, religion is continuous with science, and tries to helpfully supplement science. Why would science need supplementing? Theology Beyond The World argues that supernatural hypotheses are required in order to provide satisfying answers to the ultimate questions about the universe as a whole. Such ultimate cosmic questions include "Why did the universe start to exist, instead of just nothingness?" and "Why does the universe have these laws of nature and not others?" Theology Beyond The World demands that these kinds of questions must be asked, and must be answered. Naturalism cannot really stand on its own. A new working compromise emerged by the 1700s: science is responsible for knowing natural reality, and religion is responsible for knowing spiritual reality. Religious scientists could still appreciate their assigned role of understanding nature as god's creation, tracing out the divine blueprints for the physical architecture.

According to Theology Beyond The World, naturalism's reliance on science now becomes its weakness. Does science have satisfying answers to these ultimate questions about the cosmos? Scientists themselves confess that the current knowledge of nature hasn't penetrated very far into these matters. In fact, theologians suggest, science might never be capable of finding satisfying answers, because of science's own intrinsic limitations. The science of cosmology, which discovered the big bang origin of the universe and studies the universe's subsequent evolution, has now turned its attention to even more ultimate questions. Can cosmology ever deliver on its promise to explain the universe? Science may be very good at explaining how some part of nature is responsible for creating some other part of nature, but science may be incompetent to answer the question of the very existence of nature itself. With regard to the laws of nature, science has proven adept at identifying the basic laws of nature, but how could science ever explain why the universe has just these laws of nature and not some other set of laws?

Unless and until science supplies naturalism with good answers to these ultimate questions, naturalism appears incomplete. Can religion do better? Theology Beyond The World offers its own explanations for these tough questions, involving a supernatural creator. There is no question of religion replacing science – science does its own job well, right up to the edge of nature. Where science can go no farther, out on the edge of knowledge, why shouldn't we turn to other sources of knowledge to supplement science and complete our understanding of reality? Theology still has a job to do, following up on science's knowledge of the universe's big bang origin and the universe's fundamental laws. Where science's hypotheses halt, religion can carry on. The religious hypothesis of a supernatural god, responsible for creating the natural universe and for designing its laws, is an available explanation for the universe. Theology Beyond The World has two primary arguments for god. The "existence of nature" argument, that the universe has a divine creator, and the "fine-tuning" argument, that this god designed the universe's laws, together try to explain what naturalism apparently cannot.

If these two arguments succeed, then Theology Beyond The World would have a huge advantage over naturalism. Accepting an available explanation for an unavoidable question sounds more reasonable than dismissing perfectly reasonable questions and ignoring promising answers. What could prevent supernaturalism from satisfying curiosity when science cannot? However, Theology Beyond The World can't deliver on its promise, because its two arguments have too many problems, fail to support their conclusions, and only arouse more questions and more mystery. Theology Beyond The World only amounts to "pseudo-cosmology." There is simply too little information and too much mystery beyond the world to permit any single hypothesis about creation to decisively prevail over the rest. We don't take seriously other pseudo-cosmological notions that the universe was created by a race of super-aliens, or that the universe is only a software simulation inside some hyper-computer. Such dreamy speculations give "metaphysics" its bad reputation for hopelessly abstract conjectures. Theology doesn't have to float off into such airy metaphysics, even if the lures of curiosity feel irresistible.

By simulating cosmology's efforts to explain mysteries surrounding the universe's origin, a religious pseudo-cosmology only appears to be fulfilling the requirements of rationality. Pseudo-cosmology cannot help any religion defend its theological vision of the supernatural. How many different religions (and how many other metaphysical speculations) could equally well propose their god, or committee of gods, as the best explanation for the universe? There may not even be any need for a supernaturalistic hypothesis. For all we know, out there beyond our universe there might only be more nature, so supernaturalism is not the only option.

If Theology Beyond The World is judged as pseudo-cosmology for failing reasonable standards of explanation, can theology defend supernaturalism in any other ways?

2.5 Theology In The Know

Theology has traditionally been about showing how religious knowledge can meet standards of reason. Theology From The Scripture, Theology From the World, and Theology Beyond The World struggle to meet these standards. But why should theology have to accept Western logic and scientific method for its standards of reason? Maybe there's a different kind of reason, with appropriately distinct rules of rationality, appropriate for religious matters. The advantages of discerning this religious rationality would be enormous, and perhaps could decisively shift the advantage to supernaturalism. If naturalism decides that supernaturalism can't pass its rational test, perhaps that's only because naturalism is applying its own chosen rationality, and has begged the question against theology. Theology would then be free to justify religious knowledge on its own terms.

How can theology figure out what sort of rationality is the best match for supernatural religion? Christian religion by itself is not much help. After all, the tablets of Moses didn't mention any rules of logic. There are plenty of rules about which foods can be eaten, and what deeds you should and shouldn't do to your neighbor, but the Bible is silent about avoiding fallacies or constructing valid arguments. Well, Christian theology has other sources of inspiration. The Greeks invented syllogistic logic and Western epistemology, the study of proper rules for distinguishing the sure knowledge of truth from the hasty belief in error. From its tentative beginnings, Christian theology took logic and epistemology quite seriously. When combined with selected notions adapted from Platonic, Aristotelian, and Stoic philosophical systems, some resulting theological systems (such as that of St Thomas Aquinas) were as powerful as any naturalistic competitor until the Enlightenment. Enlightenment sciences and theories of knowledge raised serious challenges to traditional theology, and theology responded by rethinking its theory of knowledge.

If post-Enlightenment theology could abandon the logical and epistemological framework that had made Christian theology possible in the first place, where could this radical new theology turn next? Theologians didn't suddenly start studying ancient Hindu logic (despite its impressiveness). Instead, Theology In The Know tried some reverse engineering. By discerning precisely which rational principles were obstructing theology and lending skeptical atheism and naturalism support, these suspicious principles could be disconnected, thrown away, and replaced with new ones. Theology In The Know condemns the most troublesome logical and epistemological principles as stained by "naturalism" and proclaims their exact contraries as necessary for Christians. With a new set of principles of knowledge fitting Christian dogmas, theology could have its own religious foundations for certain knowledge of god.

During the twentieth century, Theology In The Know was most powerfully developed by two schools of thought: fundamentalism and presuppositionalism. These movements had some considerable interchange and overlap. Fundamentalism was a mutated form of Theology From The Scripture, which incorporated principles of pseudo-history in order to elevate stories from scripture to the status of reliable fact. Presuppositionalism agrees in large part with fundamentalism, and then adds portions of Theology From The World and Theology Beyond The World, incorporating principles of pseudo-science and pseudo-cosmology in order to make knowledge of god necessary for knowledge of anything else, including reason itself. Neither fundamentalism nor presuppositionalism can be justly categorized as theologies of blind faith as if no justified knowledge is involved. From a standpoint of traditional rationality, of course, Theologies in the Know must appear to abandon justifiable knowledge for sheer dogma. However, the point of Knowledge In The Know is to ensure that the commitments of religious faith consist of secure knowledge for believers.

Contrasted with traditional theology, Theology In The Know is only pseudo-theology. Traditional theology instructs believers and persuades nonbelievers using commonsense rational principles which everyone already accepts as authoritative. Pseudo-theology instead appeals to new principles intelligently designed to only do one thing: conveniently justify the religious dogmas already held by believers. Skeptical criticism can still try to expose this theology's self-contradictions, double standards, or irrationality. However, when the basic rules of reason are at stake, neutral ground for fair criticism is hard to find. Even theology was divided by controversy over this issue of knowledge, and another modern type of theology sought an entirely different way to do theology. Perhaps theology is still making a mistake in pursuing confident religious knowledge about god.

2.6 Theology Into The Myst

According to this type of theology, religion does not have to answer to science or even rationality. Religion just has to be faithful. Contemporary fideism and mysticism are paradigm examples of Theology Into The Myst. For Theology Into The Myst, supernaturalism is not required to explain much, and supernaturalism is immune from all possible counter-evidence and any method of reasoning. Some extreme fideistic examples of Theology Into The Myst proclaim that the best religious faith is precisely a faith in the irrational and absurd. After all, theologies entirely resting on alleged miracles or revelations are not really worried about defying rational explanation. Theology goes "Into The Myst" in more than one sense: into the "myst" of veiled obscurity where god cannot be clearly seen; into the "myst" of mysterious experiences which reveal something of god; and into the "myst" of mythical traditions with inspirational narratives about god.

Fundamentalism, a Theology In The Know, is often confused with fideism, which is a Theology Into The Myst. A fideistic Theology Into The Myst might better be described as "mysterianism" because it so sharply emphasizes our lack of knowledge about god. Fundamentalists tightly cling to their narrow scriptural dogmas and formulaic definitions of their god. Mysterians generously free their god from restrictive categories so that god lacks any specific conceptual form. Fundamentalists know a lot about their god; mysterians claims that god is fairly unknowable. Fundamentalists prefer specific creeds, while mysterians prefer a vague god. Fundamentalists are impressed by the way that personal conviction in a detailed proposition can seem just like knowing an objective truth, so that one's certainty that some biblical passages are literally true can withstand any contradictory information. Mysterians are impressed by the way that personal certainty that some sort of god exists can seem just like believing in any objective reality, so that one's belief in god can stand right alongside the existence of anything and everything else. Fundamentalism elevates religious dogmas to a level higher than any other knowledge, while mysterianism elevates a vague god above the existence of everything else. It is easy to recognize a fundamentalist appeal to the Bible, but mysterianism has no definite creed. Some mysterian views of god are so abstract that only a philosopher or theologian could admire them, while others easily appeal to the average person. "My god is the formless ground of all being in and for itself." "My god is pure love." "My god is this big reassuring presence with me all the time." Fundamentalists aren't at much liberty to form their own conceptions of god, while mysterians have the freedom to conceive of god about any way they like.

At its best, Theology Into The Myst is a liberal and liberating exploration of the breadth and depth of human experience. At its worst, akin to Theology In The Know, it amounts to defensive reaction protecting the community of believers from the distraction, doubt, and disappointment of rational criticism. Risks abound for both types of theology. Theology Into The Myst, like Theology In The Know, tends to schismatically shatter the body of lay people into opposed camps who select different views of god, and it sometimes segregates religious intellectuals into esoteric cliques that can't communicate with each other anymore. Fundamentalists dislike nothing more than another group of fundamentalists who contradict them on a crucial creed, but at least they all can see what the disagreement is about. Mysterians can barely follow the academic notions of one favored theologian of the day, but they can arrogantly dismiss the speculations of another theologian who dares to speak of god in different but similarly vague terms. The camps of theoretical mysterians can seem more like esoteric cults. Ordinary believers only feel more lost when a third theologian must be summoned to explain the precise difference between "god is the formless ground of all being in and for itself" and "god is the mystery of the self-evident that is wholly present."

Although Theology Into The Myst may have the most resources for appreciating profound experiences of faith, distilling any clear description of god for the formulation of religious belief is not easy. Theology Into The Myst is a serious defense of faith, but it may not be able to specific the object of believers' faith. What sort of faith in god can't really say much about god? Are we still talking about faith, the sort of doctrinal faith that traditional theology sanctioned, or just an inarticulate pseudo-faith? In any case, skepticism towards Theology Into The Myst is quite unlike skepticism towards the other types of theology, since arguing with inarticulate faith is impractical. Furthermore, the stances of fundamentalism, mysterianism, and skeptical atheism gradually converge on one point of agreement about religious belief. When fundamentalism and mysterianism both declare that belief in god is ultimately based on a commitment of faith, skeptical atheism can only affirm its complete agreement. That was skeptical atheism's point all along: that people's religious beliefs are not based on any objectively sound reasoning, but only personally willful faith. Skeptical atheism is still having a hard time getting even that simple point of agreement across, though. To hear believers impressed by mystery and fideism, argumentative atheists are foolish for still debating god, since no respectably sophisticated person still supposes that god would bother with so mundane a matter as actually existing (see Eagleton 2009).

Confronted by five types of theology, an atheist in the god debates has to master many critical tactics. The general strategy leading to an atheist victory would be to first refute the claims of Theology From The Scripture, and then to expose Theology From The World as unwarranted pseudo-science. Next, the atheist must oppose the pseudo-cosmology of Theology Beyond The World with the best naturalistic cosmology available. Against Theology In The Know, the atheist can muster basic logic and common sense against its pseudo-theology. Finally, Theology Into The Myst's stance on god's unknowability could help to make skeptical atheism's case against god's existence. If Christian theology can be driven into the arms of fideistic mysterianism, atheology fulfils its rationalistic mission. However, atheology is also incompetent to deal directly with religious experience and religious faith on its own terms. Atheology's reasonings only counter-acts reasoned theology, since that is all it is designed to do.

At this point, the possibility of productive debate over religion might appear to fade out entirely. We should not jump to that hasty conclusion. Some important common ground between faith, mystery, and skepticism can be marked out. Furthermore, the entire relationship between faith and reason, in the aftermath of traditional theology's decline, now demands a reevaluation. The god debates are only mutating into new interesting forms, as the final chapter reveals.

3 Theology From The Scripture

Many religions have primary foundations in scriptural accounts of historical events involving deities. A theology explaining and defending scripture, a Theology From The Scripture, can be essential for a religion's expansion. As the field of history gradually separated away from the repetitive preservation of stories and traditions, the possibility that intelligent scrutiny of religion's historical claims became possible. The religions of Judaism, Christianity, and Islam have been especially affected by the emergence of an independent understanding of history. No longer could history automatically be whatever scripture or theology said it was.

History wasn't always a science, since it only recently has been able to meet minimum requirements for a science. History for a long time was only the records of human stories, in memorized form as tales, odes, or oral histories, or in written forms like letters or books. Much history aimed at telling the truth, or at least as much truth as could be accurately retained, even if such truth amounted to little more than one person's perspective or one society's prejudices. What kept history from becoming a science for so long was not its dependence on human perspective or its distortion by social ideology. After all, a biologist's microscope observations are a kind of human perspective, and an economist's consumption statistics are made using capitalist assumptions. Perspective and prejudgment can only be

The God Debates John R. Shook

managed, never eliminated; good science intelligently controls our all-too-human efforts at reaching truth, to increase our chances of partially succeeding. History can aim at this high standard of intellectual effort.

3.1 Scientific History

Like the other sciences, history attempts to determine the truth about hidden matters not apparent to current human view. What hides historical truths from us is not spatial distances – astronomy deals with things very far away. Historical truths are not hidden from us because of scale dimensions – physics deals with very small things, while cosmology deals with the very large. Of course, it is time that hides historical truths from us, since we cannot directly perceive the past. We can indirectly observe and speculate about the past, though, because of personal memory, object permanence, and event causality. People can recall past events that they have witnessed, many things from the past survive to the present, and even those things that perish first leave causal traces down to the present.

We need a familiar example to illustrate this. Police detectives are scientific historians, in a way, since their basic task is to help learn what happened (a crime, for example) in the past. Detectives at the crime scene start from the three basic kinds of evidence: witnesses who can report what they saw or heard (like seeing a violent confrontation or hearing a gun shot), physical objects which were present at the crime scene and are still in existence (perhaps an opened money safe, or a fingerprint), and the rest of the lingering effects or "clues" caused by events at the crime scene (such as a getaway car washing up days later down the river, or a photograph of the victim discovered on a suspect's cellphone).

For events that happened too long ago for any living person to remember, historians are left with lasting objects and causal traces. Before dying, a witness may "record" his memories in other people (well, in their nervous systems), and they in turn can repeat the memories to others, down to the present. Technically such memorized records fall into the category of causal traces, along with the recordings of people's memories in letters or books. For convenience, we can label all such personally-inspired causal traces as "stories." For events in the distant past, the trail of oral repetition grows cold and lasts down to the present only if memories are eventually recorded in some physical medium more permanent than human nervous systems, such as a painting or a book. The historian of the distant past who wants to know the truth about some event really therefore has only two kinds of evidence: physical remains dating from that event, and causal traces from that event.

Stories are a special kind of causal trace that must be treated with special precaution. Stories told sincerely and authoritatively can affect readers positively, arousing a higher level of credibility than they perhaps deserve. We know from both common sense and careful examination that stories are always a little less than the whole truth, and frequently at variance with nothing but the truth. Stories can both intentionally and unintentionally deceive. The scientific historian (and the police detective) follows these common-sense principles:

- H1 A single eyewitness's testimony is only somewhat reliable evidence, even under ideal conditions.
- H2 Only if many eyewitnesses agree on pretty much the same facts can their testimony become reliable evidence.
- H3 If a story has been told and retold by several people over long periods of time before getting recorded in writing by an author, errors and distortions tend to increase dramatically as time passes.
- H4 If the author of an oft-told story has both good opportunity and strong motivation to change the story, his writing cannot be trusted as evidence.
- H5 If an author is not recording another's testimony but only attesting his own belief in that testimony's truth, this is not another instance of additional testimony, but merely a testimonial, which is irrelevant to the truth.

The other sorts of causal traces that can count as good evidence similarly get distorted and disappear with the passage of time. The smoke and powder from a gunshot may last months; the getaway car will last many years before disintegrating; but the passage of a century suffices to complete erode away almost all causal traces of an event save for those of large magnitude such as a devastating fire or terrible flood. As for physical evidence directly present at an event, that too erodes and disintegrates all too quickly. For events in the distant past, it requires archeological investigation to uncover the physical remains. Historians must be cautious when trying to verify a theory about a past event. Some further basic rules of common sense apply to history:

- H6 Only causal traces that almost certainly must have originated in an event count as good evidence for that event happening.

- H7 If there are one or more plausible alternative origins for a causal trace allegedly from an event, it cannot count as good evidence for that event happening.
- H8 If one or more people have good opportunity and strong motivation to artificially create a causal trace allegedly from an event, it cannot count as good evidence for that event happening.
- H9 Only physical objects that almost certainly must have been present at an event count as good evidence for that event.
- H10 If there are one or more plausible alternative origins for a physical object allegedly from an event, it cannot count as good evidence for that event happening.
- H11 If one or more people have good opportunity and strong motivation to artificially create a physical object allegedly from an event, it cannot count as good evidence for that event happening.

Additionally, in order to establish that an event did not in fact happen, a historian can appeal to a special category of causal trace: the "negative" trace of nonexisting evidence. If a certain causal effect must have been created by an event, but that effect does not exist, then that event probably did not happen. For example, a postulated event such as a murder by pistol fire can be conclusively ruled out if no trace of a bullet wound can be found anywhere on the dead victim's body. Something else must have killed the victim, and so other clues must be sought. For events in the distant past, such reasoning by "negative" evidence quickly becomes highly probabilistic, since it becomes difficult to verify the nonexistence of some expected causal trace. For example, the Holy Grail from which Jesus is said to have drunk wine at the Last Supper cannot now be identified to exist, but from this fact it cannot be inferred that the Last Supper never really happened. There are plenty of reasonable commonsense explanations for our inability to find the Holy Grail after so much time has passed. When it comes to negative evidence, the science of history must follow this principle:

- H12 A piece of nonexisting evidence counts against an event only if there is no plausible explanation why that evidence should now be impossible to locate.

With these twelve simple rules of scientific history in place, it is possible to rebut the common arguments given by Christian apologetics that claim that divine beings have existed and supernatural miracles have taken place.

3.2 Scientific History and Scripture

It must be emphasized from the outset that none of the rules of scientific history expressly deny that divine beings could exist or that miracles could occur. Scientific history is not scientific in the exaggerated sense that a complete naturalistic worldview must be assumed as correct. None of H1–H12 require or assume that only natural causes may be postulated, or that natural laws govern all events, or any such similarly naturalistic principles. Furthermore, while science has a deserved reputation for establishing knowledge, sometimes scientific inquiry decides that something cannot yet be known, because available evidence is inconclusive. Scientific history is quite capable of concluding that we can't know whether an event happened. We have seen too many detective dramas that reveal the real culprit; real trials often end by exonerating the suspect without ever discovering the criminal. Similarly, scientific history frequently concludes that one version of an event probably didn't happen, without proving that some other event happened instead. That's why scientific history does not have to first prove one account about the past in order to establish that some other account is unlikely. Deciding that there is not enough evidence for some event does not require first proving that some other event happened instead. Indeed, prejudicing an investigation into one event by assuming that some other event must have happened instead is unscientific. It is the assumption that God must exist which is unscientific, not the withholding of faith.

H1–H12 are quite suitable for historical investigations into religious claims about past events involving a god. They are equally applicable to any religion where that religion makes claims about historical matters and can be applied to any sources of such history from tradition, legend, mythology, or scripture, although they are most applicable to the sorts of concrete detailed accounts that scripture can provide. Scientific history is scrupulously neutral. It is utterly indifferent to whether a religion's sacred scripture is inspirational or imperious, easy or hard to understand, delightfully aesthetic or ploddingly pedantic. We now apply scientific history to Christian scripture, but the methodological lessons and skeptical results would equally apply to any religion's claims about historical activities of a god.

To repeat, scientific history approaches Christianity with a neutral attitude without begging the question for or against the existence of god. H1–H12 are entirely silent about whether Jesus was divine or not, or whether miracles around him did occur. If H1–H12 lead us towards skepticism about the Bible's Jesus stories, it is because we lack enough evidence to ever be confident about what a historical Jesus actually did say or do. H1–H12 do assume that all of the testimony about Jesus originates from people, with the same sorts of human bodies and human fallibilities that we all share, and that no additional miracles since Jesus' day are required for gathering adequate evidence for Christianity's claims. Again, scientific history approaches the whole question of Jesus from an entirely neutral standpoint, prepared to logically examine all potential evidence. Begging the question either way would make both scientific history *and* scriptural apologetics pointless from the start. Scriptural apologetics, if it really would attempt to reasonably persuade and convert nonbelievers, must not presume supernaturalism either. Both sides must show restraint. Scientific history will neither assume naturalism nor assume supernaturalism. Similarly, while appealing to the Bible, scriptural apologetics cannot require extra assumptions from the outset to the effect that Jesus really had divine powers, or that some of Jesus' followers had supernatural powers too, or that extra miracles were required to create the gospels or the early church. Theologies that do demand faith prior to talking about scriptural evidence abandon traditional apologetics and proceed directly to Theology In The Know or Theology Into The Myst.

The New Testament is a fascinating collection of Jesus stories. Scholars have produced detailed historical analyses of these stories (Wells 2009). Here we will only deal with that portion of Christian apologetics that deals directly with New Testament passages about Jesus' life and miracles involving him. Some Christians believe that there have been additional revelations, mystical contacts, and miracles since Jesus' time. Since such beliefs persist only because Christians first and foremost believe in Jesus' divinity, we will focus our attention there. Skepticism towards Jesus' divinity, or skepticism whether Jesus ever really existed at all, is sufficient for skepticism towards the God of the New Testament. After all, Jesus is the central figure of the New Testament, and there is surprisingly little information provided about God outside of God's relationship with Jesus. If Jesus was just a man, or if Jesus is just a fable constructed from pieces of other religions, then the New Testament must be entirely unreliable about God as well. Many historians have constructed a fascinating case that the Jesus of the New Testament never even existed. That there existed a Jewish man claiming better knowledge of God's wishes than Jewish leadership, who died (permanently) for preaching that message, may yet be the more probable explanation for Christianity's origins. In any case, what matters most about Christianity as a supernaturalistic religion is whether Jesus really was divine as Christianity claims.

Indeed, we may focus our attention even more narrowly, to the capacity of New Testament testimony to confirm just three matters: Jesus' ability to perform miracles, Jesus' resurrection, and Jesus' bodily appearances to people soon after his death. The evidence for these three matters is very narrow, since no causal traces of these events are detectible today, no physical objects from these events are now available to us, and there are no non-Christian testimonies of the veracity of these miracles. There are non-Christian histories and texts mentioning Christianity that report upon what Christians affirm, but of course these do not count as evidence for the miracles themselves. Furthermore, there is a wide variety of facts about mortal people, historical places, and widely known events reported in the New Testament which can be more or less confirmed by non-Christian sources and archeological discoveries, but this has no bearing on Jesus' divinity. The ability of the New Testament to frequently and accurately describe features of the Palestine world in Jesus' day is not surprising and certainly not miraculous, since early Christians would have been familiar with these mundane matters. A gospel author's ordinary ability to correctly spell the name of an obscure town is irrelevant to whether that author is correct about an astonishing miracle. Additionally, no later religious experiences of visions or voices of Jesus are relevant to the question of these miracles, since they would have to be divinely caused, and whether they could be divinely caused is a question for Theology From The World, not scriptural apologetics.

Christian scholars are mostly agreed on all these points, and so secular historians are content to concur as well. It all comes down to biblical passages directly concerning Jesus' divinity; specifically, his ability to perform miracles, his resurrection, and his bodily appearances to people soon after his death. It would nice to precisely know how Pontius Pilate was involved in Jesus' death, where Jesus' cross is, where Jesus' tomb is, or whether the Shroud of Turin could really be Jesus' shroud. Serious Christian scholars and theologians no longer rest their case on any of these things, for two simple reasons. First, those alleged stories, physical objects or causal traces cannot pass the test of rules H6–H11. Second, neither a Roman official nor a tomb nor a cross nor a shroud can support the notion that anything supernatural ever really happened involving Jesus. If Jesus had been just a man condemned to die on a cross, there could still have been an executioner, a tomb, a cross, and a shroud. In fact, the resurrection is not sufficient to prove Jesus' divinity, since God is credited with performing that miracle, so only God's divinity is needed to explain the resurrection, not Jesus' divinity. What is ultimately required for scriptural theology is good evidence that a god once walked the earth and that he performed miracles. Christians are not wrong for supposing that surviving scripture is the firmest physical evidence available for these matters.

An immediate difficulty confronting scriptural apologetics is that original New Testament texts do not exist now. Only shards and segments of some books are older than the third century. The oldest complete New Testament still in existence dates from the mid-fourth century (the Codex Sinaiticus manuscript) and the annotations and corrections of scribes are evident. Naturally, Christians would want to believe that this New Testament is an identical duplicate of the originals from three centuries earlier. That hope violates the rules of H1–H12. Furthermore, other old Bibles dating from the fifth and sixth centuries read a little differently in many places, and it is impossible to accurately decide which variations correctly duplicate the lost originals. When the difficulties of translating the original Greek into Latin or English are added to the situation, it is impossible to avoid the judgment that human transcription and interpretation pervades the Bibles that Christians read today. If a Christian declares confidence that the scriptural Word of God is literally and absolutely true, the immediate response should be: which Bible? A Bible that no one can read? One of the early manuscripts? (Which one?). Which later edition and translation?

Even if we set aside the fact that available Bibles are thoroughly dependent on centuries of human involvement, where is relevant testimony about miracles surrounding Jesus in the New Testament? We may at once set aside the letters attributed to Paul, despite their vehement tone of conviction. Although the earliest of Paul's letters date from around 50 CE, earlier than any other book of the New Testament, they contain no reliable evidence for miracles surrounding Jesus. Paul never claims to be personally acquainted with Jesus; he apparently was not in Jerusalem during those climactic times, only arriving in Jerusalem later to persecute the followers of Jesus. He does claim that he was originally Jewish and that he knew much about Christianity since he helped to persecute Christians for their beliefs. His conversion experience, a few years after Jesus' death, consisted of a bright light and the voice of Jesus. This may be a miraculous event, of the sort considered by Theology From The World. However, since Paul's vision was not about Jesus' miracles, his death, or his bodily resurrection, only his reports about others' beliefs on these matters are possibly relevant.

Paul says that he did not go to Jerusalem until three years after his conversion (Galatians 1:18) but Luke reports Paul's story that he immediately returned to Jerusalem to pray in the temple after recovering in Damascus, but quickly fled Jerusalem when another message from Jesus told him to preach to the Gentiles (Acts 21:17–21). In any case, Paul eventually made his way back to Jerusalem for meetings with the Jewish Christians, and presumably heard many first-hand accounts from followers and others who knew Jesus. Despite this presumed excellent access to living witnesses, he has no original specifics to offer in any of his letters. Paul's versions of the resurrection and bodily reappearances are second-hand and quite vague. He repeats stories in other gospels, and doesn't present his versions as anything like fresh evidence. He stresses his ability to faithfully repeat what the early Christians around Jerusalem have been saying for years, perhaps in order to enhance his own credibility and stature. Similarly, none of the other New Testament letters, all recorded after 50 CE, provide direct testimonial evidence, but only repeat what early Christian churches had been claiming for many years. We must therefore look to just the first five books of the New Testament.

Scholars have largely settled on the view that the Gospel of Mark is the oldest gospel, composed around 70, two generations after Jesus' death. If Mark did compose the gospel bearing his name, Mark may have been a later Christian follower of Peter, and he was certainly too young to recall Jesus personally. Indeed, Mark never claims to have witnessed any miracles involving Jesus. By legend Mark is supposed to be repeating Peter's direct testimony, making his gospel veridical on all crucial points, but Mark's own gospel makes this legend dubious. Peter and the other disciples are portrayed as continually misunderstanding Jesus and Jesus' purpose; neither Peter nor any of the disciples witness Jesus' death because they abandon him; Peter is particularly ashamed by his repeated denial of Jesus (a story also told in Matthew and Luke); Peter does not see the empty tomb (Luke's gospel says that he does); Jesus does not appear to Peter or the disciples after his death (the second ending to Mark 16:9–20, had a much later origin and Luke's gospel also has to add a story about Jesus appearing to Peter at 24:34); and finally, Jesus' elevation of Peter to head his church occurs in Matthew, not Mark. A disciple of Peter would be expected to treat Peter better, but, even more importantly, he should have some solid information on Jesus. Despite having a supposedly unimpeachable source in Peter, Mark's gospel is nearly useless concerning Jesus' birth, death, resurrection, and reappearance.

The Gospel of Matthew offers no direct testimony either. It repeats many of Mark's passages about Jesus nearly verbatim, adds key passages which also end up in the Gospel of Luke, and offers no strikingly original testimonies either. This should not be surprising, since the author of the Gospel of Matthew was not in fact the apostle Matthew. Scholars have mostly arrived at the conclusion that the author was no personal witness to Jesus either, but lived much later and assembled his composition around 90 to 100, or even later. Luke, who may have authored both the Gospel of Luke and Acts of the Apostles, could not and did not claim to be a personal eyewitness, just like Mark and Matthew. Luke was a follower of Paul, and he may have had a good opportunity to collect stories about Jesus as he traveled with Paul for many years. Christian scholars typically argue that Luke and Acts were composed around the same time as Matthew, but recent critical scholarship places its composition into the early second century.

Turning to the Gospel of John, it contains a handful of verses that seem to imply that the author personally knew Jesus. Nevertheless, modern scholars cannot agree with church tradition that whoever authored the Gospel of John was a witness to those times (in any case, Acts 4:13 says that the disciple John was illiterate). The Gospel of John, like that of Luke, dates from the early second century, perhaps as late as 120. The Gospel of John is the most philosophical and theological of the four gospels, recounting only a few miracles performed by Jesus (usually by copying earlier gospels), only a couple of sermons, and no parables at all. Its author was evidently learned in Greek philosophy and rival religions, and far more concerned with advancing the theological agenda of the emerging unified church in the early second century than accurately reporting testimony from the uneducated and poor people closest to Jesus. In any case, nowhere does the author of the Gospel of John assert that he personally witnessed miracles surrounding Jesus.

To summarize so far, none of the gospels or letters can provide first-hand testimony about Jesus. Their second-, third-, and fourth-generation "testimony" was collected and preserved from a wide variety of oral traditions from many Christian communities only after many years have passed. This explains why there are many important contradictions in the testimony about Jesus throughout the New Testament, which further weakens its claim to provide serious evidence. From the tone and content of these writings we can easily see how their authors were strongly motivated to support (1) their own credibility, firm faith, and spiritual authority, and (2) their own versions of what Jesus did, what Jesus commanded, and how

Christians should behave. Principles H1–H5 of scientific history indicate how the Gospels probably cannot provide much first-hand testimony for Jesus' ability to perform miracles, Jesus' resurrection, or Jesus' bodily appearances to people soon after his death.

Perhaps the collective testimony, taken together as a whole from the Gospels, could rise to a level of credibility. Where they agree, their reliability can increase; of course, where they disagree, their reliability must be questioned. The four gospels, Acts, and the letters display many divergences and disagreements about such central matters as how Jesus died, how he was seen after his death, and what his teachings were. Minor disagreements and factual errors may be attributed to ordinary causes such as the different perspectives of the authors, and the distances, in both time and space, between the authors and their subject. Major disagreements, such as whether Jesus' ministry lasted for one year (synoptic gospels) or three years (John), or who first sees the empty tomb and who first sees Jesus, illustrate how a gospel can stray from older traditions or simply fabricate stories when the narrator is working with a fragmentary or confusing narrative.

These differences are about what should be expected from writings dating from 50 to 150 which try to gather together and make sense out of several generations of oral traditions from relatively isolated communities scattered around the late Roman world. Some of these communities spoke Aramaic (Jesus' own tongue), others spoke Hebrew, most used the Greek tongue common throughout the eastern Mediterranean world, and a few used the Latin of Rome. These Christian communities of the first and second centuries had deep and long-lasting disagreements about such fundamental issues as whether Jesus had risen from the dead three days after the crucifixion to announce a new kingdom or was still awaiting a triumphant return to claim his throne; whether Jesus was fully human, partly human and partly divine, or entirely divine without definite human form; whether Jesus commanded obedience to the Jewish Law or whether Jesus urged abandoning Judaism entirely; whether Jesus intended to only reinvigorate Judaism or to establish a new religion for the whole world; and whether Christian communities should be free to maintain their own traditions and dogmas or whether all Christian communities must obey orthodoxy decided in bishop councils or by the Bishop of Rome. Over time, the top priority of a Christian community was no longer accurately recalling its own version of what precisely Jesus said or did. Priority instead went to defending that community's views on fundamental issues, and oral and written traditions were modified to suit that new priority.

The fact that so much of one gospel gets repeated nearly verbatim in the other gospels is sometimes used by Bible novices to argue that these gospels must be successfully reporting the same veridical facts. However, near-verbatim repetition actually means that there is no independent testimonial verification occurring at all. The three synoptic gospels are not providing accounts having similar perspectives on the same events, expressed in their own unique way, as would be expected from independent testimony. These gospels frequently recount the same stories, in identical ordering, and using exactly the same words. Since the sixth century, church historians and theologians have all recognized this repetition, and have produced many explanations for how the authors of Mark, Matthew, and Luke would have had both motive and opportunity to borrow from each other and from other possible sources of sayings (that did not survive in writing) allegedly from Jesus. Setting aside this theological problem, only a handful of prominent examples of New Testament disagreements about Jesus need be examined here, to illustrate how there never was consistent Christian testimony or an early unified Christian church.

Let's start with Mark, supposedly the earliest and hence most reliable account, and consider just the essential questions of who was Jesus and what he did. Mark offers nothing about Jesus' origins. Luke briefly asserts that Jesus was from the House of David, and Matthew begins with an exhaustive genealogy of Jesus back to David and then describes Jesus' miraculous birth. The Gospel of John, characteristically, ignores mere human genealogy and launches with a theological account of Jesus as the Divine Logos, the Word, co-eternal with God. The miracle stories in the gospels have little to do with each other; only where one gospel copies a story from another is there any agreement, and only one specific miracle by Jesus appears in all four gospels (Jesus feeds 5000 people in Matthew 14:15–21, Mark 6:35–40, Luke 9:10–17, John 6:1–14).

According to Mark, Jesus was not born a god, never became a god, and he repeatedly makes it abundantly clear that he did not want to become known as a god. There are two instances in Mark where Jesus seems to admit his divinity, but they are ambiguous. Peter calls Jesus the Messiah, but Jesus immediately tells Peter and the apostles to speak no more of the matter. Then Jesus seems to admit that he is Son of God to the high priest at Mark 14:62, but some early manuscripts of Mark only have Jesus reply with his enigmatic "so you say" phrase (like Matthew 26:64). Jesus' overriding concern for secrecy about any divinity notions is diminished in Matthew, almost disappears in Luke, and is positively reversed in John, where Jesus delights in pıoclaiming his divinity. Mark's Jesus performs miracles by invoking God's power and does not proclaim himself a perfect god. Indeed, Jesus seeks John's baptism for the forgiveness of sins (Mark 1:4), says that no one is good except God alone (Mark 10:18, echoed still in Matthew 19:17), and prefers to be called the Son of Man rather than the Son of God. Nowhere in Mark does Jesus say that he is the Son of the Father and the phrase "Son of God" doesn't even appear in the earliest manuscript of Mark. Demonic spirits don't care about Jesus' preferences, at Mark 3:11–12, and 5:7–8, but such evil spirits can't be reliable sources. The mission of Mark's Jesus is to proclaim the kingdom of God to all nations, to call for repentance, to question strict Jewish Law and custom, and to inaugurate a radically egalitarian and simple life. Jesus consistently calls for people to righteously obey God to receive salvation in fear of God's wrath; Jesus doesn't expect the multitudes to understand his parables (Mark 3:10–12).

Turning to the mission of Jesus' life and death, there is no developed atonement doctrine in Mark. Only once does Mark say that Jesus' life is a ransom (Mark 10:45) and the covenant made at the Last Supper only says the Jesus' blood will be shed for many (Mark 14:24). Jesus is supposed to die and soon rise again, but there is no promise of immortality or forgiveness of sins for believers in Jesus. Jesus does predict the coming Kingdom of God, which everyone alive now will live to see but not even Jesus can know when (Mark 13:30–32). Mark's gospel offers no reason for Jesus' death beyond the animosity of the Jewish and Roman authorities towards a blasphemous and dangerous threat to their status.

Matthew relies so heavily on Mark that about 94 percent of Mark gets repeated in Matthew. The verses which supplement Mark and contradict Mark are therefore quite noticeable and significant. Matthew's Jesus repeatedly urges repentance and obedience to God, as does Mark's Jesus, but then Matthew's Jesus surprisingly counters Mark's Jesus by pointedly affirming Jewish Law and custom with few exceptions. Matthew's Jesus is most clearly quite Jewish, wanting his followers to obey the Jewish Torah, interpreting Mosiac Law as carefully as the Pharisees, and concerning himself only with reforming Judaism. Jesus declares that they shall preach only to "the lost sheep of the house of Israel" and not to pagans (10:5–7, 15:24). Only after Jesus is raised, does he show up briefly to tell the disciples to preach to all nations what he has taught them (but this is likely a later addition to Matthew). Matthew's doctrine of atonement is only a little more advanced that Mark's. Matthew's Jesus promises eternal life with God to those who obey the basic Jewish commandments. Jesus' covenant made at the Last Supper repeats Mark's phrase "which will be shed for many" and then Matthew adds "for the forgiveness of sins" (26:28). Like Mark, Matthew does not directly connect faith in Jesus' divinity with salvation through Jesus' sacrifice. For both Mark and Matthew, salvation is earned by those who repent to God and obey Jesus' version of God's commandments. Mark and Matthew portray Jesus as the harbinger of God's impending judgment, requiring fast repentance. Jesus proclaims that "The kingdom of God is at hand" (Mark 1:15) and he calls out, "Repent, for the kingdom of heaven is at hand" (Matthew 4:17). Mark's Jesus emphasizes the looming Kingdom of God and there is no plan for an organized church, while Matthew predicts a second coming relatively soon, although Jesus has to leave orders for how a Christian church should operate (Matthew 18:1–35).

Coming to Luke, the most notorious feature of his writings is compromise. Almost two-thirds of the gospel of Luke repeats passages already in Mark or Matthew. Luke also tells us that he has relied on other writings about Jesus (1:1–4) that are now lost to us. Luke's careful selections from his sources are quite revealing. Luke's Jesus urges repentance and promises eternal rewards by God to the obedient. However, Luke's novel addition is the way that Jesus' injunction to faithfully believe that he is the Son of God and to recognize him as Lord becomes more central. The message that only moral righteousness will bring salvation, so essential to Mark and Matthew, is moved to the background. Luke's Jesus repeatedly says to both Jews and Gentiles that one's faith in Jesus brings salvation (3:6, 7:50, 8:48, 8:50, 17:19, 19:9). The sharp controversy between Mark and Matthew over whether Christians must keep the Jewish Torah and whether they should preach to the Gentiles is entirely swept away in Luke. Jewish Law is not irrelevant, but it has become a positive danger in the hands of overzealous Jewish priests. By surmounting the older controversies, Luke has a far grander and more inclusive plot in mind. Luke's Jesus is a scripted episode in God's plan for the salvation of all mankind. For Luke, the second coming may not come for a long time and no one can know when it will happen (Jesus has to explain this in parables at 12:40 and 19:11). The urgency to repent in the face of impending divine judgment has been replaced in Luke by the urgency to submit to the Church which rules during this intervening period between Jesus' death and his second coming.

Luke continues his account of the meaning of Jesus' life and death in Acts. Acts makes one great departure from the gospels: the apostles don't hear from the resurrected Jesus the command to preach to non-Jews. Instead, only after Paul has begun his own independent mission, Peter receives new revelation that they should preach to the Gentiles (Acts 10 and 11), contradicting Mark, Matthew, and even the Gospel of Luke (Luke 24:47). Acts is focused on resolving the disagreements between Peter and Paul in decisive favor of Paul, and then reunifying the early church. The necessity of receiving Jesus' grace through faith for salvation (Acts 15:11) and the injunction to Gentiles that they can be Christians if they merely obey four basic Jewish rules (Acts 15:13–29) is made decisively explicit and authoritative for all Christians, both Jewish and Gentile.

The Gospel of John sweeps away most of the doctrinal issues clouding the synoptic gospels. Jesus is a divine being, co-eternal with God, who briefly took human form. John expressly states that a person's faithful belief that Jesus is God's Son is essential to salvation (John 3:16–18, 3:38, etc.). Paul's letters similarly elevate faith in Jesus over righteous obedience to any law. Only in Luke, Acts, John, and some letters does the atonement doctrine emerge that Jesus died for humanity's sins so that humanity might have salvation. Among these books, Paul goes the farthest to explain that faith in Jesus is entirely sufficient to deserve partaking in Jesus' sacrifice, and John goes to great theological lengths to justify this creed. The nature of Jesus' sacrifice is yet another cause for disagreement among the New Testament books. Mark and Matthew are concerned to represent Jesus as a worthy Jewish heir to Moses, David, the prophets, and their prophecies. The idea that Jesus is inhumanly pure and divinely innocent, a worthy sacrifice sufficient to atone for most or all of humanity, only gradually emerges in Luke and Acts, and receives fullest development in John's and Paul's letters.

Consistent with this emergence of atonement in the later writings is the curious way that Jesus' form becomes less and less human. Mark and Matthew present a most human Jesus, complete with ordinary emotions and physical limitations to complement his extraordinary abilities. Luke says that Jesus passes through a crowd unseen (4:28–30) and that after the resurrection two men don't recognize Jesus at first (24:13–16) but later he abruptly vanishes (24:31). John similarly says that Jesus' human form is not obvious. Mary does not recognize Jesus at the empty tomb (John 20:14–15), and the disciples cannot recognize Jesus at John 21:4. Notoriously, Paul believes that Jesus can appear to people without any bodily form at all. Since Jesus' atonement makes sense only if he is far more god than man, it gradually became theologically necessary to sharply separate Jesus' temporary and irrelevant human form from his true divine being.

Other major disagreements among the gospels can be pursued, but we may stop at this point. It is quite an understatement to say that the New

Testament books do not present the same message about the origin, nature, mission, or ultimate purpose of Jesus. This scriptural diversity was reflected in Christian communities. According to the New Testament's own accounts, there were many different kinds of Christianities scattered around the eastern Mediterranean within two generations after Jesus' death. Although non-Jewish populations spoke Greek and shared to some degree in Greek speculative thought, the religious environment was extraordinarily complex, as the Roman Empire at that time tolerated considerable religious diversity. Within the first thirty years after Jesus' death, four major divisions had already arisen among Christians: Jewish Christians who kept the Torah Law and regarded full Judaism as essential to salvation; Jewish Christians who had Greek culture and respected Jesus' new Law; Gentile Greek Christians who converted to Jewish customs in order to join the new faith; and Gentile Greek Christians who rejected all Jewishness and expected Jesus to conform to Greek theological standards. Clearly, Matthew's Jesus and Acts' Peter are strongly sympathetic towards the Jewish Christians, while the rest increasingly send Jesus' mission on towards the Greek-Gentile world.

The story in Acts of the compromise between Peter's mission to the Jews and Paul's mission to the Gentiles is crucial to the expansion of early Christianity. In a sense, Paul's mission was more successful, since there were far more Gentiles than Jews. However, the Gentiles viewed Jesus through their lenses of Greek philosophy and whatever other religious notions they already held. Several of the New Testament letters directly testify to the annoying vitality of divergent versions of Christianity already flourishing in the late first century, and the problem only grew worse. For example, Gnostic Christianity was among the largest and most vibrant versions of Christianity within 100 years, gaining followers by portraying Jesus as an angelic messenger of salvation who can rescue specially chosen people from an evil universe. The Gospel of John represents a partial compromise with Gentile Greeks who had no prophet tradition but could appreciate a divine embodiment of a philosophical principle who promptly preaches to non-Jews. Endless variations upon the possible combinations of Jewish and Gentile expectations quickly erupted everywhere that missionaries went. Paul's own letters adequately testify how frustratingly independent and rebellious the new Christians could become.

Not surprisingly, these dozens of Christian communities each preferred to venerate and follow their own special set of holy writings. By the end of the second century, dozens of additional writings about Jesus had surfaced, for the most part designed to defend one or another version of Christianity. Bishop Eusebius, who helped to write the Nicene Creed in 325, recorded in his *Ecclesiastical History* some of the extensive difficulties of the early church in deciding the canonical list of books to be included in the New Testament. He supplies his own conclusions about this matter in Book 3, chapter 25, "The Divine Scriptures that are accepted and those that are not."

> Since we are dealing with this subject it is proper to sum up the writings of the New Testament which have been already mentioned. First then must be put the holy quaternion of the Gospels; following them the Acts of the Apostles. After this must be reckoned the epistles of Paul; next in order the extant former epistle of John, and likewise the epistle of Peter, must be maintained. After them is to be placed, if it really seem proper, the Apocalypse of John, concerning which we shall give the different opinions at the proper time. These then belong among the accepted writings. Among the disputed writings, which are nevertheless recognized by many, are extant the so-called epistle of James and that of Jude, also the second epistle of Peter, and those that are called the second and third of John, whether they belong to the evangelist or to another person of the same name. Among the rejected writings must be reckoned also the Acts of Paul, and the so-called Shepherd, and the Apocalypse of Peter, and in addition to these the extant epistle of Barnabas, and the so-called Teachings of the Apostles; and besides, as I said, the Apocalypse of John, if it seem proper, which some, as I said, reject, but which others class with the accepted books. And among these some have placed also the Gospel according to the Hebrews, with which those of the Hebrews that have accepted Christ are especially delighted. And all these may be reckoned among the disputed books. But we have nevertheless felt compelled to give a catalogue of these also, distinguishing those works which according to ecclesiastical tradition are true and genuine and commonly accepted, from those others which, although not canonical but disputed, are yet at the same time known to most ecclesiastical writers – we have felt compelled to give this catalogue in order that we might be able to know both these works and those that are cited by the heretics under the name of the apostles, including, for instance, such books as the Gospels of Peter, of Thomas, of Matthias, or of any others besides them, and the Acts of Andrew and John and the other apostles, which no one belonging to the succession of ecclesiastical writers has deemed worthy of mention in his writings. And further, the character of the style is at variance with apostolic usage, and both the thoughts and the purpose of the things that are related in them are so completely out of accord with true orthodoxy that they clearly show themselves to be the fictions of heretics. Wherefore they are not to be placed even among the rejected writings, but are all of them to be cast aside as absurd and impious. (Translation from *The Nicene and Post-Nicene Fathers*, Series II, Vol. 1)

Despite the best efforts of Christian scholars like Eusebius to help judge the many candidates for orthodoxy, it was not until the Council of Rome in 382 that the church finally converged on the list of books now in the New Testament. Around this time, major theological problems about Jesus' divinity, his human form, his relationship with God and the Holy Spirit, and the atonement doctrine were settled by councils that adopted trinitarianism and condemned as heresy any theology which disagreed. In the course of selecting and cleaning up the books for the New Testament, the third-century trinitarian and atonement dogmas were only partially imposed on much older writings, explaining why most of the New Testament books yield no clear help with these problems.

The principles of scientific history can establish reasonable doubt about the New Testament's ability to yield reliable evidence of Jesus' divinity. All the same, the New Testament books themselves, without any assistance from scientific history, display precisely the sort of mutual dependencies, stunning divergences, and sharp disagreements that would naturally be expected from a diverse patchwork of Christian communities each trying to make their own sense of Jesus. It would have been tremendously convenient for scriptural apologetics if the New Testament books clearly described the same important events, if the apostles and Paul had one coherent story about Jesus to tell, and if early Christians had received one consistent message about Jesus' purpose and what he expected of them. But none of these things actually happened, as the New Testament books themselves more than amply testify. Instead, as early church history also amply testifies, the task of artificially creating and imposing a clear, coherent, and consistent account of Jesus required an enormous amount of time and effort by highly motivated, powerful, and smart church leaders. By around 450, the task was largely done. The universal primacy of the Bishop of Rome and the Latin Vulgate translation of the fixed Bible was assured, and only from this time forward is it possible to speak of the Roman Catholic church. After that time, heretical Christians and their writings were eliminated with high efficiency, explaining why so little of the early period of Christian diversity has survived down to the present.

The absence of any original texts of the New Testament might be highly convenient. Some Christian theologians propose explaining the wide discrepancies in the New Testament by blaming later copyists who introduced mistakes into Bibles. This sort of rescue plan for biblical inerrancy suffers from two major problems. First, why would God permit the destruction of his perfect Word, after going to so much trouble over Jesus? Second, why would copyists depart from the originals concerning such crucial matters such as Jesus' miracles, Jesus' own words, and Jesus' death? The discrepancies in the New Testament which cause the most problems are doctrinal issues, where gospels don't manage to tell the same story about the meaning of Jesus' life, his relationship with God, and the way to salvation. The copyists must have been theologians themselves to invent such imaginatively sophisticated departures from any original account of such central doctrines. The right answer is that theologians were indeed involved, carefully selecting from many preserved writings only those that best fit with dogmas settled by councils hundreds of years after Jesus.

We shall not examine the vast theological effort to render the New Testament into coherent form sufficient to justify the system of dogmas constructed in fourth- and fifth-century councils. It suffices to say that this system has ready answers to all of the issues and problems raised here, and many more. But these dogmatic theological patchworks are entirely irrelevant to the fundamental question raised here, whether adequate evidence for Jesus' divinity is presented in the New Testament. Since these theological patchworks were composed in the spirit of complete conviction and faith that the New Testament books are accurate about Jesus, they cannot generate any independent evidence for Jesus either.

We may therefore leave behind dogmatic theology, and ascend to more speculative theological arguments designed to elevate New Testament testimony to levels sufficient for proof of Jesus' divinity. Against these arguments, the skeptic need only use the familiar principles H1–H12 of scientific history, simple rules of logic, and some common sense.

3.3 The Argument from Divine Signs

The argument from divine signs is common in both technical theology and popular defenses of religion. This argument starts from various signs of divinity and the need to fully explain these signs. Then the hypothesis that Jesus must be divine is advanced as the best explanation for these signs, leading to the desired conclusion that Jesus is divine.

The argument from fulfilled prophecies has this basic structure, with two premises of scriptural apologetics:

SA1 The Bible accurately recounts various signs of Jesus' divinity, including:
- (a) fulfilled prophecies made in the Old Testament about Jesus;
- (b) fulfilled prophecies made by Jesus in the New Testament;

(c) miraculous acts performed by Jesus.

SA2 Only Jesus' divinity can adequately explain how these signs could happen.

Conclusion. Jesus is divine.

Since premise 1 cannot be known to be true, the divinity explanation of premise 2 is not needed. There are plenty of ordinary explanations for allegedly "divine" signs.

In chronological order, let's start with the Old Testament. Dozens of verses in the Old Testament are supposedly prophecies about Jesus. The later books of the Old Testament are replete with doomsday prophets predicting either God's new kingdom or the arrival of a messiah to overthrow Israel's oppressors. If either the real historical Jesus or his later followers viewed the task at hand to be the fulfillment of Old Testament prophecy, it is little wonder that they would appeal to the Hebrew scriptures. Viewed objectively, however, none of these "prophecies" are any more compelling than the typical horoscope prediction which occasionally "comes true." The most well-known Old Testament prophecy about Jesus must be Isaiah's prophecy that supposedly foretells his virgin birth. Isaiah 7:14 in the King James Version (1611) reads: "Therefore, the Lord himselfe shal give you a signe: Behold, a Virgine shall conceive and beare a Sonne, and shall call his name Immanuel." Viewing this verse as a "prophecy" depends on tearing this single verse out of its context, mistranslating "virgin" from the original Hebrew word for "young woman," and then ignoring how Matthew (1:23) simply claims that Jesus is this Immanuel but no one calls Jesus by Immanuel or Emmanuel anywhere else in the New Testament. The Revised Standard Version (1946) corrects the translation and supplies the context:

> [10] Again the LORD spoke to Ahaz, [11] "Ask a sign of the LORD your God; let it be deep as Sheol or high as heaven." [12] But Ahaz said, "I will not ask, and I will not put the LORD to the test." [13] And he said, "Hear then, O house of David! Is it too little for you to weary men, that you weary my God also? [14] Therefore, the Lord himself will give you a sign. Behold, a young woman shall conceive and bear a son, and shall call his name Imman'u-el. [15] He shall eat curds and honey when he knows how to refuse the evil and choose the good. [16] For before the child knows how to refuse the evil and choose the good, the land before whose two kings you are in dread will be deserted. [17] The LORD will bring upon you and upon your people and upon your father's house such days as have not come since the day that E'phraim departed from Judah – the king of Assyria."

Clearly God is threatening Ahaz, the wicked king of the southern kingdom of Judah *c.*720 BCE, with the destruction of his kingdom within just a few years (from the infancy to the young childhood of a random boy). This prophecy didn't come true, as Ahaz passed his throne on to his son Hezekiah while the Assyrian Empire was conquering the northern kingdom of Israel instead.

Prophecies made by Jesus about his death and his resurrection cannot be regarded as any sort of evidence either. We have already established how little confidence could be placed in the things Jesus allegedly says in the gospels since their testimonial value is so low. Gospel composers had plenty of opportunity and motive to write verses to make Jesus seem divinely prescient. One of Jesus' more impressive prophecies, that the Jerusalem Temple would be destroyed (Matthew 24:1–8), isn't so impressive when it is realized that Matthew was written after the Temple was destroyed in 70 CE. Even if Jesus actually said some of things attributed to him, the most important prophecy of all, his prediction of his own resurrection, cannot be judged a correct prophecy since evidence that he actually was resurrected is so inadequate.

Since the descriptions of Jesus' miracles cannot be judged to be legitimate testimony either, they cannot be signs of anything, much less signs of divinity. Attributing miraculous works to one's favored prophet or magician, especially acts of healing the sick and exorcizing demons, was the all-too-typical way to impress gullible uneducated people. There were many would-be prophets and miracle workers wandering the eastern Mediterranean during the period from 200 BCE to 200 CE. It is not necessary to picture the apostles themselves inventing miracles stories after Jesus had died. The far more likely possibility is that rumors of extraordinary acts by the prophet Jesus just spontaneously erupted everywhere he went, so that many legends of miracles had become a sort of "public fact" widely believed even while Jesus was still alive. The rural Jewish people had been doing this sort of thing for centuries.

In Jesus' day, the followers of John the Baptist had already formed a cult of worship around him, treating him as either Elijah returned or the herald of Elijah, and a nasty rivalry between them and Jesus' followers had erupted. Matthew reports that John the Baptist himself was skeptical about Jesus' powers and sent his own disciples to challenge Jesus (Matthew 11:2–6). Why was John so skeptical? How did John fail to notice God's approval of Jesus when John baptized him? The probable answer is that John the Baptist never did recognize Jesus as the fulfillment of his own prophetic call for the coming Messiah. Competition between the two factions continued even after Jesus' death, and John the Baptist's movement actually carried on for centuries. It must have been important to Jesus' first followers to offer some sort of truce. That explains why substantial passages of Mark, Matthew, and Luke go to great lengths to simultaneously build up John the Baptist as critically important for fulfilling Isaiah's prophecy of a voice in the wilderness and depict Jesus as the divine heir to John the Baptist's human mission. Matthew's Jesus even says that John the Baptist is the greatest man alive and that he is the returned Elijah (Matthew 11:11, 17:12–13). It seems doubtful that John the Baptist's followers were impressed by this Christian olive branch of peace. The Gospel of John, from the early second century, still has to pointedly put John the Baptist back in his proper place as just a witness bearer and not even a returned Elijah (John 1:8, 1:20–21). It was imperative for the early Christians that only Jesus did miracles, since only Jesus was the true Messiah.

It seems significant to track where miracles occur, and who gets them. In Mark and Matthew, most miracles occurred in rural locations in front of local Jews; only Jews got personally healed by Jesus; several cities were not impressed by Jesus including his home town (Mark 6:1–5, Matthew 11:20–34); and Mark's Jesus performs no miracles in Jerusalem. The expectation of signs can be sufficient to inspire stories of signs. Jesus would not have had to do anything himself beyond impressing the uneducated rural populations with his religious fanaticism and righteous demeanor. On the other hand, Jesus could have done a little "faith healing" in the timeless manner still practiced to this day in churches and on television. It may not be a coincidence that so many of Jesus' impressive healings were done to people suffering from afflictions now known to typically have a psycho-neurological component, such as loss of consciousness, speech impairments, ear and eye trouble, loss of limb control, convulsions and behavioral disorders, and the like. Mark's Jesus even says that other miracle workers invoking Jesus should be tolerated (Mark 9:38–40) – perhaps as a professional courtesy? But Matthew's Jesus condemns these frauds (Matthew 7:22–23).

It is clear from biblical and non-biblical sources that faith healing was common enough during that era. News of anyone performing "miracles" truly out of the ordinary would have spread throughout the region, reaching the ears of both Jews and non-Jews and penetrating into nearby major cities for Greek-educated people to remark upon. There were plenty of politicians, scholars, and scribes active in regional cities writing down local events and sending off letters through the regular channels of communication so plentiful throughout the Roman Empire. But there is not one single mention of Jesus anywhere in all the preserved writings dating from before Jesus' crucifixion. No one found anything remarkable in Jesus' activities besides the local Jews of Galilee and Jerusalem, and no one bothered to record anything about Jesus during those days (not even his own followers, who were all illiterate in any case). Jesus' crucifixion and the political disturbances caused by Christians are only mentioned by a couple of late first-century and early second-century historians, but their veracity is questionable too. For example, the mention of Jesus in Josephus' *The Antiquities of the Jews* appears to be crudely inserted by some later Christian scribe. If Jesus' "miracles" and disruptions in Jerusalem were truly so impressive, why is there no contemporary record of them anywhere? Numerous histories and collections of letters by Jews and Romans during the decades of Jesus' life are still extant, and they make no mention of any figure like Jesus of the New Testament. Wandering miracle workers were common enough in those days, but Jesus' disturbances in and around the Temple and appearances before Jewish and Roman leadership before his crucifixion would have been so extraordinary that somebody would have recorded those events. If Jesus even existed, he must have been only a local phenomenon among his own native people.

There are remnants of a humbly human Jesus still perceptible in some New Testament books. Mark's Jesus surprisingly says that no sign shall be given to his generation (Mark 8:12). To supplement their use of Mark, the gospels of Matthew and Luke borrow from another early source (called Q, from the German word for "source"), but those passages are only wisdom sayings and sermons of Jesus, with not a single miracle among them. If Q was descended from early Greek-speaking Christians, as most scholars agree, then miracles would indeed have been far less impressive to that more educated and urban segment of the population. That also explains why Paul, a highly educated Greek-speaking scholar, never intimates that Jesus ever performed any miracles. Paul even ridicules the Jewish expectation of signs at 1 Corinthians 1:22. Many early Christians did not suppose that Jesus needed to do any miracles. To them, his religious fanaticism about God, or his resurrection by God, was more than sufficient for faith. For Paul and John, faith was far more important than evidence in any case, setting the stage for later debates within Christian theology.

3.4 The Argument from Apostolic Faith

The argument from apostolic faith is quite similar to the argument from divine signs. The amazing fact that the apostles became devout missionaries after the death of their leader, with many of them ending up as martyrs, is something demanding explanation. Is Jesus' divinity the best explanation? This argument proceeds as follows:

SA3 The New Testament accurately recounts the enormous energy and life-long devotion to missionary work displayed by the apostles soon after Jesus' death.
SA4 The only sufficient explanation for such apostolic devotion is their tremendous faith in Jesus' divinity.
SA5 The only sufficient explanation for such apostolic faith is that Jesus did reveal his divinity to them in the resurrection and his appearances to them afterwards.
Conclusion. Jesus is divine.

This argument is quite interesting because it appears to place the burden of explanation on the skeptic. "Just try to explain the early church without a god," the argument says, "since our explanation fits the evidence so well!"

We should first take a look at the biblical evidence, indeed. To take the most charitable approach towards the New Testament, we shall even ignore the fact that the earliest complete copies of its books date only as early as the fourth century, thus overlooking how those 300 years permitted the church to rewrite any of them as it pleased without us ever finding out how. Is there a good explanation for the establishment and growth of the early church that does not presume Jesus' divinity? Actually, there are many possible accounts (such as Crossan 1998) and some accounts suggest that Jesus didn't need to have actually lived (for example Wells 1988, Price 2004). The proposed account which follows stays close to the New Testament without presuming Jesus' divinity or any other divine acts.

The New Testament's Acts of the Apostles and Paul's letters recount many stories about the missionary activities of early Christians after Jesus' death. These books are mostly harmonized on main points, which is not surprising since Luke was working from a collection of Paul's letters. The overall picture of early church activities has three main phases: from Jesus' death to the conversion of Paul (*c.*30–35), from Paul's conversion to the

Jerusalem council some fourteen years later (in the late 40s), and the subsequent division of missionary labor which sent the apostles preaching to Jews and Paul preaching exclusively to Greek-speaking Gentiles until his own death in Rome *c.*62–67. Paul's eruption on the scene as a Christian upon the scene changed everything. The early Jewish Christian church would probably have never grown into a large religion on its own, and it only had about forty years to survive anyway. It faced serious competition from other rival factions within Judaism which already had their own answers to the problems of religious observance, earning God's approval, and dealing with Roman oppression. After the Jewish communities were scattered by the First Jewish–Roman War (66–73) and the Jerusalem Christian church was wiped out, many of these Jewish Christians survived in tiny obscure sects for decades and centuries as "Nazarenes" who did accept Jesus' divinity, as "Ebionites" who viewed Jesus as a great prophet, and other small sects. The vast future for Christianity lay with Paul, who was playing a major role from the church's beginnings.

If Acts is at all reliable, during the first phase of the early church some of Jesus' closest followers remained in Jerusalem, led by Simon Peter (Cephas) and James the brother of Jesus (Acts 8:1). They continued to preach the good news of Jesus of Nazareth and the immanent coming of the kingdom of God. They required full observance of Jewish Law and custom, and had some success at sustaining interest in Jesus as a Messiah among Jews in Judea, Samaria, and Galilee. However, this initial phase did not expand far, since it was limited by its mission only to people willing to be strict Jews, and it was harshly persecuted by Jewish and Roman authorities, including Saul (to be known as Paul after his conversion). Within a handful of years, interest in Jesus had spread to cities neighboring the Judean region, such as Damascus, and they had attracted a few Gentiles to convert to their movement. Already, we need to introduce Paul to the narrative.

After becoming a Christian, Paul always proudly stressed his Jewish heritage, but the versions of his biography in Acts and his letters are oddly contorted. He consistently and proudly declares that he was a Pharisee. If so, then he would have left his native Tarsus for Pharisee training in Jerusalem (tutored by the Hillel Pharisee Gamaliel) during his adolescence, as was customary (he confirms that he grew up in Jerusalem, Acts 22:3). By the time of Jesus' ministry, Saul had already returned to Tarsus, where he would have heard about the Jewish disturbances over Jesus' death. It is clear that he wasn't in Judean territory as a witness during Jesus' activities, as his letters say that he only saw and heard Jesus in visions. However, Saul sped to

Jerusalem soon after Jesus' death and offered his services to the Sadducees in time to approve of the stoning of Stephen (Acts 8:1).

If Saul did really gain authorization to help persecute Christians, as he repeatedly claims, then he was in close cooperation with the Sadducees, who could obtain legal sanction from the Roman authorities for holding trials and executions. The Sadducees rejected resurrection, were somewhat laxer towards the Law, and in Jesus' day their political power was owed to their alliance with the Roman overlords. The Sadducee revulsion towards resurrection, and their continued worry that talk of a returning Messiah would be politically disruptive, amply explains why the Sadducees immediately persecuted the apostles (Acts 4:1–3, 5:17), with Saul's help. Saul was now operating in a strange gray zone: he was proud of his unequaled Jewish righteousness as a Pharisee (Acts 22:3, Acts 23:6, Philippians 3:4–6); yet his Pharisee mentor, Gamaliel, did not approve of such persecution (Acts 5:34–40); but he eagerly sought and received Sadducee approval to expand his persecution to other cities such as Damascus. When the time eventually came for his own trial in Jerusalem as a blasphemer, Paul did seem to have fair knowledge of Jewish politics and the Pharisee/Sadducee rivalry in Jerusalem, since he could play them off against each other (Acts 23:6–10).

It is clear that Saul was a proudly self-righteous Jew. But then came his conversion on the road to Damascus, *c.*33 CE. Why did the new Paul remain so closely connected to Judaism? Paul's recognized status as a Pharisee was evidently crucial for his Christian missionary task. This makes sense, since solid Pharisee status helped to support Paul's claims that he had practiced Judaism as rigorously as possible, that he had little trouble accepting Jesus' resurrection, and that his acknowledgement of Jesus as the fulfillment of Jewish prophecy must be unquestioned among both Jews and Gentiles. Pharisees were well known and quite popular among the people for their scrupulous adherence to the Torah Law (arousing Jesus' complaints) and they also believed in resurrection, unlike the Sadducees. Also, it may have been expedient for him to stress a Pharisee connection as a Christian since his persecution work was done as a Sadducee. In any case, at first the Jewish Christians in Jerusalem (who were not actually called Christians themselves, but probably "Nazarenes" instead, see Acts 25:5) were not impressed, by Paul's Jewishness or his newfound Christianity. The apostles were shocked to hear about Paul's revelation from Jesus and his evangelical work preaching salvation through Jesus to the Jews both in Jerusalem and around Judea (Acts 9:26–30, 26:20–21) and also to the non-Jews of nearby cities such as Damascus (Acts 9:19–22, 26:20) and Antioch, where a group of the converted first called themselves Christians (Acts 11:26). By the time that Paul got around to personally preaching in Jerusalem, three years after his conversion (Acts 9:26–30, Acts 21:17–21, Galatians 1: 18), the apostles knew about many new Gentile Christian churches and had formed grave concerns about Paul's methods.

Paul's arrival in Jerusalem touched off the second phase of early Christianity. The Jewish Nazarenes were suspicious and hostile, quite alarmed by Paul's abandonment of the Jewish Law, especially concerning circumcision and Jews eating with Gentiles. The Nazarenes were barely surviving against both Jewish and Roman suspicion only because they retained their formal Jewishness, legally tolerated under Roman law. As long as they maintained an image as a non-disruptive reforming Jewish community, albeit with odd beliefs about Jesus' resurrection, they could quietly attract converts among both Jews and also Gentiles who would effectively convert to Judaism first by circumcision and obedience to Jewish Law. Paul's first visit to Jerusalem was brief yet eventful. He met with Peter and James, who seemed cautiously receptive, and he openly preached to Greek Jews for a few days until Jewish death threats forced the apostles to restore tranquility by sending Paul away (Acts 9:26–30). Paul headed north to Asia Minor and Greece, founding his churches in Greek cities and encountering Nazarenes scattered by the Stephen incident already there who were preaching about Jesus (Acts 11:19–30). Then Peter conveniently received new revelation that they should preach to the Gentiles too (Acts 10 and 11:1–18). However, unlike Paul, the apostles still demanded full Jewish conversion first, which from their perspective launched a serious confrontation over custom and morality. During this second phase of the early church, Paul's preaching to both Jews and Gentiles touched off religious chaos that reverberated up and down the eastern Mediterranean for many years. Jewish Christians spread their version north into Paul's territory, provoking Paul's condemnation of these false "super-apostles" (2 Corinthians 7:5, Acts 15:1–2) including even Peter himself (Galatians 2:11–14). Paul had to repeatedly invoke his authority as a genuine apostle too, as he tried to keep his young Greco-Christian churches from reverting back to some variation of Judaism.

The dire need for a truce is eventually realized. Paul goes back to Jerusalem *c.*48 CE to secure his unrestricted mission to the Greek-speaking Gentiles (see Acts 15:6–21 and Galations 2). The third stage of the early Pauline church then commences, and the growth of the church continues in impressive fashion until the death of Peter and Paul by the mid-60s and the destruction of the Jerusalem Temple in 70 CE during the First

Jewish–Roman War. There is precious little solid information about the progress of the Jewish Christian church during this third phase, as conflict with Paul subsides. What is clear is that only Paul's Greco-Christian version had a real future. The next century of church growth did not have to contend with any Jewish entanglement, but rather with internal theological issues involving Greek and Gnostic philosophies.

To understand why Paul's version of Christianity was genuinely and frighteningly radical to the Jewish Christians, we should be reminded how Paul preached three essential doctrines based on his mystical experiences of Jesus. First, the one true God, the God of the Jews, created the world and gave humanity its basic moral rules. Second, Jesus was God's Son, who preached the good news of God's forgiveness for sincere repentance, before being crucified and resurrected. Third, Jesus is both a sacrifice for our sins and a path to our salvation, if we faithfully accept the first two doctrines (e.g. 1 Corinthians 15:3–5, 1 Thessalonians 1:9–10). Notoriously, Paul required neither Jewish Law, custom, nor circumcision, which helps to account for his success among Gentiles. It also accounts for the puzzle Paul bequeathed to the later church, whether good works or faith alone brought salvation. While skirmishes with Jewish Christians over the importance of morality and customs was annoying enough, Paul's real missionary difficulties were mostly theological. The "one true God of the Jews" doctrine was met with skepticism among the Greek-minded Gentiles, who either liked monotheism but doubted that the God of the Jews could be the one, or liked polytheistic and syncretic philosophies which seemed so intellectually superior to any Semitic tribal cult (see Paul's debates with philosophers in Athens, Acts 17:16–34).

These theological difficulties for Paul are reflected his organization and direction of his churches. During the early years of Paul's ministry, he instituted just one Christian ritual: the Lord's Supper. (Interestingly, Paul discouraged continuing the Jewish practice of baptism at 1 Corinthians 1:17 but without success, since later letters not actually written by Paul keep approving of baptism.) The Lord's Supper was a creative variation on the Passover meal and its echo in the Sunday "agape feasts" that the early Christians shared together as a community. Mark's version of the Lord's Supper (Mark 14:22–24) is around twenty years older than its first recording in Paul's first letter to the Corinthians (11:23–26), which dates to *c.*50 CE. Therefore, it is highly significant that Paul does not say that he acquired the Lord's Supper directions to eat Jesus' body and blood from the Jerusalem Nazarenes, but instead he says that it was received from the Lord

(1 Corinthians 11:23). Considering that Jews regarded eating any blood as a terrible sin against Mosaic Law, it cannot be surprising that the Jerusalem church couldn't have perpetuated such a horribly anti-Jewish Lord's Supper. Paul obviously did not seek Jewish approval for his version of the Lord's Supper. Luke does not contradict Paul on this point, although he could easily have credited the apostles with maintaining the Lord's Supper from the start, as there is no mention of the Lord's Supper anywhere in Acts of the Apostles. Instead, Luke's gospel inserts the simplest version possible of the blood and body invocation (Luke 22:17–19), which omits the religious significance of Jesus' body and blood, unlike the fuller Pauline versions in Mark 14:22–24 and Matthew 26:26–28.

Where could have Paul gotten the Lord's Supper from? His own answer of "more revelation" has everything to do with this section's ultimate purpose: to offer a non-miraculous alternative account of the growth of the early church. We need to piece together four highly significant facts gleaned from our fast survey of events. First, Paul had figured out a powerful recipe for attracting monotheistic-minded Gentiles already infused with Greek ideas and other religious notions common across the Middle East from older Roman, Egyptian, Syraic, and Persian traditions. Second, Paul continually relied on personal mystical revelation direct from Jesus/the Holy Spirit to justify his message. Third, all the other gospels were finally composed long after Paul had been establishing churches for over twenty years; the youngest gospel of Mark was assembled around forty years after Paul's first preaching. Fourth, the original gospel of Mark records no appearances of Jesus after the resurrection to anyone (disregarding its extended ending, which was added in the fourth or fifth century). The original Mark simply ends with three frightened women fleeing a man in white in an otherwise empty tomb. If there ever was more to Mark, it disappeared at some point for a reason, since doctrinally acceptable scriptures got carefully preserved by the early church.

Let's start with Mark and find some point of agreement with Paul. From Mark, we must conclude that either the apostles never witnessed a risen Christ and only the testimony of women (which Jews then considered worthless) supported the resurrection, or some other disturbing ending of Mark was deliberately eradicated. Either way, no one ever witnessed the risen Jesus! Matthew tacitly confirms this. In Matthew, only women could testify to the missing body (a helpful point since any apostles at the scene would get accused of having stolen it first); the plausible story that the body was stolen gets elaborated at 28:12–15 but goes unrefuted (why indeed would Matthew repeat this legend, unless, as he says, many Jews believed it for good reason); and the final vision of Jesus to the apostles is only a vision and not any sort of interaction with an embodied Jesus (Matthew 28:17–18). Remember too that Matthew is by far the most Jewish of the gospels, echoing parts of a Jesus tradition going back to the Jewish Nazarenes. What did the apostles actually think had happened? They didn't really see Jesus, any more than the women. There remains another strong possibility: they had no idea where Jesus' body was, they did sincerely hope that Jesus had indeed risen from the dead, and they persistently preached his second coming with the immanent kingdom of God. It is not hard to imagine a few dedicated apostles carrying on for a couple of years with Jesus' message of repentance without having personally seen a risen Jesus. Their stubbornness was sufficient to attract the persecution of the Sadducees. Yes, they had impressive faith, but this was merely the continuation of the faith they had while Jesus was still alive. However, you'd have to imagine that such strong faith couldn't last too long. Actually, such faith didn't have to; don't forget about Paul.

On this "No Reappearance of Jesus" theory, how did the story ever get started that the apostles could see Jesus? The apostles probably got that notion from Paul. The narrative of Acts is all about how Paul successfully grafted his religious devotion upon the legitimacy of the faithful disciples left behind in Jerusalem. But Luke was a resourceful compromiser, determined to tell a version favorable to Paul's agenda. Luke couldn't have revealed the probable truth, even if he suspected it: that the apostles in Jerusalem began claiming that they had seen Jesus only after they heard reports about Paul's claim to have seen Jesus. Why didn't Paul ever let on that he probably was the first person to have seen a vision of Jesus? He never knew, or if he suspected, he didn't really care. Sure, when he was Saul the persecutor, he wouldn't have heard the apostles claiming visions of Jesus, as that only got started after the converted Paul had gone to Damascus. Paul explicitly says that he made no contact with any of Jesus' followers for three years after his conversion, giving the apostles plenty of time to spread rumors that they had seen Jesus first, before Paul. Paul had every incentive to permit the Jerusalem apostles to be as convincing as possible, because he needed their Jesus legend of resurrection to be as secure as possible. Paul might have even believed their accounts of seeing Jesus when Paul first visited Jerusalem, since it was probably reassuring that he wasn't the only one.

The stories about apostles and others seeing Jesus in Matthew, Luke, and Acts were roughly standardized during the second phase of the early church (though their wide differences remain intriguing, as more evidence that there was no original singular story from the apostles), while Paul's

Greco-Gentile Christianity and Peter's Jewish Christianity struggled for control of the movement. During this second phase, Paul also invented the Lord's Supper and the doctrine of Jesus' resurrection, borrowing heavily from older religious traditions involving resurrected gods and pagan rituals in which believers symbolically ate their god. Additionally, a highly useful function of Paul's Lord's Supper and resurrection doctrine would have been to effectively drive away troublesome Judaizers who kept disrupting his young churches. Requiring Jews to eat blood, eat with Gentiles, and believe in resurrection would have had the combined effect of screening out most ardent Jewish proselytizers. Almost twenty years have passed by the time Paul wrote 1 Corinthians, where he recounts Jesus' appearances to the Jerusalem faithful (15:5–7), and Paul has proved victorious and can consolidate his victory. And merely having visions of Jesus and visitations from the Holy Spirit turned out to not be enough. By Luke's era, it was imperative that the apostles witnessed Jesus in full bodily form, perhaps in order to make a more secure foundation of testimony to the risen Jesus than any of Paul's mystical revelations. On this speculative version of events, the "No Reappearance of Jesus" theory, there is never any need to suppose that Jesus was raised from dead.

It is time to summarize the proposed counter-argument against this "Argument from Apostolic Faith." Premises 3 and 4 may go undisputed here, as any theory about the early church might as well start from them without skeptical scrutiny. They may actually be incorrect, but it suffices to refute this argument that premise 5 is surely incorrect. Jesus' divinity is not the only sufficient explanation for such apostolic faith. Another sufficient explanation, sketched above, is apostolic hope combined with Paul's strange visual experience on the road to Damascus. This example of scriptural analysis (however amateurish, unoriginal, and flawed) is nevertheless able to construct a plausibly non-supernatural version of events from the New Testament's more reliable components. Apostolic hope does not require Jesus' divinity, as has been explained already, and Paul's traumatic psychological episode has little evidential bearing on Jesus' divinity.

Possible retorts by Christian theologians to this rational refutation fall into three main categories. First, it could be argued that Paul's strange experience in fact suffices to prove Jesus' divinity. However, the question of whether mystical experiences are good evidence for supernaturalism is not a matter for scriptural apologetics, but for "Theology From The World" (discussed in the next chapter). Second, it could be argued that sufficient evidence for the "No Reappearance of Jesus" is similarly lacking, by the scientific historian's own principles H1–H12. This is correct, but the rejection of premise 5 is merely accomplished by raising a plausible alternative theory that explains as many solid facts as any other. No fully proven theory about Jesus will ever be established, in all likelihood. The issue raised by the "Argument from Apostolic Faith" is whether we are rationally forced to conclude that Jesus was divine, and we obviously are not. Third, it could be argued that belief in Jesus' divinity is required in order to ever correctly interpret New Testament scripture. If so, then a skeptic would be disqualified from engaging in the sort of scriptural analysis performed above. However, requiring faith in Jesus' divinity from the start only betrays the entire point of scriptural apologetics: to rationally persuade the non-believer with evidence. The kind of theology which is here termed "Theology In The Know" does require faith as a presupposition for doing theology, and it also receives its own chapter.

3.5 The Argument from Divine Character

Defenders of Christianity often appeal to the virtuous traits of Jesus and the church. No other religious figure or institution, they proclaim, possesses such obviously divine perfections. The following argument brings together their most impressive qualities:

SA6 The New Testament accurately describes Jesus as a morally perfect and sinless being.
SA7 The New Testament accurately portrays Jesus as neither a lunatic nor a liar, but as completely truthful about his divinity and relationship with God.
SA8 The only sufficient explanation for the moral perfection of Jesus' commandments is his divinity.
SA9 The only sufficient explanation for the church's supremely virtuous character is that it was instituted by God through a divine Jesus.
Conclusion. Jesus is divine.

This argument fails because none of its premises can be known to be correct. We may easily doubt premise 6, since we have no reliable evidence from the New Testament about Jesus' perfections. Actually, Mark's Jesus seeks John's baptism for the forgiveness of sins (Mark 1:4) and he says that no one is good except God alone (Mark 10:18). Previous sections have discussed how the divinity of Jesus gradually built up over time through the gospels. There is no way to be confident that attributions of sinlessness to Jesus correspond in any way to an actual historical Jesus.

Similarly, premise 7 can only be doubted as well. We can't reasonably conclude that Jesus really did claim his own co-divinity with God. Nor do we have to conclude that Jesus was any sort of mentally disturbed individual. The previous section has amply explained how an entirely human Jesus could stand behind all the legends. The notion that a skeptic towards Jesus' truthfulness must first prove him to be a liar or a lunatic is a completely false trilemma. No one is forced into a harsh choice between Jesus as liar, lunatic, or Lord. There are plenty of other alternative human Jesuses, and some actually make a better fit with the overall course of the New Testament.

Premise 8 assumes that Jesus' commandments are morally perfect. The books of the New Testament are notoriously at variance with each other about what precisely his commandments are. Perhaps six commandments (Matthew 19:16–19), or only two, loving God and each other (Mark 12:28–31)? Or just one, to simply believe in Jesus? In any case, the church has frequently been internally divided over whether moral virtue can deliver salvation anyway (for example, recall the Protestant cry, Faith alone!). Setting that puzzle aside, let's return to alleged perfection of Jesus' moral code. How could we know that it is morally perfect? Presumably Christians who believe so are already pretty impressed by Jesus, so their opinion of his commandments can't constitute any sort of evidence about Jesus. Nor does it help matters for Christians to propose that faith in Jesus reveals the perfection of his ethics. Suppose a non-Christian did conclude Jesus' moral code to be the perfection of morality. This judgment would have nothing to do with having to agree with Jesus' divinity. Either non-Christians could judge for themselves that Jesus' code is morally perfect, in which case they don't need Jesus or his divinity at all, or they cannot judge for themselves whether Jesus' code is morally perfect, in which case they cannot be driven to accept premise 8. Either way, there is no rational imperative to accept premise 8.

Premise 9 cannot be taken seriously. The church has perpetrated or permitted some of the most horrific moral evils and crimes ever committed in the history of humanity. Defenders of Christianity naturally claim that a human institution like the church couldn't be morally infallible anyway. This claim is all too true, and explicitly confesses that the church in fact lacks supremely virtuous character, so premise 9 is false. Wait, wait . . . that's not what Christian defenders wanted to admit, of course. They still want to believe that the church's virtuous intentions has always been to follow Jesus' perfect moral code. But that line of thought simply returns the issue to premises 6 and 8, whether Jesus or his morality is morally perfect, and those have already been discussed. There are plenty of alternative explanations, none of them involving a divine Jesus, that more than sufficiently explain the Church's unsteady conduct over the centuries.

3.6 The Argument from Pseudo-history

The limitations of scriptural theology set by reason do not destroy the religious value of scripture. Liberal modernism, discussed in Chapter 8, accepts these rational limitations and envelops scripture in interpretative contexts far richer than literalist readings. However, scriptural theology has always been tempted to engage in what may be called "pseudo-history." Pseudo-history is a method of "verifying" historical claims that only appears to be consistent with sound historical methodology, but really only protects special historical claims from scrutiny. Religious pseudo-history turns principles H1–H12 entirely upside down in order to fully protect principles SA1–SA9 used in the arguments discussed so far in this chapter.

If successful, pseudo-history can make the church's version of history still look like historical inquiry. Pseudo-history defends the faith by rejecting scientific history, so that doctrinally crucial parts of scripture can serve as the bedrock foundations for theology's version of Christianity. The basic principles of scriptural apologetics at the core of theological pseudo-history are:

SA1 The Bible accurately recounts various signs of Jesus' divinity.

SA3 The New Testament accurately recounts the enormous energy and life-long devotion to missionary work displayed by the apostles soon after Jesus' death.

SA6 The New Testament accurately describes Jesus as a morally perfect and sinless being.

SA7 The New Testament accurately portrays Jesus as neither a lunatic nor a liar, but as completely truthful about his divinity.

Theology From The Scripture can in turn use these principles to support five more general principles of pseudo-history:

PH1 Scriptural revelation accurately describes Jesus' divinity and relationship with God.

PH2 Only someone already unable to accept Jesus' divinity would apply scientific history to question the New Testament's veracity, so scientific history cannot render belief in Jesus unreasonable.

PH3 Unless it can be proven that Jesus was human, the New Testament evidence for Jesus' divinity must be sufficient evidence, so scientific history cannot render belief in Jesus unreasonable.

PH4 Regardless of evidence either way, no inquiry of scientific history can disprove Jesus' divinity, so scientific history cannot render belief in Jesus unreasonable.

PH5 The New Testament's account of Jesus' divinity remains truthful despite scientific history.

This connected pseudo-historical argument from PH1–PH4 to the conclusion of PH5 drives the question of Jesus' divinity entirely out of the reach of scientific history. Indeed, it drives Jesus' divinity out of history altogether. Let's examine the four premises PH1–PH4 to see how this happens.

We have already amply explained the many problems with the arguments attempting to show that PH1 is correct. Regardless, the theological pseudo-historian stubbornly clings to PH1.

PH2 is false because scientific history can be properly used regardless of whether someone personally accepts Jesus' divinity. Still, Christians can understandably feel like the whole question gets begged against them. PH2 asserts that the scientific historian by definition cannot adequately judge New Testament veracity, since scientific history's skepticism towards Jesus' divinity makes it impossible for the scientific historian to take claims about Jesus' divinity seriously enough. For example, if the scientific historian wonders if gospel verses saying that Jesus is the Son of God or that a resurrected Jesus appeared to Peter are really true, then the scientific historian seems to be already throwing out terrific evidence relevant to the case. With the scientific historian continually discarding all the best evidence, it is little wonder that only skepticism remains. However, scientific history never "throws out" relevant evidence from the start. To repeat, the principles of scientific history H1–H12 do not require assuming that Jesus was not divine, that miracles cannot happen, and the like. Scientific history is not prejudicially skeptical towards gospel itself, but only demands that gospel pass some entirely reasonable and commonsense standards for ordinary believability. Is reading the New Testament really just like reading testimonial depositions from crime scene witnesses nowadays? If there is any good reason to think that a gospel verse about Jesus' divinity has been perfectly transmitted from numerous witnesses through decades of oral traditions and then a couple of centuries of textual composition and reediting, the scientific historian is eager and ready to learn of them. As it turns out, there aren't any good reasons, and scientific history therefore reaches its skeptical conclusion.

PH3 is false because scientific history only concludes that we cannot reasonably establish Jesus' divinity. That means that scientific history cannot prove that Jesus was only human, either. That is why skepticism is the proper conclusion about Jesus and not any sort of certainty. However, on the presumption that there was a real historical Jesus, it does seem far more probable that this Jesus was only a human being, since that simpler hypothesis is more consistent with all the reliable evidence. The burden of proof should be on those claiming Jesus' supernatural divinity, since that truly is the extraordinary claim. At this point in our debating, we have again encountered the theological complaint that scientific history is just naturalism in disguise. But this simply is a false accusation.

PH4 is a desperate assertion that an extraordinary claim is reasonable, regardless of evidence for it, so long as it can't be proven false. One wonders whether any Christian would approve of other religions helping themselves to this same generous standard. So many religions all ending up so reasonable! In any case, since PH4 violates common sense and strains sanity itself, we have evidently transcended scriptural apologetics. In fact, PH4, along with PH5, is already within the territory of Theology In The Know.

Accepting these five principles of pseudo-history effectively places God's involvement in the world, Jesus' divinity, and Jesus' resurrection entirely beyond the competent range of scientific history. What other sort of history is there? There are two alternative kinds of theological pseudo-history, and theologians have been sharply divided between them. First, those theologians who stubbornly believe that Jesus' resurrection really was a historical fact defiantly base their staunch faith in God on this belief. In their hands, scriptural apologetics effectively ceases to be a method for persuading nonbelievers and only serves as a way to reconfirm existing faith. Second, those theologians who can leave historical facts to the scientists defiantly claim that Jesus' resurrection stands outside of history, whatever that could mean. In their hands, Jesus' resurrection stands to subsequent history as the big bang stands to our universe: an event outside of normal space-time where supernatural beings do mysterious things. These two modes of pseudohistory are exemplary cases of Theology In The Know.

If scientific history was based on a presumption of naturalism, scientific history's inquiries into Jesus could be disqualified as too prejudiced from the start. However, scientific history only embodies reasonable common sense and logic, which are themselves neutrally sufficient for establishing reasonable skepticism towards Christian scripture. Not surprisingly, as its own chapter explains, Theology In The Know rebels against the presumed neutrality of reason and logic as well.

4

Theology From The World

Theology from the Scripture aims to explain scripture just right so that it points to Jesus' divinity. In a similar fashion, Theology From The World aims to explain nature just right so that it points to god. Reading nature correctly, by this analogy, permits the intelligent mind to understand god's involvement with the world. Theology From The World emerged within early Christian theology as an effort to keep pace with pagan philosophies, especially the Greek worldview grounded in Plato, Aristotle, and the Stoics. Theology From The World then had to adapt during the Renaissance to deal with new experimental sciences, which were also seeking liberation from Greek metaphysics and cosmology.

This chapter describes how Theology From The World has continued to adapt, under great pressure from modern sciences. After carefully distinguishing pseudo-science from genuine scientific explanation, the last three sections carefully discuss theological attempts to explain religious experiences, morality, and human conceptions of god. Because religion has long claimed these three phenomena as their own special provinces demanding theological explanation, naturalism must offer persuasive rival explanations.

4.1 Theology and Science

The new sciences making the most impressive advances from 1400 to 1700 were astronomy, physics, and medicine. Primitive but powerful, these sciences based their credibility first and foremost on their scrupulous and honest methods of observation. Astronomy used advanced sextants, armillary spheres, and mechanical clocks to track heavenly objects with remarkable accuracy. Physics also used clocks and many other measuring devices to study the regular motions and interactions of earthly objects. Medicine examined the construction of the human body with artistic eye to diagram the organs open to view. Humbly aware that speculative theories about nature's hidden powers and laws can abruptly fail when confronted with what nature actually does, experimental scientists placed their greater trust in the observable facts.

Theologians were slow to similarly trust the evidence before one's eyes. For too long they trusted Aristotle, Ptolemy, and other ancient authorities. They denied that the earth revolved around the sun; they refused to see the sun's spots and the phases of Venus's and Jupiter's moons; they resisted new medical discoveries. By the 1700s, however, a truce developed. Theologians could accept the empirical phenomena that experimental science tracked with undeniable skill, but they believed that theology was still required to fully explain the facts. How did the solar system get organized so optimally for a habitable earth? God must have formed it. Why are living organisms so different from non-life? God must have specially created all life. What makes humans so spiritually different from the animals? God must have given us conscious souls. How can people strive for ethical ideals? God must have given us morality. So many important questions! Science obviously needed help. From this perspective, science and religion are not only compatible, but positively supportive.

According to Theology From The World, supernatural hypotheses should attempt to explain special features of the natural world, like the earth, life, the human spirit, and morality. If hypotheses about the supernatural provide better explanations than any naturalistic hypotheses, then belief in the supernatural would be reasonable. This theological strategy, traditionally labeled as "natural theology," seemed plausible during medieval times, remained strong for centuries, and lasted into the 1800s with hearty approval from many scientists as well. This Enlightenment compromise, characterized by the philosophers René Descartes (died 1650) and

Immanuel Kant (died 1804), assigned separate responsibilities to the sciences and to theology. The sciences are capable of only studying the physical world of ordinary matter, while theology explains the spiritual world of the human soul. Descartes divided all reality into the material world and the mental world, following his Catholicism, and declared that the sciences are incompetent to deal with anything except what can be physically quantified and measured. Kant similarly divided all reality into the natural and the rational, confirming his Lutheran faith, by declaring that science could never understand human free will, reason, and ethics.

By the early 1900s, the Enlightenment compromise was breaking down. Neither astronomy, physics, nor medicine needed any assistance from theology any more. Astronomy was discovering the immense size of the universe and the uncountable number of stars and galaxies, vastly beyond the scale of anything Christianity had ever dreamed. No gods were needed to explain the formation of stars or the growth of galaxies, and it became easy to see how the earth was probably not such a unique place. Physics had discovered how energy transforms while being conserved in every event from cause to effect, and chemistry tracked matter's energies down to the atomic level. Biology teased apart the organic tissues to the cellular level, and used Darwinian evolution to learn the story of how single-celled organisms evolved into the proliferation of complex higher life. Medicine's therapies and drugs gave doctors novel life-saving powers formerly deemed miraculous. Perhaps most importantly, every aspect of the human being was receiving scientific examination. Psychology probed the mechanisms of the mind and began identifying the brain's parts responsible for our consciousness and intellectual powers. Sociology and anthropology treated morality like any other cultural phenomena, treatable with the same empirical methods that explained the diffusion and diversity of our languages and cuisines and technologies. Philosophy wrested reason itself away from the theologians by grounding rationality in simple logical principles of common sense acquired in childhood.

So many unexplained features of the natural and human world became understandable through science as the twentieth century progressed. Did theology still have anything to contribute to knowledge of the world? Scientists no longer thought so. It had been centuries since theological thinking had even offered an interesting new approach to a tough natural problem. Descartes' reformulation of the soul as the conscious mind was about the last prominent example. Theology From The World can try to survive on lingering mysteries in the universe.

A mystery by definition is awareness of the absence of knowledge. Three different kinds of mysteries should be distinguished at the outset. Ordinary mystery arises when some common sort of event happens which remains stubbornly resistant to satisfactory explanation. The experience of consciousness, shared by all, is a good example; also, many people have mystical experiences. Scientific mystery arises when special scientific investigation uncovers some new phenomenon that has not yet been satisfactorily explained. For example, the quantum entanglement of subatomic particles across vast distances has been experimentally confirmed but physicists cannot agree how to understand this phenomenon. Religious mystery arises when a religion requires dogmatic belief about a supernatural being's character or power or action which defies ordinary reason and knowledge. For example, Christianity requires belief that God raised Jesus from the dead, which contradicts medical understanding that death is permanent.

Theology From The World ideally operates by offering a religious *explanation* for either an ordinary mystery or a scientific mystery. Too frequently, however, theology instead offers a religious *mystery*. Substituting a religious mystery for an ordinary or scientific mystery is not any sort of satisfactory explanation, since mere substitution of mysteries does not increase understanding. Religious-minded people, of course, happily burden religious mystery with "explaining" what science can't, since any increased dependency on religion brings great satisfaction to them. That easy satisfaction is precisely what exposes mystery-substitution as not really any sort of explanation at all. Feeling secure in a religious mystery, satisfied by this lack of knowledge, a religious believer is not increasing knowledge at all by connecting one mystery with another. Merging two mysteries into a bigger mystery may be psychologically economical and convincing for some people, but this has nothing to do with real knowledge.

Here is a sampling of "mystery merging" that pervades simplistic theological "explanations."

1. Life is quite mysteriously different from non-life.
2. God would want his creation to include life.

Conclusion. God must exist to have created life.

3. The earth is an amazingly wonderful habitat for us.
4. God loves us so much that he would want to design a fine habitat for us.

Conclusion. God must exist to have made the earth.

5. Our lives would be meaningless and amoral if we lacked free will.
6. God needs our lives to be meaningful and moral.

Conclusion. God must exist to have given us free will.

7. We couldn't enjoy experiencing the world without consciousness.
8. God would want us to experience the world.

Conclusion. God must exist to have endowed our brains with consciousness.

9. We would be mere animals without rationality.
10. God needs us to gain knowledge through rationality.

Conclusion. God must exist to have given us rationality.

The first premises of these five god explanations – 1, 3, 5, 7, and 9 – express our wonder and curiosity about the mysteries of life, the earth, freedom, consciousness, and reason. There indeed are things well worth wondering about. The second premises of the five god explanations – 2, 4, 6, 8, and 10 – may seem simple and easily believable, to religious people. All the same, they too express mysteries. Why exactly would a god want to create life? Is this earth really such a great habitat for us? Why would a god get so concerned about our moral lives? How would a god link a physical brain to a spiritual consciousness? Why is knowledge important to a god?

These questions require good answers. They require elaborate answers, in fact, and theologians have been busy inventing a wide variety of answers that require volumes and libraries. What exactly does god want, and why would god want that? A vast number of sophisticated theologies have been formulated, by hundreds of Christian denominations and churches that cannot agree, with fresh versions arriving with every new generation of thinkers. Obviously, it really cannot be a simple and easy matter to credit god with "explaining" mysteries of nature when the god "explanations" themselves additionally require such immense labor to explain as well. It doesn't help the cause of theology either when a theologian eventually resorts to saying, "and then god performs a mysterious miracle."

Throwing a god mystery at a natural mystery doesn't really help much. It amounts to explaining a serious mystery with a convenient miracle. Learning from the above bad examples, we can set down a couple of ways that a theological "explanation" is exposed as a fraudulent pseudo-scientific explanation:

PS1 Use as a premise something like the claim that "God would want X to exist in nature."

PS2 Use as a premise something like the claim that "God would want us humans to have Y."

A genuine explanation is able to increase knowledge about reality by connecting what we already know together with we want to know. Scientific explanation is the most careful intellectual form of genuine explanation yet invented.

The most common sort of scientific explanation is used to account for some particular fact or event by appealing to established scientific knowledge. For example, why did this steel beam bend and fracture – because the tension forces upon this beam exceeded its tensile strength. These ordinary sorts of explanations rely on prior knowledge of matters like tension forces and tensile strengths. Our philosophical issue here is to discuss how scientific knowledge is first established.

A scientific explanation in general has the following form: These facts are known to be the case now; if some presently hidden thing really exists or did exist, then the known facts would have to be true; therefore, some presently hidden thing really exists or did exist. Scientific explanations offer hypotheses about nature's hidden aspects. All fully scientific theories grow from careful observation and mature by proceeding through these six steps: a natural pattern is noticed; that pattern is isolated and carefully observed; a hypothesis is proposed about some hidden thing responsible for that pattern; further observable consequences of that hidden thing's existence are deduced; experimental tests are designed to test for those consequences; and the outcomes of the tests judges the likelihood that the hidden thing really does exist.

While simplified for use here, this account of science's logical steps does not miss the essence of sound scientific inference. Highly influential accounts of scientific method rightly emphasize science's overriding concern for experiments that could disprove a hypothesis with novel evidence (see Popper 1959, Kuhn 1962). While science places its confidence in theories that have long survived rigorous testing, the many sciences have developed their own specialized techniques for observation, hypothesizing, and testing. Each of the six methodological steps have substeps, depending on the particular science, and substeps can vary enormously between sciences (see Giere et al. 2006). For example, postulating a hypothetical cause of climate change is quite different from the manner of postulating a hypothetical cause for the universe's origin, and confirming the efficacy of a new explosive differs from confirming the efficacy of a new drug. Coherence among related theories within a scientific field is critically important to develop a comprehensive view of its subject matter. Sometimes great theoretical advances are gained by reconciling inconsistencies within a theory or among theories, although proposed harmonizations must still proceed through the experimental phase for further confirmation. When several theories contest for the best explanation, further direct or indirect experimental contests can be designed to try to throw the balance of evidence towards one or another competitor. The six general stages offered here only form the basic logical structure of scientific method and do not pretend to describe the many actual efforts of scientists to invent, promote, and defend their theories. These six stages are by themselves necessary but not sufficient to account for dramatic paradigm shifts between old and new theory. The logic of scientific method is not the same as the rhetoric, sociology, or politics of scientific practice, which can be as nonlogical as any human endeavor. Nevertheless, sound scientific method tends to reassert itself in the long run, as even detractors of science must agree; their complaints of science's deviations from strict rationality only presume the existence of sound scientific method.

A couple of good examples for proper scientific method, much simplified by omitting interesting details, can illustrate the six-step scientific process. In astronomy, the discovery of Neptune occurred in 1846 because astronomers sought an explanation for small deviations in the orbit of Uranus (step one). This regular pattern of deviations, calculated by comparing Uranus's actual observed orbit with the orbit it should have according to Newtonian laws of motion and gravity, attracted attention from astronomers (step two). If another unseen planet orbited the sun beyond Uranus, they hypothesized, its gravitational pull on Uranus would cause the observed deviations (step three). When astronomers calculated where this unknown planet should be (step four), the race to perform the experiment of telescopically searching the night sky around that location (step five) was started and soon completed when Neptune was observed (step six).

In physics, the discovery of the positron occurred because physicists were attempting to explain the behavior of subatomic particles in terms of both relativistic physics and the wave mechanics of the new quantum physics. When Paul Dirac formulated a relativistic version of the Schrödinger wave function in 1928 to better explain the known behavior of electrons (steps one and two), his new formula required two solutions, yielding not only the understood properties of the electron, but also the properties of an as yet undiscovered particle having the same mass but the opposite charge of an electron (step three). Carl Anderson then sought evidence for this new particle, the "positron," by studying high-energy cosmic rays. A charged particle produced by such rays, including this hypothesized positron, should leave a characteristic curved path of condensation in a cloud chamber filled with a magnetic field (step four). Anderson's cloud chamber experiments in 1932 (step five) did reveal this path of condensation, which precisely matched the predicted path of a positron (step six).

To summarize, a genuine scientific hypothesis is a hypothesis that is designed to explain a natural pattern already scientifically observed, and is testable by the scientific method, outlined above. There are many ways that people can prevent their hypothesis from being genuinely scientific. In addition to PS1 and PS2 mentioned already, more prominent signs that someone is actually promoting a pseudo-scientific hypothesis are the following:

PS3 Offering an explanation for phenomena that have not been scientifically observed.
PS4 Refusing to deduce predictions from the supposed existence of the postulated entity.
PS5 Ensuring that any predictions are vague, unsurprising, impossible to test, or ignorable when false.
PS6 Modifying the hypothesis just enough to be able to afterwards 'predict' a bad experimental result.

To summarize, a pseudo-scientific explanation involves a hypothesis that fails to be genuinely scientific according to any of PS1–PS6. As we proceed to examine some prominent arguments by Theology From The World, we shall see how these arguments eventually appeal to pseudo-scientific explanations.

4.2 Arguments from Nature

All plausible arguments that start from nature in order to establish the existence of god must take either the deductive or abductive forms. An inductive argument for god would only succeed in begging the question, since some pattern of divine events would be needed to show that a god now exists. Of course, the real issue is whether there have ever really been any divine activities affecting nature.

A sound deductive argument for god from nature would ideally have something like the following general structure:

1. A natural phenomenon X has no scientific explanation now, and may never get any scientific explanation.
2. X has a theological explanation that avoids PS1–PS6.

Conclusion. God exists.

This sort of argument undertakes two huge challenges: first, it must plausibly show that some natural X will probably never get a scientific explanation; and second, it must ensure that a theological explanation avoids falling into mere pseudo-science. Proving that something natural will never be explained by science cannot be easy. Scientists can honestly admit when they don't yet have a scientific explanation for something. But no scientist should proclaim that science could never explain some natural phenomenon, since that very claim would require scientific evidence in support, the sort of evidence which everyone admits is obviously lacking too.

Some philosophers and theologians, on the other hand, do occasionally announce that science must forever fail to explain some things in nature. These thinkers must know a whole lot more about reality than the sciences, and they must know much more about science than scientists as well. Where could they obtain such impressive knowledge? All the same, defenders of supernaturalism often do claim that science is forever incapacitated from explaining some matters going on in the world. Only a few prominent cases can be discussed in this chapter; theological accounts offering god's activity to supplement nature range across most scientific fields (useful surveys are Drees 1996 and Southgate 2005). The most popular mode of argument is still about design: the apparent design of things in nature (for Theology From The World) and the apparent design of the universe as a whole (a topic for Theology Beyond The World). The recent emergence of intelligent design theory attempts to cover both kinds of explanation (see, for example, Dembski 1999, 2004).

Science's confessed inability to explore the supernatural is an entirely different issue; here we are discussing science's capacity to explore and explain natural things. Modern experimental science has been around for only about 400 years. No one can justly say that in the far future science will still be unable to explain some things. Popular contemporary examples of science's limits include problems explaining the complexities of organic DNA and evolution, the nature of consciousness, and quantum phenomena. Biology, psychology, and physics have not explained everything in their fields, yet these inadequacies cannot demonstrate the need to postulate a god that only adds to the mystery.

Darwinian natural selection's vast capacity to explain the historical fossil record and current distribution of related species needs no recounting here (see Dawkins 2009). The coherent synthesis of natural evolution, genetics, and the chemistry of DNA tells a near-complete story of how organisms descend from ancestors in diverse new species. Dramatically losing its monopoly on explaining life's evolution, religion can still find opportunities to inject divine action and intelligent design into the story of life. The high complexity and apparent design of life forms still inspires supernaturalism. There are important remaining questions about how the first life arose from organic molecules, how genetic material can convey information sufficient for self-replication, how intermediate forms of bodily organs can function sufficiently for an organism's survival, and how genetic mutations are responsible for new species. A few scholars who are fairly well informed about the way biology is trying to answer such questions remain convinced that it will never succeed on purely naturalistic grounds (a broad treatment of biology's issues is Dembski and Wells 2007). For example, it is argued that the odds of a new complex arrangement of an organ's components actually working are so small that supernatural forces or divine guidance may be required (see Behe 2006, 2007). For all the complaints about what biology cannot presently explain, no given example of such "irreducible complexity" has withstood critical scrutiny; such examples typically depend on ignoring available evidence and Darwinian explanations. Even religious scientists complain about such severe problems, preferring only a god who sets life's initial conditions (Collins 2006, Miller 2008). The field of Intelligent Design at this point amounts to traditional supernatural creationism rather than a respectably scientific research program (Forrest and Gross 2004, Shermer 2006). Biology's astonishing progress explaining the complex features and evolution of life will doubtless continue, and estimates of where biology must halt before a mystery are highly premature.

A widespread tactic for religion's defenders consists of first defining some problem so that no natural explanation seems ever available. For example, special definitions of the physical and the mental can leave them without anything in common, so any connection seems necessarily mysterious. Modern philosophers, especially those with supernatural worldviews, were especially adept at this tactic. Descartes, Locke, Leibniz, and then Kant (all religious thinkers) judged that any connection between mind and body cannot be explained naturalistically, leaving room for the supernatural soul. Another suspicious strategy in the mind–body debates is for the religion defender to define naturalism as the attempted reduction of everything to "nothing but" the smallest particles and their laws. Another widespread depiction of naturalism is that what naturalism cannot reduce, it eliminates as illusory and unreal. When the intellect rebels at any satisfying reduction or elimination of consciousness, religion can claim a false victory. However, some sensible varieties of naturalism are not pure reductivism or eliminitivism worldviews (for examples see Ryder 1994). The sciences can study mental awareness, and science's evident capacity to show the intricate and constant connections between mental activity and brain activity actually exposes their mutual interdependence. This interdependence suggests that mind and brain are tightly interconnected orders of nature or they are aspects of one common reality (nonreductive approaches have proliferated, including Davidson 1980, Searle 1992, Chalmers 1996, Putnam 2000). Scientific evidence provides for an excellent argument, an argument of positive philosophical atheology, that all mind is intrinsically connected to some physical embodiment. The supernaturalist notion that soul/spirit/mind can exist independent of body is therefore highly improbable.

Another example of defining a mystery so that it defies rational explanation is theological misuse of quantum physics. A variety of consequences of quantum physics have been understood as pointing towards god. Quantum physics suggests that particles are often better understood as waves instead, provoking the theological notion that ultimate reality is chaotic or mysterious enough to hide god's activities behind appearances, and that science is no better at deciding ultimate reality than religion. The mysterious properties of particles have suggested that two objects once joined somehow remain simultaneously linked despite their separation across wide distances that light cannot traverse in time to supply a causal explanation for the link. Quantum physics has even been understood as proposing that the universe isn't really composed of particular things but rather large wholes instead, and perhaps nature must consist of one fairly indivisible whole. It is not clear that quantum physics requires such radical revisions, since the frontiers of scientific discovery are constantly shifting and uncertain. All these suggestive possibilities at most indicate that quantum physics is gradually modifying older understandings of the physical world, demanding some modifications to naturalism's worldview to keep pace with science. But naturalism itself is untouched and untroubled by this progressive evolution; naturalism is precisely the worldview designed to incorporate science's confirmed knowledge. If naturalism is forced by science to reduce emphasis on older notions of reductivism or localism or determinism, then naturalism is enriched and strengthened, not diminished. Theological suspicions that quantum physics demonstrates a few of the older naturalism's inadequacies hardly shows that anything supernatural is suggested or confirmed by science. As an example, trying to find divine or spiritual action in the supposed gaps of quantum indeterminacy cannot be scientifically verified and only adds to the mysteriousness of how a god or soul could interact with natural energies without violating physical laws in the process. There have been bold speculations entangling quantum mysteries with consciousness mysteries, suggesting that consciousness is a manifestation of quantum-level processes among brain neurons (see Penrose 1989, Kaufmann 2008). Even if quantum phenomena are involved with consciousness, this would be a new naturalistic discovery, and not any justification for spiritualist or supernaturalist notions. Other theological attempts to make room for god in the uncertain corners of quantum phenomena are equally suspicious (see the skepticism of Stenger 2009).

Theology isn't really doing any valuable work by chasing science's frontiers. Every generation of theologians who made careers predicting that science could never explain something had impressive stances right up until the time when science did explain it. Examples over the last ten centuries are assertions that science would never explain non-linear motion, the nature of stars, magnetism, light, how organisms use air, the age of the earth, the diversity of life, and the transmission of life in reproduction. Upon these mysteries and many more, believers constructed elaborate philosophical and theological systems to do what they thought science could never do. But in time, physics, astronomy, chemistry, geology, biology, and genetics have satisfactorily explained all these things. The history of such metaphysical speculations trying to outmatch science is littered with exploded and abandoned systems of thought. Does not this disappointing track record give pause to the next generation? Apparently not, since clever mystery-mongers always find their public eager to view the spectacle of science hitting a wall. Too many people overlook the critical fallacy in this strategy: science's current inability to explain something has little bearing on whether future science will become more powerful and capable. It has always been a bad bet to bet against science.

Ensuring that a theological explanation avoids pseudo-science is no easy task either. The two greatest obstacles are the temptations to appeal to what god would want to do, and to avoid making verifiable predictions about the future. These temptations are especially difficult to resist for a religion like Christianity, whose god is conceived as like a person in certain key respects. For example, Christians regard their god as an agent who does things with some plan in mind (like creating humans) and who prefers some things over others (like humans avoiding sin). If god is like a personal agent, it seems natural to think about what god would do (such as communicating with us, or punishing sin). Similarly, because Christians view god as a personal agent, they sharply distinguish expectations about what god is doing from trying to make exact predictions about what god must do. As something akin to a person, god would not be a mechanical or computational machine, or a natural force obeying strict law. People are not perfectly predictable, and so neither would god be.

If a deductive argument cannot in the end really do the job needed for Theology From The World, abduction is still available. An abductive argument for god from nature would have this general structure:

3. If God exists, then a natural phenomenon X would be expected.
4. This natural phenomenon X is actually observed.

Conclusion. God exists.

Even if premise 3 could be established without running into trouble with PS1–PS6, remember that we are here dealing with abduction. There could always be other possible explanations for X, and these explanations could prove to be entirely natural, so that a god hypothesis isn't needed.

4.3 Arguments from Design

Arguments from design are clear examples of the way that natural theology suffers when science offers satisfactory alternative explanations. Arguments from design are abductive arguments having the following general form:

5. If God exists, then a natural phenomenon X would appear to be designed.
6. This natural phenomenon X does appear to be designed.

Conclusion. God exists.

The traditional argument from design starts from something natural that is sufficiently organized and complex that it looks artificial and not natural. We can't imagine how nature could have made it, so we see design instead. A designed artifact, the reasoning proceeds, must have a maker. Abduction suggests god, and failing any other explanation, this argument's conclusion selects god. All sort of things can appear to be designed, from watches and houses to organisms and planets. Our brains have robust design detectors (see Dennett 1987), but these information processing methods can be fooled, and they often are.

The design argument is obviously fallacious because not everything that appears designed may actually be designed. Science has reasonably established alternative explanations for many things that appear designed. For example, the solar system's organization of planets in stable orbits might look designed, until the nebular hypothesis of solar system formation made it easier to see how nature alone generates solar systems that look like ours. As another example, a life form's organization from cells to tissues to organs to the entire organism can look designed, until scientific accounts of the growth and development of an organism from initial single-celled conception to full adulthood were available. Finally, life itself may seem designed, but Darwinian evolution has provided an alternative account of the development of more and more complex organisms from very simple beginnings.

It is not necessary to "prove" the correctness of any of these alternative scientific explanations in order to logically reject the argument from design. Science does not "prove" its more speculative explanations in any case, but only reasonably confirms them through rigorous testing of hypotheses against the evidence. It is simply sufficient to show that science can postulate reasonable alternative explanations, so that it is no longer necessary to resort to the postulate of a divine designer.

The argument from design can be reformulated as a deductive argument, seemingly capable of proving god's existence. This deductive version suffers from devastating but revealing errors and fallacies.

7. A sufficiently complex thing is so improbable that it can only have been created by something of greater complexity.
8. Some natural things are so complex that nothing in the natural universe can explain their creation.
9. Only a supernatural being could have created these highly complex natural things.

Conclusion. God exists.

Premise 7 simply begs the entire question against natural science's efforts to explain the creation of highly complex organisms through a long process of biological evolution. Premise 8 similarly begs the question against science. Premise 9 presumptively credits a lone divine being for the responsibility of creating nature, but there are other (equally implausible) alternatives, like a committee of divine beings. All three premises can only lead straight to pseudo-science. To avoid begging questions and throwing out natural science, the theologian would have to point to something maximally complex in the natural world which science presumably cannot deal with. How about the complexity of entire natural universe? At this stage the theologian leaves science behind entirely and proceeds to Theology Beyond The World, where arguments over the design of the universe are debated.

Furthermore, if the theologian really believes premise 7, then it applies to a god as well. Who made god? And who made god's maker, etc.? An infinite regress abruptly arises (see Dawkins 2006). The theologian can bravely accept the infinite regress and declare that the Christian God is maximally complex (an expected perfection of god, perhaps) so that nothing more complex can be conceived, ending the infinite regress with the true god. This bold move does not logically work, however. Dawkins points out that the logical corollary and true meaning for premise 7: the greater the complexity, the greater the improbability. A supernatural being must be much more improbable than anything natural. A Christian theologian's perfect god must therefore be maximally improbable! The only way to prevent this devastating counter-argument against the probability that god exists would be for the theologian to exempt god from premise 7. God must somehow be exempt from the otherwise general rule that something of greater complexity is needed for explaining things of lesser complexity. There are many specific forms that this exemption takes. For example, some theologians retreat to the notion of a necessarily existing god, while others abruptly decide that complexity is no perfection and declare god to be simple. Any such exemption to premise 7 again abandons all pretense of scientific method and retreats to Theology Beyond The World.

Besides, if the theologian is permitted to arbitrarily exempt god from premise 7, why can't others propose an exemption for biological life? In fact, that is precisely what Darwinian evolution already did, when it rejected the theological preference for premise 7 and offered a scientifically respectable alternative which explains how more complex organisms naturally arise from less complex organisms. Neither theology nor biology could be blamed for eventually abandoning premise 7; it is a primitive medieval notion that falls apart upon any inspection by theology or science. The more significant difference remains: to explain complexity biology remains loyal to scientific method, while theology is forced to abandon science.

4.4 Arguments from Religious Experience

Sometimes supernaturalism appeals to direct experience to argue that a god exists. Revelation in its general sense is taken to be a direct encounter with something divine, such as an encounter with a god, an event caused by a god, or a sign of divine presence or activity. Revelation from scripture is discussed in Chapter 3. Here we discuss two more arguments from religious experience: the first starts from collective experiences of many people, while the second only needs one personal experience.

Revelations taken collectively, from different people of the same religion, or people of different religions, obviously exhibit incredibly immense variety. Revelations can be highly mysterious in themselves rather than indicate how a god is involved, so no inferences about anything divine could be drawn. Revelations often contradict each other, lessening their credibility, and they often yield beliefs that different gods exist – unless there are a million gods, this variety dramatically weakens the credibility of any single revelation. Precisely because religious believers understand all these problems, they are tempted to resort to the additional unjustifiable claim that their own revelation is different as an exemption from such rules. Revelations taken collectively only lead to an inevitable skepticism about their ability to rationally support the existence of any god.

Religious believers can attempt to claim that only some collective experiences supply revelation evidence: the highly similar experiences of the same sort of god. Indeed, many religions are based on a small set of near-identical experiences of the same god by a small group of people, in order to avoid all the noted violations of reason. This special set of revelations can serve as an authoritative guide to proper religious beliefs, useful for instruction in the religion and for testing any new revelations for validity. Unfortunately, problems with reason remain. There is no good explanation why just this group's set of similar experiences should count as the only valid revelations. They should not claim that god approves of just this set and no others since that assumes that god exists, only begging the question. If the group claims that no other experiences belong because they are too different from the basic set, this justification is fallaciously circular by first assuming the validity of the group. If the group claims their set of revelations seem like the best about god to them, any other group could make the same sort of justification for their revelations and their god, so there is no rational support for this group. Small sets of revelations gain no more rational support than large collections.

The best theological argument from revelation should stay focused on private, personal experiences. This tactic avoids the problems already mentioned, and it makes better sense when trying to understand religions and revelation anyway. Put another way, if only collective shared common experiences count as revelations, most of the genuinely intriguing and impressive accounts of divine appearance and intervention are discarded. How could Judaism, Christianity, Islam, or Buddhism be taken seriously as religions if the private experiences of a Moses, Jesus, Muhammad, or Buddha don't really matter? Of course, some of their followers may receive impressive revelations, but that's the point: deeply loyal followers (a Paul, for example) can have some private revelation experiences too.

Because an argument from revelation is best based on personal experience, arguing over the validity of revelation must not assume otherwise. For example, demanding that one revelation must get confirmed by lots of other identical revelations doesn't make sense. Science demands plenty of common confirmations, but that is an advanced principle of science and not among the simple basic rules of reason. Without independent confirmations, can a revelation experience get validated as proof of god's existence?

Supernaturalism argues that the best explanation for a revelation experience that seems to be about god is that it is actually caused by god. Therefore, supernaturalism must prove that there cannot be any equally good, or better, explanation, for revelation experiences. The three simplest naturalistic accounts of alleged revelations are (a) erroneous perception, (b) illusion, and (c) hallucination. Naturalism therefore offers the strongest explanation for revelations to rival supernaturalism: all revelations are cases of either error, illusion, or hallucination. The ordinary method of showing that a strange experience is either error, illusion, or hallucination is to investigate the experience to discover if some natural thing was erroneously perceived, something naturally real operated on perception to cause an illusion, or nothing was in fact perceived but only internally generated by a brain malfunction. By contrast, there is no "ordinary method" of showing that a strange experience is an actual revelation of an existing god. In fact, there can't be any method at all, since we have agreed to consider only lone experiences taken singly. Common sense suggests some options: for example, verifying a revelation would consist of checking to see if god is actually present, but such checking would consist of a second revelation of god, and we are getting nowhere. Verification could track the causal relationship between god and the person having the experience, but that also presupposes god. Verification could consist of checking one revelation against other revelations already verified, but that appeals to an established group of revelations, and there aren't any justified groups, as we have already explained.

The impossibility of verifying lone revelations has been noticed by supernaturalists. Some supernaturalists therefore claim that revelations do not need any verification. They don't need verification if they have the special character of "self-verification" or "self-evidence" or "veracity." This tactic sounds like a way to avoid having to justify revelations, but that burden cannot be avoided. The supernaturalist must at least explain how to distinguish when an experience truly possesses this self-evident character and when an experience does not (for not all experiences, and not all claimed revelations, have it). The supernaturalist might claim that self-evident revelations are ones that common sense does not challenge but simply accepts until proven false. Much of ordinary experience goes unchallenged, it is true, but revelations about god are almost always challenged and questioned by some people, especially by people of other religions. Worse, plenty of religions all claim that revelations of their particular god carry such self-evident verification, so that appeal to self-evidence cannot help any religion. If a supernaturalist claims that other religions' revelations fail to carry proper self-evidence since they are not about the truly existing god, that explanation only begs the question of god's existence. When supernaturalists are required to describe what this "self-evident" character actually consists of, they are always driven back to favorably comparing a revelation with other prior approved revelations or comparing a revelation with an approved prior conception of god. Neither option supplies the needed rational justification, so the argument from lone revelation is a failure.

One interesting variation on the argument from revelation is the argument from testimony about revelation for god. By this argument, the best explanation for the existence of people's testimony about their revelations is that god exists to deliver these revelations. Since this argument must assume the existence of genuine revelations, and the argument that there are genuine revelations fails, this argument from testimony automatically fails too. Additionally, naturalistic explanations for why people make testimonial claims about revelations are numerous and persuasive to common sense. For example, people frequently do make revelation claims when they falsely believe that a revelation has happened to them. Also, people sometimes invent and lie about revelations in order to deal with great emotional stress or psychological trauma, to draw attention to themselves, to cause public sensations, or to make money. Furthermore, no religion can rationally explain why its own scriptural testimony is good evidence for the existence of its own god while other religions' scriptures are all bad testimony. No appeal to religious scripture can be used to form an adequate rational argument for the existence of a god.

Because direct arguments over revelation fail to justify the validity of religious experiences, theology has turned elsewhere. Abductive arguments have come to play a large role in theological explanations for religious experiences. For example, consider this argument:

1. If god exists, then people would occasionally experience what they believe is god.
2. People occasionally experience what they believe is god.

Conclusion. God exists.

There are natural alternatives to this god hypothesis under examination by science right now. Consider this alternative: the brain can produce hallucinations. The alternative naturalistic argument would then be:

3. If the brain can produce hallucinations, then people would occasionally experience what they believe is god.
4. People occasionally experience what they believe is god.

Conclusion. The brain can produce hallucinations.

The notion that the brain can produce hallucinations is already well supported by common sense and scientific investigation into the brain. The kinds of hallucinations providing experiences that people commonly report as "religious" or "mystical" experiences of contact with something divine may be simply caused by the brain's own functioning under various extreme conditions. Examples of extreme conditions that affect the brain's functioning are private emotional disturbances, excitations in public groups, physical stress, uncomfortable sleep, lack of sleep, sensory deprivation, and drugs.

Religions have an intimate practical understanding of the usefulness of these extreme conditions for increasing the chances of having religious experiences. Many religions teach practices, not surprisingly, that can bring people closer to these extreme conditions. From isolated meditation and church chanting, to spirit quests in nature and ingesting all sorts of drugs, religions have experimented with every possible variation on extreme conditions. Religions that do not emphasize such practices typically place less burden and expectation on their followers to have religious experiences as well. For example, mainline Protestant denominations, where stressful conditions are not emphasized, have a correspondingly reduced expectation that members regularly have religious experiences. In fact, mainline Protestant denominations for 200 years have displayed more indifference to, or suspicion towards, people having ecstatic mystical revelations than the evangelical, pentecostal, and revivalist denominations. One might even categorize all religions into three primary groups: those desiring regular religious experiences and teaching practices to reliably arouse them; those favorable towards religious experiences but which don't institute practices to aid people; and those which regard religious experiences with indifference or even suspicion.

Recent cognitive psychology and brain experiments have been able to duplicate many of the characteristics of religious/mystical experiences. Experiments have caused subjects to think that another unseen being is nearby, to feel like they are leaving their bodies, to enjoy moments of pleasurable bliss, or to hear voices that aren't really there. Religions, however they may favor religious experiences, themselves understand how people can have spontaneous hallucinations that are only caused by their minds/brains and not by god. After all, religions have long been using the idea of natural hallucination themselves, in order to explain why people report false revelations from god, or why people of other religions report revelations of other gods that don't really exist. The scientific method simply applies cognitive and brain science to all religions without prejudice. This neutrality means that scientific study of religious experiences cannot, by itself, prove whether a god exists. This ambiguity does not prevent people from supposing that scientific investigation of religious experiences and spiritual phenomena helpfully validates religious belief in god (Alper 2008, Hagerty 2009, Newberg and Waldman 2009).

It may be possible some day to apply the sciences to explain all features of religious/mystical experiences by naturally inducing people to have them. Nevertheless, even if such explanatory power were achieved, this could only reduce the likelihood that a divine power is involved, without eliminating that possibility. If science did try to conclude logically that nothing divine could be involved, only because it could induce religious experiences by natural methods, that logical argument could be equally applied to human experiences of everything else. Could a powerful brain science figure out how to induce a visual experience of your friend? If so, does that henceforth mean that your friend never really exists when you think that you have contact with her by seeing her? Consider the following general argument, which surely goes too far:

5. If science can naturally induce your brain to have an experience of an interaction with an X, then you aren't really interacting with an X at that moment, but you are only having a brain experience that seems just like an interaction with that X.
6. Science can naturally induce your brain to have an experience of an interaction with an X.

Conclusion. You have never really had an interaction with an X.

If "god" is substituted for the "X" in this argument, then science achieves its naturalistic aim: you have never really had an interaction with god. But everything else inducible by some future brain science can be substituted one by one into this argument too, such as your friend, this book, the sun, that apple, your toes, etc. Because it seems ridiculous to conclude that you have never really seen any of these things, we can detect the fallacy of the general argument. Just because some powerful science can induce an "artificial" brain experience of an X, this achievement by itself could never make it reasonable to conclude that no one has ever interacted with an X. After all, there are other reasonable ways to naturally induce a brain to generate the experience of interacting with an apple. For example, under quite normal natural conditions you can induce a person's brain to have an experience of interacting with, say, an apple, by handing that person an apple.

The general argument's fallacious attempt to eliminate contacts with god could be repaired by expanding the argument. After all, apples are not exactly like deities. Can this expanded argument do a better job of eliminating gods but not friends or apples?

7. If science can naturally induce your brain to have an experience of an interaction with an X that probably doesn't exist anyway, then you aren't really interacting with an X at that moment, but are only having a brain experience that seems just like an interaction with that X.
8. Science can naturally induce your brain to have an experience of an interaction with an X.

9. Therefore, you are only having a brain experience that seems just like an interaction with that X.
10. Since that X probably doesn't exist anyway, then science's artificial inducement of seeming contact with X implies that you have even less reason to believe that X exists.
11. You have little reason to believe that Xs really exist.

Conclusion. You have never really had an interaction with an X.

This expanded argument against improbable Xs is now logically effective against gods but not apples, provided only that apples probably exist and gods probably do not exist. Hence this expanded argument will be quite persuasive for people who already think that gods probably do not exist and who accept premise 7 as true. People who think that there is a probability (a small probability at least) that some god does exist will not accept premise 7, and therefore reasonably deny the argument's conclusion. For a science-based argument against god, this version completely fails, since it basically begs the question. It proposes to make belief in god unreasonable, but its first premise already demands one to regard god's existence as improbable from the start. Religious believers would rightly regard this argument as irrelevant (and perhaps close to pseudo-science!). Even an agnostic, who has not decided that god probably doesn't exist, could not get any help from this argument.

It is particularly ironic that advanced scientific knowledge of the brain could not even assist the agnostic on the question of religious experiences. In fact, religious believers could take advantage of this situation and offer the agnostic a potentially persuasive counter-argument based on religious experience.

12. If god's existence is not improbable, then it is possible that an existing god would divinely induce your brain to have an experience of interacting with him.
13. In general, unless the existence of an X is improbable, your experience of interacting with that X should be reasonably regarded as genuine, unless other good reasons suggest otherwise.
14. If you have an experience of interacting with god, you should reasonably regard it as genuine, unless other good reasons suggest otherwise.

Conclusion. People who experience god reasonably believe that god exists, unless other good reasons suggest otherwise.

This counter-argument aimed at agnostics is developed extensively in Menssen and Sullivan (2007). It must not be confused with a much more aggressive argument, offered by Theology In The Know, that any religious experience must be regarded as just as reasonable as any other genuine experience of the world. The above argument only wants religious experiences to be regarded as reasonable candidates for experiencing a real god. Its humbler stance is clearly indicated by the modifying clause, "unless other good reasons suggest otherwise."

Are there other good reasons, besides what science may learn about the brain's functioning, to suggest that religious experiences may not actually be of a divine being? Other sciences can easily suggest reasons to be skeptical towards interactions with god. But these skeptical methods must be applied carefully, or else they will quickly backfire and inspire counter-arguments beneficial to supernaturalism. In the following examples, the first case of each example can easily backfire into a counter argument for religion, while the second case has better logical strength against religion.

Biology Case One

Human brains have evolved to deal with the natural environment, so they would not have evolved to experience anything supernatural. However, humans around the world still commonly have religious experiences, so by evolution's own logic that useful traits universally survive, perhaps brains evolved to also have contact with god?

Biology Case Two

Humans have evolved brains that evidently work best dealing with nature since people can largely agree on what they perceive around them (making languages possible, for example). By contrast, people and religions have great difficulty agreeing on what might be perceived in religious experiences, and common languages are notoriously rare (it is hard to comprehend or compare religious experiences).

Psychology Case One

When humans try to describe features of religious/mystical experiences, the commonest features amount to little more than feeling infinite, or awed by something infinite, or feeling intense bliss/peace/love. However, humans around the world still frequently experience these basic features, so by psychology's own logic that agreement enhances validity. Perhaps the same divinity is responsible for most religious/mystical experiences?

Psychology Case Two

Humans happen to have the kinds of unusual experiences labeled as "religious" or "mystical" because a few common features can unite them into a group. This is probably an arbitrary grouping, since many other features of unusual experiences are selected by various religions as also essential to contact with their preferred divinity. There is no way to objectively figure out which features of unusual experiences are really the "valid" features indicating contact with a god.

Cultural Anthropology Case One

Humans have evolved culturally to incorporate religious beliefs, rituals, and institutions into their social systems, but the practical utility of religion does not require that any god actually exists. However, humans around the world do find that actually believing in some god provides religion with its utility and power, so by cultural anthropology's own logic that reasonable beliefs track reasonable practices, perhaps belief in some god is entirely reasonable for humans.

Cultural Anthropology Case Two

Humans happen to have cultures which incorporate religious beliefs, rituals, and institutions into their social systems, and cultures have invented an incredibly diverse number of ways to achieve the practical benefits of religion. Religions therefore display a bewildering variety of characteristics that somehow serve in some particular society or another. There is no way to objectively figure out which religion is more practical or which more correctly understands god.

The three examples of "Case Two" from these three sciences avoid generating a useful counter-example lending plausibility to religion. Instead, they suggest good reasons to be skeptical towards the idea that religious experiences are actual interactions with something supernatural. Recall premise 14 of the counter-argument for agnostics, discussed above: "If you have an experience of interacting with god, you should reasonably regard it as genuine, unless other good reasons suggest otherwise." Well, here are four good reasons suggesting otherwise:

Brains can naturally generate, or be artificially induced to generate, many features of religious experiences.
Brains don't seem to have evolved for working best with religious experiences.
Minds can't objectively sort out which kinds of religious experiences really involve a god.
Cultures don't converge on a most practical or accurate kind of religion.

If an agnostic did have a religious experience, these four reasons to doubt should make an agnostic hesitate to decide to believe in god. These reasons are together sufficient for that agnostic to remain skeptical that in all probability no god was really involved.

Religions are hardly daunted by these problems; they have long understood that immense variability among religious experiences casts doubts on the special validity of any one of them. Religions have gone further to design theological justifications for privileged religious experiences (the ones supporting that religion's beliefs, of course!). These theological justifications amount to nothing more than pseudo-science (or mutate into

Theology In The Know). Consider some typical responses by Christian theologies:

> Do brains naturally generate, or are they artificially induced to generate, many features of religious experiences? That only means that god wanted to give us brains that are quite responsive to divine contact, and therefore our brains can also generate false reports too. Just because there are some false reports, that cannot imply that all reports must be false. Fortunately, god wants to divinely induce religious experiences through our brains so that people can experience god.
>
> Do brains appear to have evolved for working better with nature than with religious experiences? That only means that over the course of human evolution, experiences of nature were far more frequent than experiences of god. Just because religious experiences are infrequent, that cannot imply that they fail to contact god. Fortunately, god wants to occasionally reveal himself to people so that they can interact with god.
>
> Do minds have difficulty objectively sorting out which kinds of religious experiences really involve a god? That only means that most people don't know enough about god to reliably figure out which religious experiences are genuine. Just because most people are ignorant, that cannot imply that everyone is. Fortunately, god wanted to reveal himself to chosen authorities who are then in the right position to judge all valid religious experiences.
>
> Do cultures fail to converge on a most practical or accurate kind of religion? That only means that few cultures enjoy the correct religion preferred by god. Just because most cultures have failed to recognize the one true god and adopt the correct religion, that cannot imply that every religion is lost in ignorance. Fortunately, god wanted to reveal himself to his chosen people so that the one true religion can be enjoyed by those cultures that decide to accept the truth.

These theological responses are obviously just more examples of mystery preserving pseudo-science that violates PS1 or PS2. More sophisticated versions defending religious experience by Theology From The World are not hard to invent, but they too eventually violate PS3–PS6. Religions, including Christianity, notoriously refuse to try to reliably predict when, how, or why god may cause religious experiences. They also refuse to define exactly how god would or should reveal himself in religious experiences. Christianity is a good example of a religion that tolerates an unpredictable, multi-faceted, and quite mysterious god. This impressive flexibility and vagueness almost guarantees that any Christian's religious experience, provided that it doesn't sound too much like the devil or another religion's god, can count as an experience of the Christian God. This wide accommodation of religious experience no doubt helps Christianity succeed as a religion, but it is no help in theology.

4.5 Arguments from Morality

There are a variety of theological arguments from morality designed to conclude that something supernatural must exist. Bringing together many of the key points made by these arguments, a concise argument from morality can be constructed:

1. The truth of moral rules requires the existence of a supernatural reality to explain their truth.
2. The ability of people to be moral requires the existence of a supernatural being to communicate moral knowledge to people.
3. The capacity for people to be responsible moral agents requires that people possess some supernatural property or be partly supernatural.
4. The motivation of people to be moral requires the existence of a supernatural being to guarantee that moral conduct is not ultimately meaningless.

Conclusion. Something supernatural must exist to explain these four features of morality.

How should the naturalist reply to this argument? The naturalist replies that all four premises are false. Naturalism can satisfactorily account for moral truth, moral knowledge, moral motivation, and moral capacity.

In support of premise 1, the theologian appeals to the existence of absolute moral truths: these truths are both universal (true for everyone) and eternal (must always be true). Only such absolute truths, if there really are any, could present a problem for the naturalist and suggest that something supernatural must be involved. An absolute truth of any sort would be a problem for naturalism, the theologian reasons, because there couldn't be anything in nature anywhere that could be responsible for making that absolute truth actually true. Natural truths, those truths about something natural, might sometimes be universal but could never be eternal. For example, the truth that "There are seven continents on the planet earth" is true for everyone (its truth doesn't depend on what any person thinks) but it is not eternal (its truth does depend on the current geology of the earth, which is constantly changing). In time any natural truth could become false, and nothing can guarantee that a natural truth won't someday be false. That is because nature is a scene of constant change. Even truths about laws of nature are only true because this natural universe happens to now exist. Every natural truth is only relatively true, relative to that part of nature which makes it truth for a while. The theologian then reasons that, if that nature cannot make an absolute truth true, then something supernatural must be responsible instead.

Even though absolute moral truths would present naturalism with a severe challenge, the naturalist has a simple way of dealing with this potential problem: simply deny that there really are any absolute moral truths. For the naturalist, every truth, including moral truths, must be some type of relative truth. The naturalist recognizes that there are many moral truths, but are any absolute? This burden of proof is on the theologian, since an extraordinary claim is asserted here. The theologian must first prove the existence of one, just one, *absolute* moral truth. Let the theologian propose some candidate, such as "thou shall not kill." A commendable moral truth, indeed, and one with which civilized people should agree. How can we know that this is an absolute moral truth? The theologian cannot just say, "It is absolute because god commanded it," since that explanation begs the question. We must find an absolute moral truth first, if there are any. Can the theologian point to the fact that this moral truth is acknowledged as absolute by many people? Perhaps it is; yet the proffered evidence just amounts to a large collection of people believing in this moral truth absolutely, which only reawakens the problem, that this truth now relatively depends on some people. An absolute truth cannot depend on just many people believing it, since people come and go and they change their minds. Similarly, the theologian cannot offer as evidence of absolute truth the relative fact that entire religions or even entire cultures accept a moral truth. In any case, finding any substantive moral rule (more specific than mere platitudes or clichés like "love thy neighbor") that most religious people believe, or even a substantive moral rule that most people in the same religion really believe and consistently live by, is a difficult task.

Consider how all religions including Christianity have modified their moral rules over the centuries, and how they have all broken apart into sects and denominations, precisely because they cannot agree on serious moral principles. Religion is a poor place to go looking for allegedly universal and eternal moral truths.

Hypothetically, even if the theologian could put forward a moral truth that every single person on the planet now accepts as true, that only makes that moral truth relative to this quite large collection of people. It would be impressive, nevertheless, to find a universally accepted moral truth. None has ever been found. A handful of prohibitions against deeds like killing innocent members of one own tribe, marrying close family members, and behaving too selfishly can be found in nearly all known human cultures. However, there is no universal agreement on whether these rules have exceptions and, if so, what those exceptions should be. If there was a god who desired all humans to follow some set of specially defined rules, this god has spectacularly failed to accomplish such a goal. Does the naturalist have an easier way to explain the near-universal acceptance of a few basic rules and the immense variation and disagreement about all other moral rules across cultures?

Friends of religion often claim that, if there are no absolute moral truths, then there are no moral truths at all, and that morality is simply whatever each person wants to be moral. This nasty alternative is called moral subjectivism. One's own subjective opinion about what is right and wrong would be, friends of religion fear, the only option left in a world without absolute moral truths. According to naturalism, there are no absolute moral truths. But morality is not simply subjective, either: most of morality consists of culturally *objective* truths, and the rest is indeed subjective. An objective moral truth is made true by the natural fact that a society of people share a common culture which includes that accepted truth among its social rules. An objective truth is still relative to people, but not to any individual person. Because cultures make most moral truths true, these moral truths are only relatively true, even if some people within that culture actually believe that some moral truths are absolutely true. The difference between objective moral truth and absolute moral truth is that such absolute truth is objectivity plus infallibility: it can never be different or wrong. According to naturalism, there are no such infallible or unchangeable moral truths, so there are no absolute moral truths.

Naturalism understands how morality is an essential part of human culture, and how a person should be moral in order to live a cultured social life with others. Only false caricatures of naturalism, often drawn by friends of religion, could suggest that naturalism's perspective on human life can only see brute selfishness. The Social Darwinism of nineteenth-century materialism was not based on sound evolutionary theory or sociology. Naturalistic accounts of morality presently emphasize the evolutionary origins of moral instincts and the cultural pressures guiding the moral development of humanity (see for example Hauser 2006, Joyce 2006, Schweitzer and Notarbartolo-di-Sciara 2009). Like the capacity for other kinds of knowledge, the human capacity for moral feelings and knowledge is part of our species, but moral rules can take diverse complex forms across cultures.

There are some vague moral rules found across most societies, but each society can only really know the specific morality needed for its distinctive culture. Culturally objective morality is not absolute, but only objective. Therefore, it is not the case that something is moral only because one's culture says it is. Permitting one's culture to dictate one's morality would make that culture morally absolute, much in the way that many religions try to make their moralities absolute. A culturally objective morality is much different. A culture's morality is objective because that morality is independent of whatever any individual person wishes morality to be. A good analogy is a country's laws. Laws are valid because they are politically objective: the law is not whatever any person wants it to be.

Culturally objective moral rules are never fixed, final, or perfect. Individuals can always disagree with some moral rules, able to subjectively prefer other rules and to desire changes. Cultures do modify their moral rules gradually over time, sometimes under pressure from lone individuals and sometimes after reevaluating them in groups. The analogy between social morality and political law remains helpful. The law can be modified after protest by a few, or after reconsideration by many, and such political thinking about law is frequently guided by higher political principles. In the same way, the people of a society can change their culture's morality after ethical thinking. Individuals can disagree with a culture's morality, of course, by appealing to a different morality or to a higher ethical standard. Any effort to thoughtfully justify or improve a culture's morality is the work of ethics. An appeal to a higher standard is an appeal to an ethical ideal. For example, why should I follow the moral rule that I should not lie to others? Because of the ethical ideal that you should not do to others what you would not have done to you. This is just an example. There are many ways that various ethical ideals can be used to help persuasively justify specific moral rules.

Naturalists, of course, do not regard ethical ideals as absolute moral truths, either. However, people do appeal to ethical ideals when they compare, criticize, and modify the moralities of cultures. From the standpoint of naturalism, it is perfectly natural to expect people to try to change a morality using ethical thinking when they see problems with that morality. And it also quite natural to expect that ethical ideals are the sorts of things that people do not agree about, and that ethical ideals also change or disappear over time. At the same time, naturalism can also explain why many civilized peoples have gradually come to agree on a few basic moral principles. These principles naturally arise from civilizations dealing with large concentrated populations, so the convergence upon some moral truths is no more surprising than the way that civilizations converged on a few principles of wise agriculture.

There is an interesting variation on the morality argument that can be proposed by the supernaturalist. Suppose that the naturalist's "objectivity" account of civilized moral principles is accurate. In that case, the emerging consensus of civilizations over millennia towards a small set of moral principles is a fact that requires further explanation. A different moral argument for god could be devised: the best explanation for emerging global objectivity is that god really exists, because only a god could explain why diverse peoples would have convergent beliefs (see Wright 2009 for a suggestive approach to this argument). Maybe a god is quietly talking to people, stirring their consciences or luring their spirits, or maybe seeking moral convergence is precisely the search for god. This convergence argument is analogous to the objectivity argument for scientific realism: objective nature exists, because this objective nature is the best explanation why scientific investigation gradually converges on one scientific theory rather than many. After all, there must be something real out there in nature beyond what scientists happen to want to believe which helps to guide inquiry towards convergence and agreement.

Unfortunately for this supernaturalistic argument, the best explanation for convergence on global moral objectivity is entirely natural: the natural experience of humans living together in a natural environment. Poor moral principles get weeded out, if not by people gaining hard experience of learning from mistakes and teaching the lessons to next generations, but also by people dying out from suffering the extreme consequences of poor moral choices. Humans are a social species trying to survive in diverse tough environments. Globally objective moral rules aim to protect the young, guard the group, promote the healthy and strong, conserve resources efficiently, and prevent reproductive unfitness. Even principles like "sacrifice your own interests for others in your group" and "be hospitable to strangers" make great sense in the long run for human tribes and clans. As civilizations have grown, they have experimented with additional moral principles, and we are in the middle of such experiments. The world's religions can have their combative war-like aspects, and their pacifying, sympathetic sides. Christianity has produced both the genocidal Crusades and the humble monk. Buddhism has produced pacifists and Zen Samurai warriors. These divergent features of evolving religions are best explained naturalistically. Furthermore, a god could easily produce much faster and firmer moral convergence. This fact arouses the problem first raised with the design argument: the moral design in evidence is poor evidence of a moral god.

Since the theologian cannot provide any clear example of an actual absolute moral truth, and naturalism can explain why cultures have culturally objective moral truths, premise 1 of the argument from morality should not be accepted as true. As for premise 2, naturalism explains how cultures, and not gods, convey moral truths to people, through education. The theologian would again appeal to the supposed existence of some absolute moral truths, claiming that only god could teach them since cultures cannot. But no god is needed to explain how people would learn absolute moral truths that do not exist anyway. Morality's rules, values, and ideals can serve quite well to guide a person's conduct, even though this person does not know whether the morality she follows is universally or eternally true.

Even religious people are left without any absolute guarantees about morality either, if they have to depend on god to know them. For example, the "divine command theory" tries to explain how there can be absolute moral truths, but it actually destroys the possibility that they are absolute in the sense required to help supernaturalism. According to the divine command theory, moral truths are true because god commands them. When the supernaturalist explains that moral truths must be dependent on god rather than humans, moral truths don't become absolute since they simply become relative and subjective for god. This is Plato's Euthyphro dilemma: supposed objective moral truths could still be different if god were different (if the divine mind changed its will, for example). Theologians may claim that god would not and could not change its will, but there seems to be no good reason to accept this claim. An unchangeable will is not really a will; the point of a person having a will is that a person can make and change a decision. If a god can will something to be true, that god cannot will something to be true. There is no guarantee that morality could have been different with a different god. Dependence on god cannot make morality any more absolute in the sense required for the supernaturalist's argument from morality.

Another variation on this theme is the "divine approval theory" of ethics, which states that the only reason a religious follower has for obeying a moral rule is that god has approved it. On this theory, like the divine command theory, the religious follower has no rational way to judge moral dictates from god – the religious follower in effect abandons all independent moral judgment when obeying god. A religious follower would have no way to judge which religion is actually morally correct, but must simply pick one religion arbitrarily. If the friend of religion complains that the naturalist lets morality be arbitrarily decided by culture, the naturalist should reply by pointing out that a religious believer simply lets morality be arbitrarily decided by religion. As a matter of fact, however, the naturalist understands how ethical thinking can judge cultures that are immoral, even one's own culture, by ethical thinking. On the other hand, the divine approval believer has no way of doing any ethical thinking to judge one's own religion to be immoral. It is the religious believer, and not the naturalist, who is unable to recognize evil in their own belief system. We may conclude that religious people have no more absolute guarantees about morality than naturalists, if they have to depend on god to know morality.

The naturalist can reject premise 3 as well. The capacity for people to be responsible moral agents does not require that people possess some supernatural property or be partly supernatural. During its early theological organization, Christianity elevated the notion that god creates every soul with a free will to the exalted status of core dogma. What sort of theological argument can be constructed to justify this dogma? Led by the idea that god designs us to be responsible for at least some of our decisions (otherwise god could not ever blame us for misdeeds), theology then considers whether there can be genuine responsibility if naturalism is true. Perhaps not, as this argument suggests:

5. If naturalism is true, then events including decisions (and intentions, actions, etc.) are completely controlled by natural causes.
6. If some event is completely controlled by natural causes, then no person is ever really is responsible for that event.
7. If naturalism is true, then no one is ever really responsible for any decision (or intention or action, etc.).

8. Unless a person is responsible for at least some of their decisions (etc.), that person cannot have the capacity to be morally responsible.

Conclusion. If naturalism is true, no one ever has the capacity to be morally responsible.

Having ruled out naturalism as incompatible with moral responsibility, the theologian can suggest the preferred alternative view of supernaturalism to save moral responsibility. The theologian could claim that god would want us to have moral responsibility and so would give us a supernatural free will, but that tactic only begs the question with pseudo-science. Even worse, this sort of supernatural free will would have some bizarre and counter-intuitive characteristics. Consider the point of this sort of free will: when active, it momentarily suspends all natural causes that would have dictated one action, so that it can decide to go ahead and choose that action, or choose some other action instead. This free will cannot be influenced by any natural cause, including whatever is going on in a person's brain. If such a free will existed, it would reveal itself in noticeable violations of the law of conservation of energy, but no such effect has ever been detected. Even worse for morality, such a free will would severely disrupt morality itself. All character, all knowledge, all moral habit laid down in the brain's neural pathways is set aside for a split second while one's free will does its work. If someone did use this free will frequently, their behavior would be whimsically erratic, rather chaotic and quite unpredictable, even from that person's own perspective. That does not seem like a solid foundation for reliable moral character or moral responsibility. Morally responsible people are reliable and dependable – if not perfectly predictable, at least more predictable than not. What would the purpose of so much moral education and training for the young actually be if we expected adults to suddenly use their mysterious supernatural free will instead? Being a moral adult does not feel like becoming more and more whimsical; having good moral character instead feels like *not* having to apply free will to every moral choice. The whole point of moral habit is that it doesn't require continual resort to a free choice.

The theologian could avoid this pseudo-scientific disaster by appealing to common sense instead. We know that we are responsible moral agents with free will, since we intuitively feel free in many of our decisions and actions. Must naturalism respond to this tactic by denying that any intuition of freedom is deceptively illusory? Many naturalists do hold that intuitions of freedom must be some sort of illusion or hallucination, and some even approve of the conclusion that no one is ever morally responsible for anything. However, that conclusion is unnecessary, since the naturalist should not even accept the validity of premise 6 and so they should reject that argument's conclusion. Premise 5 is true, since naturalists do hold that all events are completely controlled by natural causes. Naturalists do not believe in the existence of any unnatural "free will" that could somehow interfere with or override natural causes. Such a free will was never needed in the first place, since premise 6 is false: there are some events that are completely controlled by natural causes for which someone is responsible. For naturalism, what sort of events would these be? They would simply be intentional actions made by people. According to naturalism, people are organisms having their own metabolic energies and nervous systems capable of controlling behavior. People are complex thermodynamic systems of internal natural causes.

The naturalist does not accept the existence of contra-causal free will, yet believes that many people are quite capable of being responsible moral agents. How does the naturalist explain moral agency? A free will sufficient for responsible moral agency only requires that a person have both (a) partial control over current habits, and (b) partial control over the deliberate modification of habits. This partial control is not any sort of contra-causal free will, but rather recognizes humans as energetic causes in their own right, alongside external environing causes. Where people have both (a) and (b) we rightly hold them morally responsible for their actions. Furthermore, what would it feel like to be a person exercising such controls over their conduct? It seems obvious that exercising this control capacity would usually feel like being free in our intentional decisions and actions. The naturalist has a much simpler and more satisfying way of accounting for both human moral capacity and what it is like to exercise this capacity. Any sort of freedom and control over one's conduct that is worth having for moral responsibility is entirely compatible with scientific naturalism (see Dennett 1984 and 2003).

The naturalist can similarly explain what it is like for a person to be morally motivated. Does the motivation for people to behave morally depend upon their conviction that a supernatural being guarantees that moral conduct is not ultimately meaningless or without value? Consider the following argument:

9. If God does not exist, then there is no guarantee that moral goodness will ultimately prevail.
10. If there is no guarantee that moral goodness will ultimately prevail, then there is no guarantee that moral conduct is meaningful.

11. If there is no guarantee that moral conduct is meaningful, then people cannot be reasonably motivated to behave morally.
12. People should be reasonably motivated to behave morally.

Conclusion. God exists.

Naturalists agree with premises 11 and 12 of this argument from "moral motivation," and they cannot understand why Christians would view naturalism as an obstacle to people wanting to behave morally. Nonbelievers behave about as morally as anyone else (for example, the percentage of criminals who are nonbelievers is just about the same as the percentage of nonbelievers in the general population). Of course, the faithful see naturalists rejecting their god and his/her/its commands, and if they feel that the only motivation to be moral is to fear/love/appease their god, then the naturalist must seem morally unmotivated from that perspective. But this failure to understand how the naturalist is motivated to be moral is predicated on the assumption that god exists, so it cannot help justify the existence of god. The faithful may believe that they need god to be morally motivated, but this fact about them cannot be used to argue for god's existence.

Naturalists reject the false notion that, if there is no guarantee that moral goodness will ultimately prevail, then there is no guarantee that moral conduct is meaningful. The faithful who believe this notion worry that a moral action is meaningless unless its positive value is eternally guaranteed. This worry is analogous to the worry that the eventual destruction of something we create makes our creation ultimately meaningless and valueless. This is the worry of nihilism: everything might really be pointless and amount to nothing. What will our lives and our deeds really mean, one million years from now, or when the universe ends? Naturalists are not immune from this worry. Some naturalists do believe that human life and all human creations are ultimately meaningless and valueless when imaginatively viewed from any sufficiently remote perspective. A few philosophies and religions instruct us to adopt this nihilistic stance towards our lives, our deeds, and our creations: we should stoically view them as having little or no value, so that we are not attached to them and we suffer nothing when they are gone. Even if naturalism required nihilism, nihilism does not make moral conduct unreasonable and need not deprive us of the motivation to be moral. First of all, nihilism cannot imply that a person would only do immoral things. The religious person worries: without god, why should I bother being moral? Of course, if nihilism were correct and all of my deeds are ultimately meaningless, then my bad deeds are meaningless too – why should I bother being immoral either? Nihilism cannot imply anything about what a person should or would do.

Regardless of nihilism, there are naturalistic explanations for the reasonableness of preferring moral conduct over immoral conduct. The naturalist can argue that (1) possessing moral knowledge alone provides a reasonable motivation to be moral; (2) moral conduct can be intrinsically satisfying for one's self and hence is reasonable; (3) moral conduct towards another person is valuable to that person and hence reasonably creates value; (4) moral conduct can be a practical means of maintaining beneficial social relations and hence is reasonable; (5) moral conduct can be useful for survival and hence would be reasonable. Any one of these options suffices to supply a naturalistic account of reasonable moral motivations; the naturalist would assemble several of the more plausible options in order to organize a robust alternative to supernaturalism.

The naturalist can finally point out that moral motivation, moral courage, and moral character hardly depend on an assurance that "all will work out for the best in the end." Why should religious faith in ultimate victory deliver moral superiority? After all, who deserves higher approval – the person who does the right thing when the best outcome is already guaranteed, or the person who does the right thing even when the outcome appears hopeless? Righteousness even in the face of despair marks the genuinely moral person. Such a person is not unreasonable for their convictions. The naturalist may not know how it all will turn out, but the naturalist can reasonably want morality to prevail right here and now. Helping the needy, promoting peace, and protecting the weak are always morally meaningful, regardless of what may happen tomorrow.

To summarize, the naturalist concludes that there is nothing about morality that requires the existence of god or belief in the existence of god. Replacing theological explanations for morality are four basic naturalistic stances towards morality:

> The objective truth of moral rules requires cultures to sustain those rules, but people can change them.
>
> The ability of humans to be moral requires cultures teach moral knowledge to humans, and they also teach how to do ethics to change cultural moralities.

> The motivation of humans to be moral requires only the knowledge that being moral is the right thing to do now, regardless of unforeseeable long-term results or guarantees.
>
> The capacity for humans to be responsible moral agents only requires that humans partially control current habits and can deliberately modify habits (often with the help of others).

Developing these four naturalistic stances on morality is the task of a comprehensive naturalistic ethics, which is not our task here. To oppose theology, it suffices to see how the naturalistic approach to morality is able to provide a plausible alternative to a supernaturalistic explanation for human morality.

4.6 Explanations for Reason

The capacity of humans to understand and use reason is a feature of the natural world that requires explanation. Theological arguments can be constructed for attempting to show that no naturalistic explanation suffices to account for this human capacity, and that supernatural explanations can do the required explaining instead.

Any theological argument from reason must be carefully distinguished from an argument from knowledge. An argument from knowledge asks how it could be possible for an entirely natural human to gain knowledge of truths, suggesting that knowledge of truths must be impossible if humans are just collections of atoms obeying physical laws. Such arguments from knowledge are failures from the outset, since they overlook the way that highly complex organisms like humans have sophisticated nervous systems quite capable of detecting, tracking, and remembering patterns of nature in the surrounding environment. The fallacious trick of these arguments is to first depict organisms as made up of chaotically unpredictable and highly variable reactions of tiny particles that know nothing, and second to rashly assume that an entire human must be as uncaring and stupid as any of these tiny components. One might as well complain that a locomotive engine could not possibly move a train, since close scrutiny of its thousands of small parts fails to detect either the immense power or coordinated drive to pull a train. From the naturalistic perspective, although the human brain is so complex that our comprehension of its operations remains limited, there is no big philosophical mystery for the way that a human brain could keep track of the more obvious and relevant features of the surrounding environment. Indeed, the more we learn about nervous systems, the more evident it becomes that brains work best at tracking environing conditions, especially those most significant for the organism's survival. Human knowledge need be no big mystery; rather, theologians are usually more careful to focus on one aspect of knowledge: our capacity to reason.

Reasoning is the intellectual capacity to reach knowable conclusions of truth (certain truth, or probable truth) by proceeding through inferences of beliefs connected in some logical order. The three basic ways of logically connecting beliefs to a conclusion are deduction, induction, and abduction. Reasoning is a psychological process, and therefore, according to naturalism, a natural process. The difficulty for naturalism arises because a logical inference does not look like a natural process when one is actually reasoning. This is especially the case for deduction, since in a deductive inference the truth of the premises necessarily guarantees the truth of the conclusion. Here we will only pursue the controversy over deduction, because it presents the toughest case for naturalism, while naturalism's ability to account for deduction can then be applied to handle induction and abduction.

The compelling necessity of a logical or a mathematical truth, with deduction at its core, makes it virtually impossible to seriously conceive that it is false. Carefully consider the logical law that "a statement and its negation can't both be true at the same time" or the mathematical law that "$1 + 1 = 2$" – how long can you seriously sustain the conviction that these laws are actually false? Hopefully, not for long.

These laws seem to be absolute: these truths are both universal (true for everyone) and eternal (must always be true). Like an absolute moral truth, an absolute truth of logic or mathematics would be a problem for naturalism, the theologian reasons, because there couldn't be anything in nature anywhere that could responsible for making that absolute truth actually true. The validity of an absolute truth shouldn't be reducible to being only an actual deductive process of intellectual reasoning, which naturalism claims is an entirely psychological process. The theologian can construct an argument from reason against naturalism.

1. Naturalism must explain how a deductive truth is actually a psychological process.
2. A psychological process's result depends on the proper functioning of a human brain, goes in and out of existence depending on a brain's

activity, and can proceed differently from brain to brain with undetectable differences.

3. A deduction's truth does not depend on the proper functioning of a human brain, does not go in and out of existence, and does not vary at all regardless of whose brain is thinking about it.
4. A deductive truth does not share some essential characteristics with a psychological process. (From 2 and 3)
5. If a deductive truth were actually a psychological process, then they would share essential characteristics.
6. A deductive truth cannot be a psychological process. (From 4 and 5)

Conclusion. Naturalism cannot explain a deductive truth. (From 1 and 6)

Having reached this desired conclusion against naturalism, the theologian quickly offers supernaturalism as the source of alternative explanations for these evidently unnatural truths. Perhaps truths of reason are made true by some supernatural realm of perfection, and humans have a suitably spiritual part of our minds to somehow "see" or "intuit" into that perfect realm to gain deductive knowledge. Perhaps there's a little divine power in us, permitting us to know such unnatural truths. These Platonic suggestions are intriguing, and the Christian theologian makes sure that god is closely involved. Perhaps god dictates truths of reason and then instructs human minds to appreciate them, or just builds our brains with the ability to recognize them. Perhaps god just knows truths of reason (god knows everything, right?) and then supplies just the right amount of direct inspiration to human minds so that we know them when we think about them, too.

Any Christian explanation making reason too dependent on god risks its own refutation, of course. If deductive truths cannot be dependent on a personality, as this argument reasons, then it couldn't be dependent on god's personality. We cannot conceive without falling into incomprehensible paradox any way that god could know some other set of deductive truths rather than the ones we know about, or any way that god could decide to change the deductive truths we know. Could god make $2 + 2 = 5$? Assuming that a Christian theologian can avoid these problems (which is a big assumption), and assuming that the argument from reason succeeds for deduction (and by extension, for induction and abduction as well), then Christian theology can justify to another powerful principle:

PS11 Unless god exists, humans could not reason and acquire knowledge of truths.

However, this argument from reason contains a false premise. Premise 1 states: "Naturalism must explain how a deductive truth is actually a psychological process." Naturalism does not have to do this. In fact, it is a bad mistake to identify a deductive truth with a psychological process.

We have to more closely examine what a deductive process actually is. Every deduction ultimately depends on some essential connections between concepts, connections made because of the meanings of those concepts. For example, the concept of "two" essentially includes an additive relationship between "one" and another "one." Put another way, if someone thought that they had grasped the meaning of "two" but had no idea that any "ones" were involved at all, this person is quite mistaken and does not really have the concept of "two." The capacity to appreciate that $2 + 2 = 4$ is precisely the capacity to appreciate the meanings of the concepts involved. Whenever a person adequately appreciates the meanings of "one" and "two" then this person automatically can appreciate that "$2 + 2 = 4$" is a deductively necessary truth. The psychological process of having concepts, appreciating their meanings, and thereby understanding the validity of their conceptual connections is the process of knowing these sorts of necessary truths. The necessity of these truths is not some extra thing that suddenly emerges out of nowhere to land upon a truth so that a person then says, "Oh yes, now I see that these conceptual connections are true!" The necessity is immediately appreciated simply by entertaining the concepts together. To understand the meanings of a concept is the same thing as appreciating the meaningful relations between concepts is the same thing as appreciating the truth of the deduction between the concepts. These three things are all the same process expressed in three different ways. You cannot simultaneously hold the concept of "two" in your mind and fail to hold "one and one" in your mind. If "one and one" does not also occur to you, then you simply aren't really entertaining "two" in your mind, but some other concept instead.

Do not confuse this explanation of deduction with two other false ideas: (1) every time you entertain a concept in your mind, you have to also think about each deductive truth involved with that concept, or (2) every concept you possess has deductive relationships with other concepts. These two notions are false because thinking of complex concepts rarely requires following essential connections (every time you think of "15" you don't immediately also have to think "7" plus "8") and most complex concepts don't have clear necessary relationships with any other concepts (what necessarily and automatically follows from thinking about "Zen gardening" or "democracy"?). The account of deduction offered here only deals with truly deductive processes, in which clearly defined concepts have essential relations to other concepts that can be appreciated in thought. Deduction only works when and where such special concepts can already be entertained by an intelligence. Logic and mathematics takes much training of the intellect, after all, and science especially so. For science to use deduction, simple and clear concepts have to be refined from ordinary concepts. For example, the scientific concept of "water" is not the same as the ordinary notion of water. In science, water by definition means hydrogen atoms combined with oxygen atoms in a certain constant ratio, while "water" in ordinary language just means whatever is in the oceans or comes out of the tap or falls in rain.

Since deductions are special psychological processes that immediately result in the appreciation of necessary truths, the "truth" of a deduction must not be confused with the deductive process. It is a mistake to identify a deductive truth with a psychological process, so premise 1 is false. All the same, for us actual intelligences, our appreciation of a deductive truth is exactly the same thing as our undergoing that particular deductive process. It is impossible for an intellect to do one without doing the other. This fact explains why we appreciate the necessity of a deductive truth: each time we try to appreciate its truth, our intellects simultaneously perform the deduction of that truth all over again and get the identical result (and if somehow we don't, that only means that we failed to actually perform the relevant deduction and instead got confused into a different deduction). For example, when I appreciate the validity of the truth "$15 = 7 + 8$" I am instantly doing that deductive calculation over again in my mind. It is impossible to appreciate how $15 = 7 + 8$ without the mind (perhaps subconsciously and almost instantaneously) doing the fast inference. And if we suddenly stop and say, wait a minute, doesn't 15 equal 7 plus 9? – this only means that we have momentarily lost mental focus on the concepts involved in the truth. Mental slippage is nothing unusual (this is why even mathematicians check each other's chains of deductions). But when the mind stays focused, the appreciation of a necessary truth always results from the right deduction. That psychological fact creates the cognitive illusion that a truth like "$15 = 7 + 8$" is so necessarily true that its truth can't have much to do with the psychological process of deduction that appreciates its truth. When we "verify" that "$7 + 8 = 15$" time and time again, always getting the same answer, its truth can't help but seem absolutely universal and eternal. And so it must appear, in reality, to us. Otherwise, we wouldn't be performing deductions.

According to this naturalistic account of what is going on when humans perform deductions, successful deductions make their truths seem absolute to us. They seem so absolute, in fact, that it becomes hard to understand how their truth could possibly depend on mere psychological processes of human brains. The truth of a deduction is not the same thing as a psychological process of a deduction (so they don't share essential characteristics), but nevertheless, no deductive truths could exist without the trained functioning of human brains. We have the entirely natural capacity to sustain focus on the meanings, and their relations, of special concepts that we ourselves have refined. No supernatural realm or divine god is needed to explain how we appreciate the necessary validity of deductive truths of reason, or how we can reason in general.

4.7 The Ontological Argument for God

The ontological argument for god starts from the natural fact that humans can have a conception of god and humans can reason about logical connections between conceptions, and proceeds to argue that therefore a god must exist.

Sometimes ontological arguments are described as involving only pure logic, as if neither human conceptions nor even human minds are involved. It is possible to interpret some medieval ontological arguments as purely logical arguments. Contemporary examples are mostly expressed in highly technical modal logic and their success hinges on the dubious application of certain logical principles, such as Axiom S5 of modal logic: "a proposition that is possibly necessary is necessary." We will not examine examples of such purely logical arguments. While their common feature is the attempted conclusion that a "necessary" or "perfect" being exists, they are also commonly rejected as having little significance for religion. Logicians are not agreed on the validity or significance of key logical axioms, and theologians are not agreed that the conclusions are about their religion's god.

Characterizing ontological arguments as "purely logical" reasoning is probably a mistake in any case. The presumed aim of an argument for god is human knowledge of god's existence. Any reasoning to a knowable conclusion requires known premises, and human knowers. Pure reasoning by itself knows nothing and yields no knowledge about the actual existence of anything; it is just the manipulation of symbols according to arbitrary rules. An analogy is mathematics; mathematicians can prove propositions about relations between numbers or sets or geometrical figures, but no mathematical proof could ever actually show that anything really exists. Put another way, if any ontological argument omits a person actually having a conception of the god that is supposed to exist, then even a valid conclusion that "god exists" accomplishes nothing. No one would know what god is argued for, and no one could gain knowledge of this god.

In this section we will only consider versions of ontological arguments that proceed from some human conception of a god to a potentially knowable belief that a god exists. For example, if someone conceives of god as "the most perfectly possible being," and also believes that "an actually existing god would be more perfect," then this person might conclude that she ought to conceive of god as actually existing, that is to say, she ought to believe god exists. When formalized into a simple logical argument, it has this structure:

1. A person has a conception of god as "the most perfect being."
2. An actually existing being is more perfect than something that does not exist.
3. When a person has a conception of "the most perfect being" this conception must include conceiving that this being does exist.
4. When a person conceives of god, then that person conceives "the most perfect and existing being."
5. If a person conceives of god, then that person conceives of god as most perfect and as existing.

Conclusion. This person believes that a most perfect god exists.

The impressive force of this argument lies in the way that it starts from a person just thinking about god – nothing more than merely considering an idea in one's imagination – and ends with that person believing that god exists.

If this argument conceals no logical mistakes, then every rational nonbeliever, simply by thinking about god, should become a believer! But how is that possible? A nonbeliever can easily entertain a conception of god. Indeed, nonbelievers can understand many conceptions of god, all those notions of god from various religions which probably don't exist. An nonbeliever of sufficient sympathetic imagination can even conceive of what it is like to actually believe in a god, if only briefly, before returning to his usual state of disbelief. This ontological argument does hide fallacies, however. No nonbeliever suddenly falls into irrationality if momentarily thinking about some god doesn't compel acknowledgement of god's existence.

There are three main fallacies in this argument. First, premise 1 is just a definition, but it is an open definition. It permits each person to have their own notion of what counts as a conception. When many people simultaneously conceive of "the most perfect being," there is no way to ensure in advance that all these people will have the same conception. Even people in the same religion may have widely varying notions of the most important perfections god should have. Some may select righteousness, others omnipotence, or maybe lovingness. People of no religion might select any random perfection, like being beautiful or delicious, or may have no idea at all what to select. Furthermore, even if two people each select some perfection property like "righteousness," that still doesn't mean that both people mean exactly the same thing. Dictionaries allow variation in definitions, and there is no way to impose one dictionary or one single definition of "perfection" on everyone anyway. This variability in human conceptions means that the conclusion tells us almost nothing specific about what sort of god actually exists.

Second, premise 3 may not be true. Depending on what might count as a perfection, it might be that a most perfect being should not or could not exist. For example, suppose I happen to believe that one of the perfections is "controlling everything." I think that the power to control other things is a measure of perfection, and that a perfect being would control everything that ever happens everywhere, so that my conception of god would be of a being that controls everything. But I don't think that such a being should exist or could exist. Such being should not exist because, if it did, no one besides god could ever do anything; we might think we are in control, but it would really be god. While some people might enjoy that conception of god; I don't, so I would reject premise 3. Furthermore, I don't think that such an omnipotently controlling god could actually exist. The weight of the available evidence goes the other way: we have plenty of reliable knowledge that lots of things in the natural world have some control over events. For example, I frequently control my behavior, the wind controls the weathervane, and the sun controls most of the total energy available on the planet earth.

Third, the conclusion appears to be about god existing, but that is deceptively misleading. In this argument, the term "god" is just a symbolic placeholder, like the variable X in a mathematical equation. The conclusion reads: "This person believes that a most perfect god exists," but technically it should only read: "This person believes that the most perfect and existing being exists." Sure, you might want to call this being "god" if you are already religious, but if you add anything to the narrow and specific conception of the conclusion, like "who loves us," you have gone way beyond the reach of this argument. Should a nonbeliever really believe that the most perfect and existing being exists? Well, why not? Suppose my conception of perfection is just "delicious," and suppose that I live in a universe where only one delicious thing, a pizza, really exists (I call it the "Best Pizza"). By the ontological argument, therefore, I ought to believe that a most delicious and existing thing exists. And indeed I ought to, and there is no difficulty about that belief automatically being true, given my notion of perfection and the kind of universe I happen to live in. And indeed I do believe in the existence of the Best Pizza. If I live in a universe that contains many delicious pizzas, then I believe in the existence of most delicious pizza among them, and correctly so. If I don't live in a universe that contains any pizzas, but it does contain other things I would consider delicious, then my belief that the Best Pizza exists is still made true, in a way, because my universe contains a most delicious thing (but I don't know if it really is a pizza or not). (If I don't live in a universe that contains any delicious things, then I wouldn't have a conception of "delicious" anyway.) Here's another example. Suppose my conception of perfection is just "made of gold." Then when I believe that the most perfect and existing thing exists, I am only referring to the most massive body of gold in the universe (since the universe does contain chunks of gold, then there is one most massive chunk of gold, or maybe two in a tie).

This ontological argument really says nothing about what a religious person really wants to mean by "god." Logically, this ontological argument at most warrants belief in certain most "perfect" things (perfect according to each person's subjective notion of perfection) that actually happen to exist in the natural universe. There no logical way for this argument to point to something outside nature, or to something completely perfect within nature.

The theologian can try to patch up the ontological argument with answers to the logical fallacies raised here. In defense of premise 1, the Christian theologian typically says, "Come on, we Christians all know what the essential perfections are." Well, what about non-Christians? This argument would need an extra premise saying: "Only we Christians accurately conceive of god," which arrogantly prevents this argument from ever convincing a non-Christian. Even among Christians, the notion that all Christians complete agree on god's perfections is just wishful thinking. In fact, the early Church Fathers had enormous disagreements about god's essential properties and powers, not to mention how far such intellectual exercises depart from ordinary notions of god held by lay Christians. The only places where precise uniformity about god's perfections is easily found are in scattered theological arguments over god, certain decrees of religious councils, and a few papal bulls.

Descartes' version of the ontological argument gets around this problem of uniformity. He simply points to his own conception of a necessary god so perfect that only an actually existing perfect god could be responsible for Descartes' ability to have that conception. Unfortunately, Descartes cannot justify his initial claim that his human conception of god is really so perfect. After all, can it really be so easy for a mere human being to recognize the highest possible perfections of divinity when that person thinks of them? There's suddenly no human limitation or fallibility when it comes to conceiving god? Why is Descartes so special? Common sense alone would suggest that attempts to conceive god would fall short. Indeed, most of Christian theology has emphasized how we fail to fully conceive god (this point is especially emphasized by Theology Into The Myst). Disagreements among theologians aside, Descartes may claim to perfectly conceive a necessarily perfect god, but how can he justify this claim? Not by any other fallible human way of sensing or knowing or thinking. Indeed, that is Descartes' entire point: nothing in ordinary human psychology or reason could account for such a conception of a god. And that is Descartes' trap: he can't explain how he might possibly be so special that he has a perfect conception of a necessary god. He can't point to anything human for an explanation, and he can't assume that god helps here since he is trying to prove god's existence for the conclusion. Descartes is left with two bad options: admit that he might be wrong about his "perfect" conception, or beg the whole question by crediting god with help in achieving a perfect conception. And there Descartes' ontological argument collapses.

To defend premise 3, the theologian could claim that a genuine perfection by definition must always be compatible with what should exist and what can actually exist. This claim would fix the logical problem and make premise 3 much more acceptable to a nonbeliever. However, this fix actually generates a different fallacy, because "god" is now defined as something that can and should actually exist, which was the original proposition to be established by this argument. This fix therefore only permits the theologian to beg the question and assume what was to be proved.

To defend the conclusion's aim to be about god, and not just some naturally existing thing, the theologian must deal with the crucial ambiguity inherent in the notion of "most perfect." The religious person wants to read "most perfect" as "complete perfection" and not merely "the most perfect thing that happens to actually exist." To fix up the argument, an extra premise must be added that says, "By 'most perfect' everyone always means 'completely perfect.'" Yet this extra premise doesn't seem to be true. When I refer to this impressively delicious pizza as "the most perfect pizza," I don't mean to refer to "the completely perfect pizza," since I could probably think up some ways that this pizza could be even better. Similarly, when I say that a Monet painting is the "most beautiful painting" I am not trying to refer to some completely beautiful painting; I have no idea what such a painting could be like.

To summarize, a sufficiently patched-up ontological argument would have to add controversial premises that risk begging the entire question. The ontological argument goes nowhere interesting in the direction of anything supernatural or divine.

4.8 The Argument from Pseudo-science

Modern science, in just 400 years, has displayed tremendous potential for satisfactorily explaining so many of the great mysteries of the natural world. In the next 4000 years, about the typical lifetime of a great religion, what might still elude future science? For the remaining mysteries, will theology have any advantages? It is difficult to imagine how. Theology now lacks any advantages over science, and could remain stuck in clinging to mystery and appealing to pseudo-science. The limitations of natural theology set by reason need not destroy the religious value of comprehending nature. Liberal modernism and religious naturalism, discussed in Chapter 8, accept these rational limitations and experience nature with spiritual transformations far richer than scientific knowledge.

Nevertheless, theologians who remain convinced that Theology From The World can succeed with its arguments still claim to have established knowledge of god. For them, god can easily explain everything that science cannot, and god's existence cannot be scientifically tested. Among the many principles of religious pseudo-science uncovered in this chapter, we may bring together the following, suitably adapted for theological application:

PS12 A god that wants nature or us to have some feature is a good explanation for that feature.
PS13 God is a good explanation for any feature or event in nature that can't be explained by current science.
PS14 God's interventions in nature cannot be predicted or tested in any way.

Using these principles, theology can remove science as a competitor for explaining remaining mysteries in nature. If these principles are used as premises, pseudo-scientific theological arguments for god's existence can easily be constructed, such as the following:

1. There will always be many mysterious features of nature that science cannot satisfactorily explain.
2. It is reasonable to accept a good explanation for a mystery, wherever that explanation may come from.
3. The hypothesis that god is responsible for a mystery is always a good explanation.
4. It is impossible for science to show that god could not be responsible for any mystery.

Conclusion. It is reasonable to believe that god exists.

We will not pause here to consider this argument, since we are no longer in the realm of Theology From The World, but rather Theology In The Know.

There is another option for those who still think that the natural universe points to god. Perhaps theology should not try to explain features within nature, but instead refocus for a much wider perspective upon the entire universe itself. These theologians are now involved in Theology Beyond The World.

Theology Beyond The World

There are two remaining arguments for god bequeathed by traditional natural theology. They inquire into the two most significant facts about the universe: that the universe exists at all, and why this universe has the overall features and laws that it does. No longer needed for dealing with anything within nature, theology has been driven to the very edge of nature itself and the extreme boundaries of scientific knowledge.

The scientific field of cosmology attempts to understand the cosmos using the scientific method. Theology can try to compete directly with cosmology. Although theology postulates a divine power to explain mysteries about the universe's existence and its structure, does a god really explain anything? Similar to the way that Theology From The World can degenerate into pseudo-science, Theology Beyond The World can degenerate into pseudo-cosmology. Deceptively appearing to provide explanations for the cosmos, the arguments for god offered by Theology Beyond The World only increase mystery.

5.1 The Existence of Nature Argument for God

The existence of nature argument for god first makes nature's existence into a problem, and then offers something supernatural (like a god) as the solution. A simple version can be formulated as follows:

1. Everything that exists requires an explanation for its existence.
2. Nature (a collective label for all natural things) exists, so an explanation is required for its existence.
3. Nothing natural can serve as an explanation for nature, since a proposed natural thing would just count as more nature.
4. Only something supernatural could serve as an explanation for nature.
5. It is more reasonable to accept a proposed explanation than to leave something unexplained.

Conclusion. Something supernatural exists to explain nature.

Despite this argument's simplicity, an examination of the credibility of its five premises reveals the serious problems with any existence of nature argument.

Premise 1 and variations on its theme (such as "every effect must have a cause") appear to make sound common sense. Intellectual curiosity and scientific methodology spring from this basic theme, which appears to be essential to the normal functioning of our brains. It is true that the intellect is also quite good at closely filtering and quickly integrating what we observe, so that we are not perpetually curious about most ordinary routine things going on around us all the time. Nevertheless, if something unusual catches our attention, or if we just focus our attention, we can ask and often answer the "why?" question which our mind so easily arouses. Instead of pondering too deeply whether premise 1 should be trusted, let us carefully take notice that we do normally trust it. In fact, we trust it so seriously that we ought to also think that, if something supernatural exists, then there ought to be an explanation for the supernatural too, by parallel reasoning. Going further, an entire parallel argument could be assembled, demanding an non-supernatural explanation for everything supernatural – let us call this the "superdupernaturalism" argument. A child's question, "But who made god?", is echoed here. Without any way of stopping the inevitable questioning work of the intellect, an infinite series of parallel arguments now loom before us – like an infinite series of meta- and meta-meta-levels of reality, or an endless series of gods, each responsible for the next. This is a problem for the naturalist and the supernaturalist alike, although their recommended remedies differ.

The theologian has a fast and simple remedy for the problem of whether the supernatural is in just as much need of explanation as the natural. This remedy has two parts. First, a slight but powerful modification to premise 1: "Everything that contingently exists requires an explanation for its existence." Second, an additional premise (call it premise 6) must be added: "The supernatural explanation for nature is itself not contingent but necessary." In traditional theology, god plays the needed role of the supernatural and necessary being which can explain nature. Working together, the revised premise 1 and the new premise 6 depict god as just the sort of thing that needs no explanation, unlike nature. If successful, this god would put a quick stop to any endless series of explanations, since this necessary god would not itself require any additional explanation.

To see how convenient this supposed necessary god is for the existence of nature argument, we need to explain the distinction between contingent and necessary beings. A contingent existing thing happens to exist, but it could possibly not exist. There are two primary senses in which something could possibly not exist. The first sense is temporal: a contingent thing had an origin, and it will stop existing. The second sense is rational: a contingent thing can be reasonably conceived as not existing. Every natural thing fits both senses of contingent well, since every natural thing of which we are aware does pass in and out of existence and we can reasonably imagine it not existing. For example, a cloud, restaurants, and the planet Mars are all contingent things. Neither ordinary knowledge nor scientific knowledge has yet discovered any natural thing that is not contingent, but instead necessary. A necessary thing has no origin or destruction and we cannot reasonably conceive of its nonexistence. Furthermore, a necessary thing needs no explanation for its existence, since its existence is already guaranteed regardless of whatever else happens to be the case. Nothing else could possibly be responsible for, or helpful towards, the existence of a necessary thing. If god is postulated as a necessary being, this god would not require any further explanation.

Once the supernatural explanation is postulated as a necessary being, two more disputes quickly break out. First, why should a god be postulated as a necessary being? Why couldn't nature, taken as a whole, be similarly postulated as a necessary being, removing any need for a supernatural (or any other sort) of explanation? Second, why should premise 5 be accepted? Only good explanations should be accepted, and not just any explanation, especially an extravagant ad hoc god. Theology has clearly strayed into pseudo-cosmology at this point. And it is no use for theology to try to prove that a postulated necessary god must necessarily exist, since calling something "necessary" can never logically imply that it actually exists. Other versions of the ontological argument can't prove god must exist either (see Chapter 4).

Theologians offer three reasons why nature is probably contingent and not necessary. Nature did have an origin (in the big bang), it is possible to conceive of nature as not existing, and the collection of all naturally contingent things (that is, nature) must itself be contingent too. Naturalists must reply to these reasons, and it is not easy. The big bang has presented a huge headache. Some naturalists argue that even though our own universe had an origin, an even vaster (infinite?) kind of nature might have caused the big bang, and that this behind-the-scenes "megaverse" could be a candidate for the necessary being required. Other naturalists argue that the best cosmological account of the big bang indicates that the universe was somehow self-caused or was itself the origin of all time and cause and effect, so that the big bang could not have an explanation, since nothing could exist "before" the big bang. Examining this "self-caused" interpretation of the big bang is well beyond the capacity of this book and perhaps not worth the effort, since cosmology itself has busily gone on to postulate various explanations for the big bang involving more nature than just our universe. Cosmology, like all science, is powered by the curiosity of finding more and more explanations. As for conceiving the postulated infinite and eternal megaverse (all of being!) as not existing, how could that be possible? That would like trying to imagine pure nothingness instead, but what would one be imagining, exactly? Because it is far easier to conceive of our universe and our big bang as not ever having happened, naturalists are on far stronger logical ground by simply letting science explore more and more of potentially infinite nature. Finally, logicians are well aware that a whole, such as the set of all natural things, does not automatically possess a property just because all of its parts possess that property. Nature might, for all we really know, be necessary even though all its parts are contingent.

Summing up, the naturalist should argue that science should be permitted to continue inquiring into nature wherever empirical inquiry may lead. It is not necessary to postulate anything outside of nature while it is still sufficient that more and more explanations within nature can be achieved.

Cosmology avoids falling into pseudo-science by postulating only natural explanations that can be tested by the scientific method.

Theologians will not be impressed by science's never-ending exploration of nature, or by naturalism's postulate that science is exploring deeper into an infinite and necessary megaverse. Nevertheless, postulating a supernatural and necessary god hardly seems any less a stretch of the imagination and only increases mystery. Here, at the ultimate limits of human imagination, only a skeptical stand-off is reached. Neither side can prove its claims about a megaverse or about a god. Nevertheless, naturalism and its scientific cosmology can prevent the existence of nature argument from reaching any firm conclusion about god.

5.2 The Fine-tuning Argument for God

The fine-tuning argument for god is inspired by the argument from design offered by natural theology. The universe displays some organization and structure. Does it display enough of these two characteristics to make it appear designed? The earth might look designed, but planetary geology and evolutionary biology can assemble a natural history of the earth that requires no miracles. The solar system might appear to be designed, with small rocky planets near the sun and gas giants further out, but astronomy has put it in its proper context. Now that we can image other nearby stellar systems and their planets, our own solar system isn't unique and represents one example of many variant configurations of planets. Does our Milky Way galaxy appear to be designed? A swirl of stars determined by gravity, one galaxy strewn among hundreds of billions of galaxies scattered across the visible universe, doesn't seem too unusual. No single aspect of the universe appears quite designed any more. Where plenty of examples of something can be surveyed, be it a planet, a solar system, or a galaxy, from that objective standpoint none of them seems so special.

However, two features of the universe still strike us as quite interesting: the order of life and the order of the cosmos. Life is highly complex, while the universe as a whole is pretty simple. Life requires chemical thermodynamics, organic metabolisms, and continual reproduction. The universe only needs a handful of laws and constants. Taken separately, theology can construct design arguments for each. However, Darwinian evolution is well on its way to explaining naturalistically the complexity of life from simple chemical conditions, so the intelligent design theory is probably not needed (as we discussed in the previous chapter). And the universe with its basic laws doesn't seem very complex and organized, and at large scales it appears more chaotic than constructed. Each design argument has excellent naturalistic competition. But connecting life in the universe together into one big question – why is there a universe that contains life? – can give theology some fresh energy.

The easiest answer to the question of why our universe contains life is to reply that this question needs no explanation at all. Recall the distinction between contingent things requiring explanation and necessary things needing no explanation. It is necessary that *our* universe contains life. After all, we are asking the question! The universe that any life observes must necessarily be a life-supporting universe. It is not as if there could possibly be a life-forbidding universe in which some life form asks, I wonder why it is impossible for me to exist here. Therefore, our universe must necessarily be adequately organized to host us. This "anthropic principle" sensibly says that no special explanation is required for the fact that we now live in the universe during the period of its evolution which is quite favorable to life's emergence. We simply couldn't have existed during the universe's youth, when rocky planets were not forming around metal-poor suns. Only supernovas can fuse and spray elements like carbon, oxygen, and iron into space, so several generations of stars are required first. Looking forward as the universe ages, galaxies will have fewer and fewer main-sequence suns capable of sufficiently warming their planets. Statistically speaking, the odds of the universe supporting intelligent life happen to be the greatest for a modest middle period of roughly 10 to 100 billion years, and our existence not surprisingly falls within this period. The universe did not gradually adapt itself in order to produce life. Quite the opposite. During favorable conditions during the universe's expansion, life spontaneously emerged and adapted to the universe. From this naturalistic perspective, the universe is not designed for life; life is naturally designed for the universe.

Our universe *must* have developed in such a way as to permit our existence. All the same, that a universe exists which contains life is not also a necessary fact. It is still possible to imagine this universe not existing, or this universe having quite different laws, or another universe inhospitable to all life existing instead. Alternatively, we can imagine that the universe evolved quite differently after the big bang, so differently that no life could ever emerge within it. It is therefore a contingent matter that this universe, with its particular structure, did come into existence and include life. The only way to return to necessity would be to discover that the only possible outcome of a big bang is precisely the arrangement of natural laws that we currently observe. On this surprising scenario, cosmology would effectively determine that every universe, if it comes into existence like ours did, would have the same basic laws as ours. We need not ponder this unlikely scenario for long. Naturalists should accommodate themselves to the contingency of our universe, even if it is special because it is ours.

Many cosmologists themselves are chasing a quite different scenario, that our universe erupted from some more fundamental kind of reality that is capable of creating other universes too. Unwilling to take this universe as some sort of necessary or unique thing, scientists hypothesize theoretical explanations for the existence of our universe. This effort, essentially consisting of "multiverse" speculations, postulates that many universes could exist, each having it own characteristic sets of basic laws (see Calle 2009). The extravagant notion that a nearly infinite number of universes exist, with nearly every possible combination of kinds of basic laws represented among them, cannot be asserted with much confidence. It could turn out that the production of universes is constrained by the fundamental properties of whatever kind of reality is generating them, so that a much narrower range of universes can be created. The multiverse scenario at its most reasonable, and many cosmologists are finding it more reasonable (see Carr 2007), still permits us to consider our universe as quite contingent.

The natural contingency of this universe is particularly displayed when we specifically ask how this universe supports intelligent life. There are two basic factors: our universe had to have been guaranteed a long-enough lifespan, and it had to provide locations of stable energies needed for organic metabolisms. Current cosmology now knows enough about the development of the universe to see how a small number of natural laws have ensured that the universe has met these two requirements. For example, the cosmological constant and the force of gravity both determined that the universe could expand properly to reach a great age; only very slight variations to either of these magnitudes would have prevented the universe from sustaining life. Other examples include the strengths of the four basic forces of nature, and masses of protons, neutrons, and electrons. A significant variation of any of these magnitudes would prevent any elements besides hydrogen ever existing, or prevent stars from ever forming. Many natural contingencies are involved with permitting life to even have any chance of emerging.

The hypothesis that god created a designed universe requires first knowing that the god hypothesis is needed to explain the universe. We have already looked at arguments that we don't need god as a creator, so we don't need god as a designer either. But the theologian thinks that the universe is specially designed to have the natural laws that it does. What evidence is offered to show that was specially designed? The theologian appeals to current scientific knowledge that a delicate arrangement of some basic laws of nature permits life to exist in our universe. Supposedly, any minor divergence from these basic laws forbids life. Since life does exist, the universe might look "fine-tuned" (by a divine creator) to ensure that just the right basic laws prevail in our universe.

It is interesting how this fine tuning argument is based on current scientific knowledge. Unlike religion, however, science constantly revises its theories in light of new evidence. That means that this fine tuning argument is precariously based on current scientific knowledge of the laws of nature involved with the big bang. Cosmological understanding of the big bang is in its infancy; calculations of the "probability" of our universe's laws are highly speculative and revisable. There's been much talk lately about the "fine-tuned" cosmological constant, perfectly balancing the vacuum energy density, permitting the universe to expand big enough to support stars and planets. It can look to us like an incredible coincidence, but you have to wonder about whether cosmology will make new discoveries that erase this "coincidence." For example, some cosmologists are already wondering whether the universe's vacuum energy density is really a phenomenon caused by some other basic feature of the universe, so that this accidental "coincidence" collapses into a natural law that hasn't been discovered yet. All this talk about fine tuning is really premature. You also have to watch out for exaggerated numbers manufactured by choosing the units of measurement. For example, Michael Jordan was a great basketball player, so great that he looks fine tuned. After all, if he had been 1 part in 10 to the 16th of a light year shorter, he wouldn't have been so great. That's a joke, because 1 part in 10 to the 16th of a light year is about 1 meter, and Jordan would have been only 4 feet tall (Stenger 2007 provides this example). Miracles don't look so miraculous if you get your scientific perspectives right. Most of the items listed by theologians as incredible fine-tuning examples actually collapse when you account for the choice of units of measurement. There are a few natural constants that appear to be important for life like ours. However, up-to-date calculations show that several basic constants such as the strengths of basic forces and the masses of subatomic particles could vary by as much as 15 to 20 percent and some life could still be possible (again, Stenger 2007 is good reference).

Theology just doesn't have good enough evidence of fine-tuning. Furthermore, current big bang theory implies that most of the universe created by the big bang is beyond our visible universe, having exploded off in other directions so fast that its light can never reach us. For all we know, basic physical laws may vary widely across the entire universe and we happen to live in a portion hospitable for the emergence of our kind of life. Also, this design argument only considers life like us. Other kinds of life, unknown to us, might be possible in other parts of the megaverse, or in different kinds of universes, so this universe did not have to turn out just right for us. In other words, we emerged as we did to survive in this universe, and if the universe had been different, other life-forms may have emerged in those. There may be nothing special about our form of life, and getting this universe "just right" for us does not need to be viewed as anything special requiring explanation. There's an analogy with planets. Once upon a time, the only planet we knew was Earth, and it seemed uniquely special. Now we are discovering planets all around neighboring stars, all kinds of planets. We still see how we live on a special planet, at least special to us because we evolved on it. But planets are not special at all, and it is easier to see how we happened to evolve on a "lucky" planet that was not designed for us. Similarly, in the future we may come to see how we live in a lucky corner of one immense universe among other different kinds of universes. Religion cannot prove this possibility false, and so it can't demonstrate that we even need a god hypothesis in the first place.

Finally, because we may be an accidental natural product and may not be special at all, this design argument specifically proposes a supernatural creator that personally cares enough to intentionally and intelligently ensure the creation of a universe for life like us. The design argument is therefore actually an argument designed to support a theistic creator god (rather than just any "god", such as Hinduism's impersonal Brahman or Taoism's Tao). However, the evidence can't support the existence of a smart and caring god. Our universe is actually highly hostile towards the emergence, survival, and growth of life. Only a tiny, tiny, fraction of the immensity of the universe looks livable, and it won't be livable in the long run (as universal expansion and entropy eliminate heat sources over the next hundred billion years). It is pretty easy to imagine a more hospitable universe for our kind of life. And on our own little planet, Darwinian evolution has been incredibly wasteful. Just producing humans has taken a very long time with thousands of discarded extinct species along the way. The evidence that we have shows us a universe incredibly wasteful, highly hostile, and quite indifferent to life. This universe looks much more like a universe not pre-designed for life, at least for any kind of life similar to ours. The naturalism hypothesis can much more easily explain our available evidence. For all these reasons, any "fine-tuning" of the universe is probably not anything special requiring explanation, since life doesn't seem special from any universal perspective.

To summarize, even if there was dramatic evidence of fine-tuning that cosmology cannot account for, the supernaturalist would have to first assume three things: (1) that current science is fairly accurate about the big bang and all natural laws; (2) that no other kind of life could exist in other sorts of universes; (3) and that the universe looks exactly like what god wanted in order to create life like ours. It is hard to see how a theologian could show that all three points are correct. Let's take a closer look at the way a supernaturalist can try to make argumentative room for god's existence.

Both naturalistic science and religious theology regards this life-hosting universe as quite contingent, requiring explanation. The conclusion to be established by Christian theology is that a supernatural creator god is entirely responsible for the natural universe's existence and structure. (We set aside other hypotheses that the universe is actually a part of god, or that god and the universe are co-extensive.) The basic "fine-tuning" argument for god has this form:

1. If god exists, then it is highly probable that this universe would permit life.
2. This universe is organized to permit life.
3. On the naturalistic "multiverse" theory, it is not highly probable that this universe would permit life.
4. It is more reasonable to accept the theory that makes it more probable that this universe exists.

Conclusion. God exists.

Premise 2 is a statement of fact. Premise 3 is complete conjecture, for Christians and naturalists. Some naturalists are enthusiastic about the way that the multiverse theory would permit so many universes that a few would naturally be life permitting, just on the sheer odds. There is a convenient analogy between the diversity of planets, which may be so plentiful in the universe that our planet is a naturally random result, and the diversity of universes so plentiful that our universe is a naturally random result, too. In this context of diverse plentitude, "random" does not mean "highly unlikely," but rather the reverse: among so many planets (or universes), any particular random example becomes highly likely. My surprise at repeatedly flipping a coin to get ten straight heads is much smaller if I had been flipping that coin for an hour. The greater the plenitude, the more likely that any random result will occur. This logical point doesn't help the naturalist too much here, because current cosmology has no way of guessing whether multiple universes exist or how many exist, so no probability could be reasonably assigned. The real problem confronting the naturalist in the fine-tuning argument is the task of making sure that the multiverse theory could at least offer a rival speculation, so that the god hypothesis doesn't automatically carry the argument by offering even a slightly more probable explanation. Of course, we must first determine whether the god hypothesis of premise 1 is even plausible. If it is not, then the fine-tuning argument fails anyway, and we are left in a skeptical standoff between supernaturalism and naturalism, unable to know why our universe permits life.

Christians really want premise 1 to be correct, and it might appear plausible even for naturalists. Sure, naturalists might say, your god is supposed to make life, if your god even exists. But let's slow down and reconsider this odd premise. In order for premise 1 to be believable and possibly acceptable, it must offer an explanation for the universe that makes some sense. We are all entitled to ask why a god would create *this* universe. Without a good answer, premise 1 cannot offer an explanation worth even considering. We need to know more about this god, and about why this god would bother creating a life-permitting universe like ours.

In order for premise 1 to offer a genuinely explanatory hypothesis, the meaning attached to "god" makes all the difference. This premise would not offer any explanation if it were assumed that "god" is already conceived as a being who would want life to exist. Such an assumption is akin to the pseudo-scientific mistake made by theologians who only offer "god wanted to do that" stories. To illustrate the potential logical problem here, if your conception of god already includes "our creator who loves us," then premise 1 effectively says: "If our creator who loves us exists, then it is highly probable that this universe would permit life." This now-explicit premise really doesn't offer a serious explanation any more, since the "explanation" is conveniently too easy. By analogy, your doctor might tell you: "If the Blue Flu exists, then it is highly probable that your high fever, headache, and nausea will last three days." But if the doctor then says that what he means by Blue Flu is just "that high fever, headache, and nausea last three days," then your doctor isn't really explaining your illness at all. It amounts to saying: "The disease causing those symptoms will cause those symptoms."

To ensure that the god hypothesis of premise 1 actually has some explanatory power, the definition of god intended cannot essentially include wanting to create life. This explanatory requirement can be easily fulfilled by Christian theology. For example, if god is defined as "that supreme infinite supernatural power" the premise does offer an explanation, since "wanting to create life" doesn't automatically follow from that definition. Whether this explanation is a good explanation is another matter, but at least it becomes possible for a theologian to explain more about why such a god would create our life-permitting universe and create us. With a conceptual gap between the definition of god and god's creation, theologians have a place to fill in explanations for this god's actions. What sorts of theological explanations are possible?

5.3 Why Would God Create?

Considering typical Christian views of god, some explanations for god creating the universe can spring to mind. They are not all equally satisfactory; indeed, some may sound ridiculous after some thought. However, we must be sure not to omit obvious possibilities even if they seem odd. The reader may add more to the list below; we only need some examples to watch how theology works on its explanatory gap in the fine-tuning argument.

What characters of god can explain why god creates? Noticeably missing so far in the fine-tuning argument are two traditional theological attributes of god: omnipotence and omniscience. Neither can help explain life, since supreme power alone lets god create any universe, and omniscience by itself has no connection to creation. But there are other typical ideas about god that might help:

> Because god is so spiritual, god would create more spirits, and we are just those sorts of spirits.
>
> Because god is so alive, god would create more life, and we are just that sort of life.
>
> Because god is so personal, god would create more personalities, and we are just those sorts of personalities.

> Because god is so good, god would create more goodness, and we have just that sort of goodness.
>
> Because god is so free, god would create more freedom, and we have just that sort of freedom.
>
> Because god is so powerful, god would create creatures with their own powers, and we have just those sorts of powers.
>
> Because god is so righteous, god would create creatures capable of righteousness, and we are just those sorts of creatures.
>
> Because god is so worshipful, god would create worshippers, and we are just those sorts of creatures.

Each of these eight explanations can take on three basic modes, for a total of twenty-four specific explanations. The three modes are:

> God must necessarily create life, because it would logically contradict god's essential traits if god did not create us.
>
> God means to create life, because creating us is the best way to achieve something that god must want.
>
> God might choose to create life, because creation is a free gift from god to us.

For example, the first explanation taken in mode 3 would be "Because god is so spiritual, god might freely create more spirits, and we are just those sorts of spirits."

We can immediately notice a problem with mode 3. Recall that these sorts of explanations are supposed to help support premise 1: "If god exists, then it is highly probable that this universe would permit life." But any explanation in mode 3 permits god to freely decide, if and when he does decide, to create life. Does that divine freedom make it "highly probable" that the universe would permit life? Or does it make it somewhat improbable, or at least incalculable? Does this proposition make sense: "God might choose to create life, making it highly probable that life exists." If this proposition appears at all plausible, we are trying to imagine god as eternally deciding not to create life, and then suddenly creating our universe at some random moment. With an eternal god, any choice god might make would seem almost inevitable, since god would presumably get around to affirming just about every decision he would freely make (unless he really did not want to do it at all, ever).

This manner of imagining god just passing the time away, toying with the notion of creating life, and then abruptly figuring, what the heck, why not? – is this how we should imagine a god making decisions? First of all, wouldn't god have some pretty good reasons for everything he does, so if creating life had good reasons from the start, why would god hesitate for a while? Second, if god did have good reasons for waiting, and then good reasons for suddenly creating life, then we have actually transitioned into mode 2: god creating life as a means to fulfill some purpose. Third, why are we talking as if time passes for god? Christian theology usually prefers god to be eternal in the sense that god is beyond time, so that the ordinary notion of time doesn't apply to god. We can't go into all the reasons why most theologians have preferred a "timeless" god, although it is not a coincidence that an eternal god couldn't be depicted as waiting around before doing whatever a god must do. Although Christian theology sometimes portrays god as "freely" choosing to do things, it is inconvenient to think that god does things on a whim, for no proper reason. Maybe god didn't have to create us. Maybe our creation is a free gift from god. Maybe we'll never really know why. That's all fine for the religious imagination, but then this sort of thinking can't make it "highly probable" that we exist. For all we know, god could have just as easily decided against our kind of universe and our kind of life.

For all these reasons, mode 3 explanations about god's freedom can't supply the sort of persuasive support that premise 1 requires. That leaves modes 1 and 2. Let's proceed with mode 1: God necessarily must create life. That certainly would make it "highly likely" that life exists, but recall that premise 1 is about not just any life, but our kind of life. Why must god *necessarily* create us? Here the immense gap between us and a supreme deity is hard to imagine, much less justify. Even if good spirits must have spirited company, why us? Even if the powerfully righteous must have righteous company, why us? Of course, we may not be alone in this universe and god may not be alone in heaven. Indeed, it is far easier to imagine god creating diverse kinds of beings to fill the gap between us and god. Is that the point of angels? We have no difficulty imagining all sorts of creatures with more spiritually advanced or more morally advanced natures than us. By combining god's omnipotence with god's creativity, one might hypothesize that god must create virtually every possible kind of creature, so he got around to us too. Such divine plenitude and overabundance makes it highly probable that we'd get created, but this extravagant hypothesis has little available evidence to support it. We live in a universe that is fairly hostile to life as we know it, and if there is much of it, it is scattered very widely and frugally across galaxies.

We feel alone in the universe for a reason, and this bothers us deeply. Like any child, we'd love to believe that of course god wanted exactly us, and nobody else. But we need more than wishful thinking to prop up the fine-tuning argument. We find it difficult to figure out why god would want creatures just like us to exist, when god could make any creature he wants. Without good answers here (and who really can dare to claim they have the answer?), how can we be confident that it is "highly probable" that god would make *us*? If you feel lucky and privileged and grateful that a god would bother creating you, that is quite understandable. But there is no reasonable support in such emotions for premise 1's claim that it is highly probable that god would make us.

Mode 2 explanations, crediting god with using us as a means to gain something god wants, presupposes that god wants to accomplish certain things, or needs to gain something. Aside from a repetition of the same problem we detected in mode 3 explanations, that we can't see why god must make *us*, mode 2 adds the problem that god is less than perfect. A completely perfect god would lack nothing, right? How could a perfect god have any wants or needs or goals to achieve? The main point of mode 3 explanations was accommodating a perfect god's free gifts, which god doesn't need to do. But in mode 2, god has wants and needs. Older mythologies dreamed of gods that used humans as playthings for amusement, or as workers for labor, or as soldiers for a cosmic battle. But the more impressive a god gets, the less there is any reason that it needs us. Nevertheless, mode 2 explanations have far greater explanatory power than mode 1 or mode 3 explanations, at least for Christians. It's not hard to see why. After all, the Christian god is a personal god with some anthropomorphic characteristics that allow god (and Jesus) to make and pursue plans, get into emotional relationships, and pass moral judgments. While many Christian theologians have pursued god's perfections to such lofty heights that any divine personality fades from sight, Christianity as a distinctive religion would not last long if the laypeople followed the theologians. For typical Christians, it makes good sense that, even though god couldn't get lonely and couldn't find us useful for anything, god would still prefer something to exist besides himself. God at least wants relationships. Don't we all? Is that not the essence of being a personality – wanting relationships with other persons? And what sorts of relationships would a Christian god want? Here, at the very limits of human imagination, we still fall short of figuring out why god needs us so badly that a universe just like ours, and lives just like ours, are highly probable. Mode 2 explanations can't do the needed work to support premise 1 either.

Although each of the three modes of explanation separately fail to provide the needed support for premise 1, there must be some reason why Christians find premise 1 so plausible. I suggest that a blending of all three modes of explanation energizes the Christian understanding of god's relationship with us. A personal god *must* have relationships; a morally good god *means* to create persons capable of righteous relationships; and a free god might hence create persons just like us. From mode 1, to mode 2, and then mode 3 – each step of explanation brings the divine closer, gradually explaining how god would create just us. This suitably sophisticated and specific hypothesis about god's creation of us might bridge the vast explanatory gap in the way that premise 1 requires. Unfortunately for the fine-tuning argument, this sophisticated vision of god still leaves us well short of seeing how it is "highly probable" that our specific universe would exist. It remains too easy to imagine that god could have just as easily (and more efficiently) created other kinds of universes and other kinds of creatures to more satisfactorily fulfill a divine being's plans. If god wants great relationships, why create such moronic and pathetically limited insects like us? If god wants devoted ethical followers, why create such willful and happily disobedient rebels like us? If god wants spirited free wills, why create us only to continually harass us with commandments and judgments?

There are only unsatisfactory answers every which way one turns. No possible combination of explanations and modes will satisfactorily bridge the vast chasm between us and a god. Any theologian who confidently expects a sophisticated story full of mysteries about god to rival scientific cosmology is engaging in more pseudo-cosmology. That's why many a wise theologian (or just a sympathetic minister) will simply admit the impenetrable mystery and recommend a humble gratitude and reverence towards a god that would put up with us. As for the fine-tuning argument, it must be judged a failure. We can't credit premise 1 with enough plausibility, and we can't discredit premise 3 for implausibility, to be reasonably confident that either the Christian or naturalistic hypothesis is more probable.

5.4 The Problem of Evil

The "problem of evil" for Christian theology is a specific example of the general problem raised in the previous section, the problem of the immense gap between god and god's actual creation. If the actual universe, and our lives within it, are supposed to serve as evidence that only a god can explain, the quality of the evidence matters greatly. As a paradigm example of positive philosophical atheology, the problem of evil could be raised in the chapter on Theology From The World, since evils are in the world as much as anything else. However, theology is well prepared to attribute any seeming evil in the world to the overall plan for all of god's creation, so we can efficiently present the problem of evil in this chapter on Theology Beyond The World.

Do we have such an impressively ideal universe and such impressive lives that only a supernatural god could explain our existence? A perfect, omniscient, omnipotent, and beneficent god, at that? Any defects in the design are the responsibility of the designer. A defective design at most requires a less-than-perfect designer (or perhaps no designer at all). A defective design cannot disprove god, but it disproves a perfect theistic god. An imperfect god, or no god at all, makes a better fit with an imperfect universe. Yes, a perfect god might freely choose to create a less-than-perfect universe. Yet such optional choices do a poor job at providing "highly probable" explanations. Yes, a god might have good reasons to need to create a less-than-perfect universe. Yet such mysterious reasons don't do any better job explaining the defects than naturalism, which can easily explain defects. Serious defects in the universe's design eliminate the plausibility of the Christian theistic god.

As was noted in the previous section, the universe looks pretty imperfect for life. Some people describe these imperfections, all the features of the world that make it really hard to live and enjoy life, as the world's "evils." Maybe it is inappropriate to call natural imperfections "evils." A pounding hurricane or a crashing comet are not evil, the way that a person can be evil to another person. We are not talking about any evils that people do to each other, in any case. The problem of evil first and foremost concerns the natural evils, evils that are necessarily part of the universe's structure, that we can imagine as not really necessary in a supposedly wonderful world created by a perfect and caring god. To take a specific example of a defect, consider a natural evil, some event that happens which seems to be just the sort of thing that the Christian god would not permit to happen. How about a horrible disease that strikes thousands of children, causing immense suffering and premature death? How about a plague that kills millions of innocent people? How about a massive hurricane that destroys and kills across a vast region? It is not hard to imagine that a Christian god (so supremely powerful and knowledgeable and good) could easily prevent each of these tragedies from happening, without disrupting the rest of the fine design of the universe.

For a theologian to make a good case that we need the hypothesis of a perfect and caring god, two alternatives must be first ruled out: either some imperfect god(s) made the universe, or no god made the universe. Although the hypothesis that a less-than-perfect god or committee of gods badly designed the universe can be imaginatively fitted to our available evidence, few religions still propose this hypothesis. A Christian theologian must explain how every piece of evidence that looks like an unnecessary imperfection must actually be the way god wants it. Yes, a perfect god might mysteriously decide to create an imperfect universe. Theologians have spent hundreds of years trying to figure out how such a nice god would make a wasteful and unpleasant universe. Theology is imaginative enough to come up with elaborate stories about god, and different religions disagree on such stories just like they disagree about everything else. One says god wants lots of people to reject god for lack of evidence so hell is full. Another says that god wants all people to eventually resort to faith for lack of evidence so that heaven is full. Endless variations on such accounts can be designed, so that people can be convinced that a great god would create just this actual world we live in. Maybe this supreme deity wants us to live short and hard lives with quickly failing bodies and slowly working minds.

A theologian proposing a perfect god must defend everything about the universe as something this god necessarily wants. If there is anything in the world that this god would not want, that evidence counts heavily against this god's existence. A theologian defending all the world's evidence has a lot of work to do. There are so many things that humans cannot understand as really good when they look so evil to us. The skeptical atheist thinks that there is enough obvious unnecessary evil to make people skeptically doubt god. If the theologian thinks that there is really is no evil because it's all good, we await an explanation for each and every evil. If the theologian alternatively says that there is evil but not that much evil, then the god hypothesis is in deep trouble, and we can wonder how much evil it would take for a theologian to begin doubting god. If there's no amount of evil, not even a million plagues and earthquakes and holocausts, that would make a theologian doubt god, then theology really isn't taking the available evidence seriously any more. Accounting for evil is the theologian's problem here, not the skeptic's. The skeptic is already confident that there is plenty of evidence of evil to cast lots of doubt on a perfect god.

The theologian trying to show how we live in an ideally designed universe is doing what is traditionally called theodicy (prominent recent examples are Plantinga 1977 and Swinburne 1998). The most straightforward theodicy would consist of a lengthy cataloging of natural evils with corresponding explanations why they are actually necessarily good. Perhaps unsurprisingly, published theodicies don't look like that. The typical theodicy has a more efficient strategy, consisting of skeptically doubting the human capacity to know god's design. This skepticism relies on a distinction between appearance and reality, starting with a claim that any seeming defect to the universe is mere appearance. This typical theodicy therefore has two claims to justify, not about the world, but about people: first, what appears to be evil to us may not in fact be evil, but a good part of an ideal design; and second, just because we think that we can imagine god easily preventing such evils does not mean that god really could or should. We should neither trust our judgments on evil, nor trust our estimates of what god can or can't do. For all we know, theodicy urges, every apparent evil is actually "good" according to god. The way that the universe is the best design is somewhat hidden from us, the theologian argues, and that is why the universe can really be ideal despite all appearances to the contrary.

This theological attempt to save the notion of an ideal universe, just right for a perfect god to explain, again falls back into sheer mystery and pseudo-cosmology. Even if this universe really is the ideal best that a perfect god could make, we couldn't know this to be true based on our available evidence. A Christian may assume on faith that this universe was ideally created, but that only begs the question. Faith might be necessary anyway, since the skeptical kind of theodicy forbids a theologian from having better powers of observation that the rest of us; and a desire to understand evil as really good is not enough. The universe that we can observe and understand is obviously less than ideal for life in general and for us in particular. Skeptical theodicy and skeptical atheism converge on agreement that the available evidence cannot justify the existence of the Christian god.

Besides, should a theologian or any Christian really want to see each evil as good? If there are no real evils, if "it's all for the best," what happens to the religious motivation to prevent evil or to fight evil? What would happen to Christianity if theology became an theodicy industry hastily producing justifications for every evil that comes along? If theology became obsessed with theodicy, continually explaining that all evils are actually good, might Christianity become complacent or even defenseless in the face of evil?

A clear example of how theology can lose its clarity on good and evil is supplied by the religious notion that human free will explains evil. Many versions of this notion abound in the history of Christian theology. The Adam and Eve story blames human free choices for all the evils of the world we inhabit. We can mention two prominent recent combinations of the free will problem and the problem of evil. Suppose god loves us so much that he wants to persuade us to have faith by any means short of violating our free will to choose to believe. Would god leave us in Eden? Presumably not, since excessively comfortable people notoriously don't need god and ignore god. But make us suffer, and the churches fill up. So suffering is actually good for us, since it freely draws us towards god. This theological argument fails since suffering is just another potent kind of coercion (that's the point of punishment after all).

An even more ambitious version of combining free will and evil also tries to explain god's mysteriousness as well. On this theological story, there is precious little evidence for god because god would not want to coerce our reason. Too much evidence and people's intellects would be coerced into rationally believing in god. That's why god only sent a Jesus once to a some illiterate Jewish peasants instead of putting Jesus on tour from Rome to London and New York City, and why god didn't place a thousand-mile-wide cross up on the moon for all to see. On this view, god does not want be believed through evidence or reason since these are not as good as committing by faith. Skeptics are unreasonable because they expect humanity to easily discern a hidden god (Friedman 1995), or they stubbornly cling to reason (Moser 2008), or they expect god to force rational belief (Novak 2008), or they ignore how evils teach how faith in god is so useful for dealing with evils (Reitan 2009). Needless to say, a theology going down this road no longer regards commitment to rationality as an important value, and has proceeded to Theology In The Know.

The naturalist has no temptation to view this universe as an ideal habitat for life. Yes, our kind of life happened to emerge in his universe, and it struggles for its uncertain existence where it can. The naturalist has no difficulty perceiving the universe and its defects clearly and realistically, and is still able to distinguish good from evil.

5.5 The Argument from Pseudo-cosmology

The Greeks contrasted the cosmos, the orderly and predictable universe, with the idea of chaos, the absence of order where anything could happen. The Greeks also proposed what we now call the principle of sufficient reason. Christianity credits god with reasonably accounting for both the universe's existence and the universe's order. Theology Beyond The World proposes that neither the universe nor its order could be possible without god. In addition, our capacity to understand anything about the universe by discovering its regular laws of order depends on god's establishment of the universe's order. None of the foundations of science would be possible – the cause–effect relation, the induction of nature's patterns, the mathematically predictable laws – without god. Theology Beyond The World argues that god is the necessary condition for the universe, for its order, and for its intelligibility.

Without question, the principle of sufficient reason must be taken seriously. However, not all explanations are automatically equal. There is a minimal sense of "explanation" that both science and pseudo-cosmology share, which starts the confusion for some people. An explanation is, in its simplest form, a story about something, A that is allegedly responsible for something else, B, such that, if A actually exists and does what it is supposed to do, then B becomes expected, instead of a surprise. Basically, A explains B in this minimal sense by making B expected. For example, if the force of gravity really exists, then the behavior of falling objects is explained. The moon's mass generates a gravitational force that explains the ocean tides. The full moon's bright glare explains the rise in suicide rates. The peculiar arrangement of planets in the sky at your birth explains your personality. The appearance of a great comet explains the amazing victory of the Byzantine king's army. The release of god's righteous wrath explains the annihilation of that tribe.

While there is this minimal sense of explanation, applied in those examples, explanations do not automatically get sanctioned by reason, not even if there is no other explanation that we can think of right now. Theology Beyond The World's proposed arguments for god explaining the universe can't pass the test of reason. Furthermore, a good explanation had better include some extra details sufficient to deal with obvious concerns. For example, if god created the universe, why did god do this? What is it about god that would cause god to create this sort of universe, and not some other type? Are there any other gods playing with their own universes? Why can there be only one god? Does god create many universes, or just one? Did god have to create this universe, or could god have decided not to? What is so special about this universe's natural laws? Couldn't god have done a better job? How can we know that we are the whole point of this universe? What or who else might have this universe been designed for? What is god going to do with this universe? If god really exists, then what explains god? What or who created god? If god didn't have an explanation, doesn't that violate the principle of sufficient reason? Theologians hasten to exhibit their elaborate theologies to answer all these questions and more, but the whole process arouses suspicion. Religions disagree so bitterly over god precisely because there's no way to rationally settle these inevitable questions. Deep mystery beyond the world is mystery enough.

Pseudo-cosmology's tangles in ever-deeper thickets of impossible questions should give everyone pause before concluding that supernaturalism has an advantage over naturalism on the edge of scientific knowledge. The mere capacity to offer explanations does not satisfy rationality. As far as rationality can tell, nature is probably all that exists and it possesses some sort of eternality similar to that attributed to a god. The limitations of cosmic theology set by reason need not destroy the religious value of explaining nature. Although strict atheism rests content with scientific naturalism, liberal theology and religious naturalism, discussed in Chapter 8, embrace nature's mysteries for enlightenments far richer than any material reward.

If Theology Beyond The World ignores the factual and logical difficulties of its arguments, stubbornly persisting in its claims that only god can explain the universe, it perpetuates a religious pseudo-cosmology. This religious pseudo-cosmology contains these principles:

PC1 Unless god exists, the universe could not exist.
PC2 Unless god exists, the universe could not possess any order or regularity.
PC3 Unless god exists, the universe could not be intelligible to anyone.
PC4 Unless god exists, the universe could not be scientifically investigated.
PC5 Unless god exists, scientific knowledge of the universe could not be gained.
PC6 There is no feature of nature that could possibly be incompatible with god's existence.

A theology using these six principles has little argumentative support, as we have seen. These principles so thoroughly connect the natural world to the supernatural world that theology might claim a victory.

However, when reminded how defenses of these principles require so many violations of evidence, reason, and science, theology is tempted to directly challenge those three foundations of knowledge. When theology decides to bypass those foundations to avoid such problems, it moves towards Theology In The Know or Theology Into The Myst.

6

Theology In The Know

Under the scrutiny of atheology, Theology From The Scripture is tempted to resort to pseudo-history, Theology From The World can descend into pseudo-science, and Theology Beyond The World amounts to pseudo-cosmology. These three types of theology failed to accomplish their aims because they tried to meet the reason-based expectations of history, scientific method, and cosmology. Some common sense, sound logic, and proper application of scientific method expose fallacies and failures of all of the theological arguments examined so far. Two more options are left for theology: Theology In The Know and Theology Into The Myst.

Theology In The Know remains confident that secure knowledge of god is available, but it holds that roles of reason and evidence have to be entirely recast. Theology Into The Myst denies that knowledge of god is possible, suggesting that our relationship with god has other grounds in experience and faith. This chapter deals with Theology In The Know, collecting together various theological stances sharing a distrust of reason's authority, logic's neutrality, or science's impartiality.

6.1 Arguments from Ignorance

If no one can know that god doesn't exist, then we can know god exists. That's a poor argument, right? Theologians rarely commit such a blatant fallacy, the "argument from ignorance," but it can be found in popular books for lay Christians. They take the general form, "Christianity cannot be proven false, so therefore it is true." Four major examples of arguing from ignorance are presented here.

The first argument of this type uses premises from pseudo-history, pseudo-science, and pseudo-cosmology. Let's call it the "nature can't disprove god" argument for Christianity. It starts out from an excessive confidence in various arguments for the Christian god covered in previous chapters.

1. Regardless of evidence either way, no inquiry of scientific history can disprove Jesus's divinity, so scientific history cannot render belief in Jesus unreasonable. (PH4)
2. God's interventions in nature cannot be predicted or tested in any way. (PS14)
3. There is no feature of nature that could possibly be incompatible with god's existence. (PC6)
4. Nothing in nature could ever serve as evidence against the existence of the Christian god. (From 1–3)
5. If nothing natural could ever disprove a religious belief, then it remains reasonable.

Conclusion. It is reasonable to believe that the Christian god exists. (From 4 and 5)

Even if the first three premises were correct (and previous chapters have explained why they are all false), this argument relies on a poor premise: premise 5. This premise cannot be accepted, for several reasons.

First, compatibility with everything natural cannot be the only test of a reasonable belief. A belief could be unreasonable in other ways, too, besides incompatibility with something natural. For example, a religious belief could contain within it a logical contradiction, or could imply a logical contradiction. Even theologians must worry about a definition of god harboring logical contradictions, especially when several perfections are attributed to god. Could god create a rock so heavy that he can't move it, or make $2 + 2 = 5$, or create creatures capable of free choices that god could not accurately predict? Preventing such logical contradictions in the Christian conception of god has kept theologians busy for centuries, illustrating the point that religious beliefs have to survive other tests besides natural tests.

Second, premise 5 is irrational because it supposes that maximal compatibility with everything natural is a fine test of reasonableness. This notion is the final culmination of natural theology driven to extremes. Natural theology was established to seek special natural features that could only point to god. Premise 5 is used here to ensure that no natural features point away from god. Natural theology's assumption that reasonable belief requires positive evidence is now abandoned; premise 5 instead says that reasonable belief only requires no negative evidence. This premise violates common sense and sound inquiry, and could not be applied in any other area of life. Would you want your legal justice system of criminal trials based on premise 5? After no evidence could be produced that you did not steal a car, you should be judged guilty of stealing a car?

Third, premise 5 is useless for theology because it permits demonstrative proof of any religious belief that can pass its test. How many other religions, similarly eager to immunize their divinities from all natural evidence, might successfully establish their reasonableness using premise 5? Actually, most sophisticated religions with their own theologies have already accomplished this relatively easy task. Indeed, many religions have even matched Christianity's ability to produce a theodicy, so that the actual natural world is exactly what each religion would expect from its divinities. If it is reasonable for Christians to believe that the Christian god exists, then those other religions are just as reasonable for their believers too. Instead of helping to narrow down the number of correct religions to just one (Christianity), premise 5 accomplishes the exact opposite result: most sophisticated religions become equally reasonable. Actually, premise 5 would permit a potentially infinite number of religions to be reasonable, since endless religions could be imaginatively designed to be perfectly compatible with nature. No theology should accept premise 5. Because this argument's first three premises are all false, premise 5 is unacceptable, and the entire "nature can't disprove god" argument proves way too much, this argument is a failure.

The second argument from ignorance cheerfully acknowledges the failures of arguments from pseudo-history, pseudo-science, and pseudo-cosmology. Let's call it the "reason can't deal with god" argument for

Christianity. The inability of human reasoning to successfully establish arguments for the Christian god covered in previous chapters is somehow taken as a sign that Christianity remains reasonable.

6. The human intellect is quite limited in the scope of its knowledge and power of its insight.
7. God is so infinite, supremely perfect, and supernaturally transcendent as compared to humans.
8. The human intellect cannot rationally prove or disprove god's existence. (From 1 and 2)
9. If there are no rational proofs or disproofs for a religious belief, then it remains reasonable.

Conclusion. It is reasonable to believe that the Christian god exists. (From 3 and 4)

This argument conveniently explains why all the arguments for and against Christianity are inadequate failures. No wonder there are so many skeptics out there. Indeed, could the existence of reasonable skeptics itself be a sign, a sign of a truly transcendent god? Perhaps god even intends and approves of skeptical atheism.

This argument's reliance on premise 9, a dubious premise, is its downfall. Premise 9 is unacceptable because there are other tests for the reasonableness of a belief besides its provability or disprovability. For example, if someone believed that the President is actually an undetectably disguised alien, common sense tells us that this belief is not rational even if it cannot be proven true or proven false. That's why we don't use premise 9 in any other area of life. Do you find reasonable every paranoia, hallucination, fantasy, or delusion in other people's minds just because they can't be proven right or wrong? Furthermore, applying premise 9 permits most other sophisticated religions to establish their own reasonableness for their believers, defeating the entire point of this "reason can't deal with god" argument favoring Christianity. Finally, the "reason can't deal with god" argument is itself another human argument for god, so, according to premise 8, this argument can't help prove god. Because this argument's first three premises strongly support religious skepticism, premise 5 is unacceptable, and the entire "reason can't deal with god" argument either proves way too much or proves nothing at all, this argument is also a failure.

Another third argument from ignorance for Christianity similarly starts from the failures of the arguments for god discussed in earlier chapters. This "god would not want proof" argument for god takes particular notice of one skeptical argument against the existence of god. Proceeding from the Christian belief that god wants most (or all) people to believe in god, the skeptic can ask why there is so little convincing evidence for god. This skeptical argument is a specific variation on the "problem of evil" argument against god. Peoples' inability to believe that god exists is presumably a kind of "evil" nonbelief when the Christian god would instead want much more "good" belief, and it is all god's ultimate responsibility anyway. However, the Christian god has other priorities, too, as this argument supposes.

10. The Christian god would want people to hold religious beliefs in ways that do not violate their free will to choose to believe.
11. Convincing reasons for the Christian god's existence would cause a person to hold religious beliefs in a way that violates their free will to choose to believe.
12. If the Christian god exists, then no one would have a convincing reason for god. (From 10 and 11)
13. The fact that no one has a convincing reason for believing in god is best explained by the existence of the Christian god.

Conclusion. It is reasonable to believe that the Christian god exists. (From 12 and 13)

According to this "god would not want proof" argument, Christians are people who hold religious beliefs about god by having less than convincing reasons. Similarly, skeptics do *not* hold religious beliefs by having less than convincing reasons. Christians may congratulate themselves for superior faith. However, skeptics reject premise 13 as unacceptable. The best explanation for the absence of convincing reasons for god's existence is god's nonexistence. No sane person could rely on premise 13 in any other area of life; someone who did rely on anything akin to premise 13 in their ordinary life would be regarded as irrational. Should we believe that there are disguised malevolent aliens living among us, since these aliens would never permit any good evidence for them? Furthermore, this argument proves too much, since any sophisticated religion about a benevolent god who admires free will could also receive reasonable justification by this argument. Because this argument can easily justify skepticism, or justify many other religions using an irrational premise, this argument is yet another failure.

These three arguments from ignorance can be bought together for a fourth general theological argument. Using the first three arguments' unacceptable premises, and adding a couple more, this general argument from "no disproof is as good as proof" for god has the following structure:

14. Nothing natural could ever make a religious belief in god unreasonable.
15. Nothing rational could ever make a religious belief in god unreasonable.
16. No lack of a convincing reason could ever make a religious belief in god unreasonable.
17. Nothing – no natural evidence, rational argument, or lack of convincing reason – could ever make a religious belief in god unreasonable.
18. If a belief is not unreasonable, then it is reasonable.

Conclusion. It is reasonable to believe in the existence of god. (From 14 and 15)

According to this general argument, you can't judge someone's religious belief in god as unreasonable or false unless you can first prove that it is true that god does not exist. This argument supplies a master response to the skeptic who demands sufficient reason for religious belief. If "no disproof is as good as proof," as this general argument claims, then we have reached a first principle of Theology In The Know:

ITK1 Nothing could ever make belief in god unreasonable, so belief in god is reasonable.

According to ITK1, the impossibility of proving that god does not exist makes it unreasonable to criticize people who do believe that god does exist. Reasonable belief in god is now utterly immune to any possible challenge or criticism from any evidence or reasoning. This sort of domination over reason and defeat of skepticism lacks sound foundations, however, since this argument's first three premises are all unacceptable.

Let us now consider more theological arguments taking a different approach to the challenge represented by evidence and reason.

6.2 Religious Epistemologies

According to Theology In The Know, the elevation of reason, logic, and science above religion cannot be tolerated. Religion should not take second place to any of them, and should no longer be judged by them, but religion need not abandon them entirely. For Theology In The Know, philosophy is not an equal partner any more. Philosophy has little to teach Christianity about the path to knowledge of god. Although the Greeks invented the notion of epistemology – an account of the methods of genuine knowledge – that historical fact cannot mean that only Greek epistemology is possible or even desirable. Theology In The Know demands a divorce between theology and Greek thought. Liberated from philosophy and its epistemology, Christianity can utilize a properly Christian rationality and epistemology instead.

What might a Christian epistemology look like? Theologians over the centuries have suggested a wide variety of approaches. To helpfully organize these approaches for discussion, we can recall how the theologies discussed in prior chapters can lead a frustrated theologian to rebel against the standards of reason, logic, and science. Since those standards are independent from, and perhaps alien to, the Christian religion, perhaps the misguided failures of theology actually point out the right direction. After all, pseudo-history, pseudo-science, and pseudo-cosmology are classifiable as "pseudo" – as false or fake – only when measured against the "true" Greek heritage. Why not reconsider their principles in a new light, the light of Christian religion? Why not place them at the foundations of a new Christian epistemology?

The principles of religious pseudo-history, the claims that scripture provides knowable truths about god and Jesus, could serve as the basis for an epistemology. This view that the Christian knows god through scriptural revelation already has the label of "fundamentalism." Basic principles of Christian fundamentalism include the following:

PH1 Scriptural revelation accurately describes Jesus' divinity and relationship with god.

PH4 Regardless of evidence either way, no inquiry of scientific history can disprove Jesus's divinity, so scientific history cannot render belief in Jesus unreasonable.

PH5 The New Testament's account of Jesus' divinity remains truthful despite scientific history.

According to fundamentalism, the Christian is the person who accepts these sorts of principles. It is not fundamentalism's position that a Christian has to become rationally persuaded of the truth of these principles, by considering the arguments for and against them. Rather, by simple definition, a Christian is the person who believes these principles as knowledge and believes in god and Jesus. Christians do not accept them because they are reasonable; Christians find them reasonable because they know them. It is firm conviction that matters here, and not any intellectual process that may or may not have been involved. In fact, some fundamentalists have held that "reasonableness" is irrelevant, scripture can directly inspire knowledge of god, and no complex intellectual process need be involved at all. Here, different fundamentalist epistemologies begin to diverge. Perhaps reading scripture suffices. Perhaps god's direct intervention with the human soul is even a necessary or sufficient condition for religious knowledge. In any case, fundamentalism requires the Christian to reject the relevance of scientific history to the issue of accepting scriptural revelation.

Fundamentalists also disagree over the question of what kind of knowledge is provided by scripture. Obviously, knowledge of god and Jesus would have to be at least as firm and reliable as human knowledge of any other fact of nature or fact of history. Otherwise, those other facts might be applied to raise skepticism towards scripture, as we saw in Chapter 3. Some fundamentalists have claimed even more for scriptural knowledge. For example, perhaps Christian religious knowledge is as certain as the knowledge of one's own name, or how many fingers one has on one's hand, or the fact that $2 + 2 = 4$. These sorts of "basic beliefs" are so foundational for anyone's body of knowledge that it is hard to imagine any other belief one could have to raise doubt in them. Staunch Christians, from fundamentalism's perspective, would sooner surrender their other beliefs than doubt god, Jesus, or scripture. Another Christian epistemology established in the twentieth century, presuppositionalism, similarly makes this sort of claim about the genuine Christian.

The principles of religious pseudo-science, the claims that nature's features are only explainable through god, could serve as the basis for an epistemology. The view that the Christian knows god through features of nature already has a label, "evidentialism." Core principles of evidentialism include the following:

PS12 A god that wants nature or us to have some feature is a good explanation for that feature.

PS13 God is a good explanation for any feature or event in nature that can't be explained by current science.

PS14 God's interventions in nature cannot be predicted or tested in any way.

Evidentialist theologians frequently strengthen these basic principles if they are especially impressed by divine explanations. Some evidentialists claim that divine explanations are absolutely required for explaining certain features of nature.

Evidentialism shares little with fundamentalism, although there would no difficulty for a Christian to hold both positions together. In fact, most Christians throughout the centuries have believed in god because of scripture and because they saw god's hand in the workings of nature. These two modes of knowledge, revelation and natural evidence, have been widely viewed as complementary and helpful towards salvation. Their differences arise from the way that reasoning is not required for revelation to establish Christian knowledge of god, while reasoning (however misused) is essential for nature's features to guide a Christian to knowledge of god.

The particular principle of religious pseudo-science regarding human reason claims that reason is only possible through god. The general view that the use of reason presupposes God's existence is a key component of a theological stance having the label of "presuppositionalism." In Chapter 4 we examined the arguments over this principle:

PS11 Unless god exists, humans could not reason and acquire knowledge of truths.

Presuppositionalists, impressed by the arguments in its favor, frequently express this principle along the lines of "God is the necessary precondition for the human capacity to reason and acquire knowledge of truths." Presuppositionalism is a broad theological epistemology with many components that go beyond this principle about reason to include much of fundamentalism, along with selected portions of Theology From The World and Theology In The Know. We will not attempt to delineate all the theologies that have had the label of "presuppositionalism." Many presuppositionalists view their epistemology as a direct competitor to evidentialism, as if a Christian must choose between them. However, the primary presuppositionalist complaint against evidentialism is only that it falls short of establishing god's existence as certain knowledge, leaving the matter open to probability estimations. Appealing to presuppositionalism need not require abandoning evidentialism; the practical Christian may simply use both. In fact, since evidentialism depends on reasoning about nature and presuppositionalism accounts for reason itself, presuppositionalism encompasses and completes evidentialism.

The principles of religious pseudo-cosmology, the claims that the universe and its order is only explainable through god, could also serve as a basis for a religious epistemology. The view that the Christian knows god through the universe's design can receive the general label of "creationism." Creationism is presently used to refer to the specific belief that god made the universe and all living things precisely as Genesis recounts. In this limited sense, fundamentalists are creationists. However, not all creationists need to be fundamentalists, in the wider sense of "creationism" used here. A creationist is persuaded by Theology Beyond The World of these principles:

PC1 Unless god exists, the universe could not exist.
PC2 Unless god exists, the universe could not possess any order or regularity.
PC3 Unless god exists, the universe could not be intelligible to anyone.
PC4 Unless god exists, the universe could not be scientifically investigated.
PC5 Unless god exists, scientific knowledge of the universe could not be gained.
PC6 There is no feature of nature that could possibly be incompatible with god's existence.

Furthermore, as the entire naturalistic worldview is based on the intelligibility of nature and scientific knowledge, the creationist theologian can easily draw another conclusion directly from PC1–PC6:

PC7 Naturalism's foundations all necessarily require that god exists.

At this point, the presuppositionalist can propose a compelling alliance with creationism. Both positions regard the existence of god as a necessary pre-condition for human knowledge. The presuppositionalist can admire the way that creationism demonstrates how the presupposition of god must ground naturalism, effectively exposing naturalism as an incomplete worldview needing supplementation with supernaturalism. The presuppositionalist would only add that its own view of reason as presupposing god fits nicely with creationism. Since knowledge of nature requires both an intelligible universe and an intelligence to know it, creationism and presuppositionalism together can fully explain all aspects of human knowledge. This combination was discovered and rediscovered by several thinkers in eighteenth- and nineteenth-century theology. In recent theology, much of this coherent synthesis is represented by Alvin Plantinga's theology (see Plantinga and Tooley 2008).

In fact, by combining presuppositionalism, evidentialism, and creationism, a highly compact and powerful Theology In The Know is established. Let's bring together core principles of these three positions:

PC3 Unless god exists, the universe could not be intelligible to anyone.
PS11 Unless god exists, humans could not reason and acquire knowledge of truths.
PS12 A god that wants nature or us to have some feature is a good explanation for that feature.

Next, considering how human rationality is a feature of nature, we can derive another PS principle that specifically applies to reason from PS12:

PS15 A god that wants us to have reason is a good explanation of why humans have reason.

Finally, to ensure that Theology In The Know is still talking about the Christian god, we add fundamentalism:

PH1 Scriptural revelation accurately describes Jesus' divinity and relationship with god.

The combination of PH1, PC3, PS11, and PS15 yields the desired result, which we will regard as the second principle of Theology In The Know:

ITK2 The Christian god created an intelligible universe and intelligent humans to understand creation and know Jesus.

ITK2 provides Christian theology with a powerful way of defending against skepticism, atheism, and naturalism. On the presumption that sufficient knowledge of god becomes available to us through scriptural revelation or reasoning, what grounds remain for the nonbeliever to mount a challenge? Scripture cannot be refuted; the use of reason itself reveals god.

This theology yields a comprehensively religious theory of knowledge: all possibility of knowledge completely depends on the existence of god. This is a mature Theology In The Know quite capable of seriously challenging the Greek tradition. However, the Greek tradition still has more to say about the contest.

6.3 Knowledge, Justification, and Truth

Theology In The Know would dominate and domesticate the Greek philosophical tradition. By placing revelation over reason, god's mind over logic, and god's design over science, Theology In The Know has turned its relationship with Greek thought upside down. The servant is now the master. Or is it?

Greek thought is not yet overcome. It possesses deeper and more powerful resources than even reason, logic, and science. The Greeks built a cosmopolitan civilization, acutely aware of its contacts and exchanges with alien civilizations and modes of thinking. In this ceaseless clash of worldviews, the Greeks were forced to cope with the inevitable cognitive tensions and breakdowns like no other civilization had ever before. How does one maintain internal mental equilibrium and external social harmony when pulled in so many directions at once? The Greeks knew well from long experience how civilizations can simply impose their worldviews at the point of a sword. Having experimented with their own alternatives to civil war, inventing democracy along the way, the Greeks dealt with the diverse claims of the multitudes in a simple fashion: what is the justification for the truth of your view? This is direct way of politely asking, "Can you persuade and teach us?"

The Greeks invented epistemology by first noticing that there is crucial difference between the psychological state of feeling completely confident in a belief and the cognitive state of holding a justified belief. The first belief state may be called "certainty" while the second belief state is called "knowledge." The essential difference between these two kinds of beliefs is not truth: a person can feel certain about a true belief, and a person can hold a justified belief in a truth as well. The question confronting Theology In The Know is this: will it accept this fundamental distinction between certain belief and justified belief? Will it understand "knowledge" as simply feeling certain about a belief, or will it still agree with the Greeks that knowledge is justified true belief? This is the "problem of justification" for Theology In The Know. The best answer for Christian theology is far from obvious, and theologians have sharply disagreed. Let's consider the costs and benefits of the options.

Theology In The Know claims that knowledge of god is achieved by Christians. There is an immediate tension between fundamentalism and the other theological epistemologies. Fundamentalism complains that the others ultimately depend on the success of some logical arguments, while fundamentalism does not. Fundamentalism is the simplest of the epistemologies involved, since reading or hearing scripture can suffice to make Christians knowers of god. In this way, basic fundamentalism denies that the knowledge of god provided by scripture requires any justification. Christians simply feel certain in their religious beliefs, and nothing more need be asked of them. Some presuppositionalists may add that there is a way to handle the justification problem: simply hold that the truths in scripture are their own justification, that their justification simply shines forth as self-evident when they inspire knowledge in the reader. There are convenient analogies for such self-justification in reason and in perception. For example, deductive inferences simply are justified in the very meanings of the concepts involved, and we don't have to look elsewhere for the justification of a deductive inference. As another example, when we clearly perceive something under normal conditions, like our hand in front of our eyes, the belief that this is my hand stands justified in its presence, as there is nothing else required to justify us in knowing that this is my hand.

This potent combination of fundamentalism and presuppositionalism describes the Christian as a person whose knowledge about god is so certain, basic, and foundational that there simply is no point in demanding any further justification from this person. The tradition of Reformed epistemology is a prominent example of this combination, and its modern form takes the Christian's personal faith that god has been revealed or that scripture is infallible to be the ultimate foundation for everything else this Christian can know. Prominent varieties of this presuppositionalism include the religious epistemologies of Cornelius Van Til (1969) and William Alston (1991). Let's refer to this Christian as the "personal knower of god" (hereafter the PKG) since this epistemology finds that a single person of proper faith and access to scripture can be a knowing Christian. Has the Greek requirement that knowledge be justified true belief been settled?

Not quite. Remember how the demand for justification is essentially an interpersonal demand that arises when worldviews disagree? The Greeks would hardly be impressed by the way that presuppositionalism portrays justification as a personally internal matter. So what if a person feels justified in their knowledge? Just another feeling, that of feeling justified, added to the original feeling of certainty, only adds up to a bunch of feelings. A series of mutually reinforcing psychological states easily explains how a person can be unshakably certain about a belief. What remains unexplained is whether two people who hold opposed beliefs can figure out which person actually has the true belief. The point of justification is not to reinforce belief, but to orient beliefs (and the people who hold them) towards the truth.

At this point the problem of justification breaks out again, as the problem of truth. This is ironic, since fundamentalism and presuppositionalism were designed to take care of truth from the beginning. Christians know the truth about god. More specifically, according to the PKG epistemology, each Christian knows the truth about god. It can't get any simpler, can it? Well, it can get complicated pretty fast. In the Greek spirit we could ask, "Does each Christian know the same truths about god? Do Christians ever disagree in their knowledge?" There are endless examples of Christians disagreeing about god. Yes, they agree that he (or she, or he/she, or it, etc.) does exist. Yes, god exists in that supremely supernatural creator way. And Jesus the son, the savior. Are there any other things that a Christian must know about god in order to be a Christian? Perhaps.

The PKG epistemologist must have a strategy for dealing with religious truth and disagreement about truth. Only four primary options are available to choose from. Perhaps disagreement is irrelevant to religious knowledge. Perhaps disagreement signals that someone isn't a genuine Christian. Perhaps disagreement means that everyone has to work harder at scripture. Or, perhaps disagreement means that everyone needs some additional help. Expanding on these four options, we can distinguish these situations:

A. The truths that any Christian (call him "Peter") knows about god are personally valid regardless of whatever other Christians may happen to know. If another person claiming to be a Christian (call him "Paul") contradicts Peter about one of these truths, Paul has no judgment to pass on Paul or on Paul's truth. Religious truths are entirely personal, and Christians can never know who other genuine Christians may be.

B. The truths that any Christian must know about god are relatively few and simple, so genuine Christians need never worry about contradicting each other. If Paul contradicts Peter about one of these truths, Peter judges that Paul is not a genuine Christian (and Paul judges Peter likewise).

C. The truths that a Christian must know about god are fairly numerous and complex, so that genuine Christians have to worry about contradicting each other. If Paul contradicts Peter about one of these truths, Peter judges that one or both of them has made an error, so a rechecking of scripture is needed to decide who is the genuine Christian (and Paul judges likewise).

D. The truths that a Christian must know about god are numerous and highly complex, so that genuine Christians have to worry about contradicting each other. If Paul contradicts Peter about one of these truths, and rechecking of scripture doesn't help, Peter judges that one or both of them may have an inadequate capacity to know what the truth is (and Paul judges likewise).

The PKG theory of religious knowledge only works with options A and B. It is not even really clear that it works with option A, since scripture should presumably have the same revelatory impact for each genuine Christian (can't god guarantee that, at least?). The PKG theory obviously works best with option B. It can't work with option C because continual rechecking of scripture might never settle the disagreement, so that disagreeing Christians are left not knowing what the truth is. For the PKG theory, a Christian automatically knows the truth; there is no possibility that a Christian, by definition, can fail to know one of the essential truths. If Peter is forced by disagreement to judge that he can't know one of the Christian truths, Peter should simply confess to not being a genuine Christian. The PKG theory can't work with option D either, since Christians by definition do not have an inadequate capacity to know the essential Christian truths. Again, if Peter is forced by disagreement to judge that he can't know one of the Christian truths, Peter should simply confess to not being a genuine Christian.

Actually, from the standpoint of the PKG theory, no Christian need ever be concerned with situations C or D, since Christians will never encounter them. Take Peter the Christian again. On the PKG theory, Peter knows the essential truths about god and there is no possibility of error. Anything anybody else may say about those truths is utterly irrelevant and Peter should never be troubled by them. Peter has a fast and easy way to judge who the genuine Christians are: those people who agree on the essential religious truths that Peter knows. For Peter, his religious knowledge is the absolute standard of who is a Christian. No rechecking of scripture is ever really necessary, since revelation is its own justification, and justification shines by its own light and not by someone else's efforts to understand scripture. Some presuppositionalists follow a Calvinist view by adding that god's own direct intervention (of grace, etc.) is required for revelation to fully complete its work of conveying knowledge to a Christian. This Calvinist presuppositionalism can then explain that people who can't appreciate revelation are the people who haven't yet been properly transformed by god.

The spectacle of Peter and Paul disagreeing over an essential religious truth, and disagreeing over who has a better relationship with god, may be dismaying to a spectator, but that is no objection to the PKG theory. If the spectator is a Christian, then that spectator will be able to judge for themselves who is the genuine Christian. If the spectator is not a Christian, then the spectator will be unable to judge who is the genuine Christian (but that raises no objection either, since the PKG theory is not an epistemology for non-Christians).

The religious epistemologist who thinks that situations C or D could arise for genuine Christians must modify or abandon the PKG theory in order to solve the problem of justification. Furthermore, the religious epistemologist could distribute religious truths among these four options. Maybe an A/B truth is "god exists," while a C or D truth could be "Jesus is begotten, not made, being of one substance with the Father" or "In the unity of the godhead there be three Persons of one substance, power, and eternity: God the Father, God the Son, and God the Holy Ghost." Serious recognition of Christian disagreements over essential religious truths forces the religious epistemologist to (1) admit that scripture might fail to resolve a disagreement over essential religious truths, and (2) appeal to more resources than just scripture, such as reason. At this point, evidentialism and creationism step in to offer their assistance, along with group deliberation. Perhaps groups of sincere Christians can learn essential religious truths together even if each person may fail on their own.

All of these epistemological options and many more are open for the religious epistemologist. What we should notice at this stage is the way that justification will stop being an entirely personal matter and become a social matter instead. If situations C or D really can occur among genuine Christians, then Christians will need some methods of justifying their disputed claims to knowledge for each other. Instead of just dismissing each other as pseudo-Christians, they will have to talk to each other, debate with each other, and try to persuade each other. Along the way, Christians will have an opportunity to persuade non-Christians, too. But all that effort of reasoned persuasion is precisely the traditional work of scriptural apologetics and natural theology.

Fundamentalism fails as soon as Christians agree to disagree about essential matters. It might well be pointed out that fundamentalism fails as soon as Christians find themselves dividing and subdividing into ever smaller sects, each accusing all the rest of no longer being genuine Christians. However, the collapse of the Christian community is not really fundamentalism's problem, of course, since fundamentalism did not promise to keep a large community of Christians together, but only to guarantee that a genuine Christian knows religious truths.

6.4 The Religious Community

What would a religious epistemology look like for a community? The kind of epistemology needed for a community is a social epistemology. A social epistemology regards the sharing and comparison of information among community members as the best way towards gaining and improving knowledge, and regards knowledge as primarily the possession of a community and only secondarily as the possession of any individual. We could not possibly discuss all the major varieties of social epistemologies, nor do we need to. From the basic definition of a social epistemology, we can immediately derive a small number of rules all society members must follow.

> You can't claim that you know something that cannot possibly be known by anyone else.
>
> You can't claim that you know something through some means or method that others cannot access or apply for themselves.
>
> You can't claim that you know something that is so true that no other knowledge could challenge its validity.
>
> You can't claim that you know two things when one contradicts the validity of the other.

More rules easily suggest themselves, but we should proceed cautiously. Perhaps of greater interest at this point is the way that a society which enforces these rules is also a society that endorses skepticism, the withholding of belief.

> You should be skeptical about someone else's claim to knowledge that cannot possibly be known by anyone else.
>
> You should be skeptical about someone else's claim to knowledge gained through some means or method that others cannot access or apply for themselves.

> You should be skeptical about someone else's claim to knowledge that is so true that no other knowledge could challenge its validity.
>
> You should be skeptical about someone else's claim to know two things when one contradicts the validity of the other.

Skepticism is a privilege of a member of a community utilizing a social epistemology. In the limited sense intended here, skepticism is simply the socially recognized capacity to withhold belief about someone's knowledge claim made under these four specified circumstances.

This social skepticism must not be confused with other kinds of skepticism having much broader scope. For example, Cartesian skepticism, in which a person should be skeptical toward every knowledge claim not confirmable by one's own cognitive efforts, is quite unjustified and illegitimate for a social epistemology. Cartesian skepticism is simply a corollary to Descartes' foundationalism prioritizing personal knowledge. A social epistemology does not reject personal knowledge, but it does make personal knowledge answerable to, and useful for, other people acquiring knowledge too. A community that takes social knowledge seriously will empower its members to hold each other to basic epistemic standards.

Having criticized personal fundamentalism, might there be a kind of social fundamentalism? Let's reconstruct a "Christian social epistemology" (CSE). Starting from the religious principle that the New Testament's account of Jesus' divinity is truthful, we can imagine a community of Christians who fulfill the four social epistemic rules.

CSE1 This community of Christians knows that the New Testament's account of Jesus' divinity is truthful.

CSE2 This community of Christians knows about Jesus' divinity through some means or method that everyone else in the community can access or apply for themselves (reading scripture, etc.).

CSE3 This community of Christians understands that repeated use of this religious means of knowledge might inspire appropriate modifications to religious knowledge.

CSE4 This community of Christians understands that any contradictions within religious knowledge would require appropriate modifications to religious knowledge.

This CSE can sustain itself over time and through multiple generations by teaching the young how to read and understand scripture and to participate in adjusting the community's body of religious knowledge. A CSE can apply multiple methods of gaining religious knowledge, as well. For example, a CSE can approve of other means of revelation (religious experiences, etc.) for gaining religious knowledge, so long as that means is accessible by everyone too. If some extra means or method is not available to everyone (for example, only some people have religious experiences conveying religious knowledge), then the community must check this extra knowledge against the community standard (scripture, in our CSE example). The level of understanding, and the amount of participation, sustained by each adult member will vary, of course. We can easily imagine specialists in religious knowledge earning greater responsibility and authority. What would destroy this CSE is a group of specialists or a lone person who acquires exclusive responsibility and authority over religious knowledge. The rest of the community would rightly be skeptical of anyone seeking such status.

A CSE has gone a long way towards solving the problem of justification and meeting the epistemic expectations of the Greek tradition. One critical question remains to be answered: the question of epistemic isolation. It is the same issue, on a larger scale, which we confronted with the personal knower of god, who isolated his knowledge from anyone else's knowledge. Will the CSE permit the possibility that some other form of knowledge could contradict its own religious knowledge, requiring its adjustment? A CSE that elevates its own religious knowledge to such a high status that no other kind of knowledge could ever challenge it will effectively isolate itself from all other epistemic communities. Foundationalism and presuppositionalism tend to encourage this sort of epistemic isolation. Indeed, in its more extreme forms, presuppositionalism urges Christians to isolate their religious knowledge in this manner.

During the twentieth century, several strands of thought converged on this notion that an epistemic community by definition regards its most basic knowledge as forever unchallengeable by any other kind of knowledge originating within that community or arriving from beyond that community. A few extreme versions of postmodernism made this same claim about epistemic communities, as did some "form of life" fideists inspired by Wittgenstein. Fundamentalists have sometimes described Christian communities in this way. Presuppositionalists have drawn upon many aspects of these developments, often adding their own Calvinist conviction that god has already chosen and inspired those capable of religious knowledge.

The idea common to all these strands of thought is that a CSE can isolate its religious knowledge from all challenge. Let us refer to this sort of CSE as a "closed" CSE, to contrast it with an "open" CSE. An open CSE regards its religious knowledge as potentially challengeable by other kinds of knowledge, which may require compromise and creative adjustments to its body of knowledge. The open CSE is precisely the sort of epistemic community encouraged by the Greek tradition. Christians who find some inspiration and enlightenment from other religious traditions, and Christians who coordinate their beliefs about god with scientific knowledge of nature and humanity, belong to open CSEs. The open CSE abandons foundationalism in favor of coherentism: all knowledge claims are potentially challengeable, so greater coherence among forms of knowledge must be sought instead. Since there is no logical recipe for uniquely maximizing coherence, a wide variety of open epistemic communities can co-exist which do not necessarily agree on their bodies of knowledge. There could never be one "correct" open CSE, or one correct open epistemic community in general. All open epistemic communities continually seek new knowledge and try to coherently adapt to it in creative ways. An "open" Christian can appreciate the debates in previous chapters, and recognize where Christian religious knowledge may be poorly reasoned or inadequate, and require adjustment. On the other hand, a Christian who clings to pseudo-history, pseudo-science, and pseudo-cosmology would probably prefer a closed CSE.

We have explored how a Theology In The Know that is capable of seriously confronting the Greek tradition is driven to make a choice among three epistemic options: personal foundationalism (the PKG); community foundationalism (the closed CSE), and community coherentism (the open CSE). The open CSE agrees with the Greek tradition, so it is not going to be interested in pseudo-theology, and we may set it aside until the next chapter. The PKG and the closed CSE would try to dominate the Greek tradition.

The PKG ultimately succumbs to the Greek tradition, since each Christian is ultimately permitted, indeed encouraged, to be extremely skeptical towards any other would-be Christian that disagrees. If Christianity were the sort of religion that provided for only a small number of simple truths, skepticism may not become a problem. However, Christianity did not evolve in that fashion. Despite the repeated efforts of peace-making Christians who suggest just a few simple religious truths for all Christians, there is something about Christianity that irresistibly lures Christians into vast numbers of complex religious truths that they feel compelled to defend at all costs. Perhaps it is the scale and complexity of Christian scripture, or perhaps it is the diversity of Christian religious experience. At any rate, every would-be peacemaker offering a simplified universal Christianity only manages to add one more divisive sect to all the rest. If PKG were the Christian epistemology, only universal skepticism would result. Universal skepticism was never the aim of the Greek tradition, and so that result would not be any sort of "victory" for the Greek tradition over Christianity. Nevertheless, the Greeks taught us what skepticism is really like, and the PKG theory would exemplify it in abundance. When Christians abandon PKG for either open or closed CSEs, they admit the wisdom of the Greek tradition. Christians who choose open CSEs join the Greek tradition.

The remaining option for a Theology In The Know epistemology seeking domination over the Greek tradition is the closed CSE. Let's set down the third principle of Theology In The Know:

ITK3 A closed CSE regards its religious knowledge as reasonable truths that cannot be challenged or contradicted by any other kind of knowledge.

Immediately the problem of justification arises all over again, at a larger scale and a higher level. A closed CSE is a group of people joined by a common commitment to a foundationalist epistemology. By what justification does a closed CSE claim to know that foundationalism is the correct epistemology? There are other epistemologies to choose from, most notably the coherentist epistemology preferred by open CSEs and many other kinds of communities. Closed CSEs stand out as highly unusual, not merely by the specific basic belief they know, but especially by the foundationalist epistemology they espouse. A closed CSE may be embedded within a larger pluralistic civilization containing many open epistemic communities, for example. How can closed CSEs explain their foundationalism? Could they return to an appeal to scripture? Scripture provides basic beliefs about religion, not about epistemology. In scripture, Christians are commanded to believe, and they are provided with revelation. Maybe that is where Christians should obtain help with their epistemology once again. Is obedience to a command, or submission to a revelation, a sufficient justification for foundationalism, or for any epistemology? Perhaps. We could not fault closed CSEs for trying to return to scripture again; that is their characteristic way. In any case, a closed CSE would have to take the foundationalist stance. When a closed CSE is combined with a Pauline view of personal revelation and a Calvinist view of human depravity, a potent foundationalism emerges. The Christian appears more reasonable than the skeptic, since skeptics by definition have not had revelation and lack god's grace to know how to respond to god (see Moser 2008). Skeptics can complain all they want about the blatant question-begging and circularity of this theology; too bad, since they aren't members of the Christian circle of knowers. The skeptic may also be forgiven for doubting whether there is a genuine epistemology behind this sort of closed CSE.

At this stage, we cannot enter into the vast philosophical contest between rival epistemologies. Needless to say, the Greek tradition posed, but did not resolve, the question of how best to determine the correct epistemology. This question remains outstanding as one of the basic issues in philosophy, so we could not settle it here. Christian theology over the centuries has closely followed the epistemological debates in philosophy, and occasionally has contributed to them (one thinks of the medieval giants Thomas Aquinas and John Duns Scotus, or Alvin Plantinga today). Christian theology has naturally been deeply influenced by philosophical epistemologies. Although in principle Christian theology has tried to be foundationalist in spirit, in practice it has been more coherentist. This coherentist practice is evident in the way that the earliest Church Fathers tried to express basic Christian dogmas in Greek philosophical formulations (describing Jesus as *Logos*, the Word, for example). Then the hundreds of bishops participating in the first eight Councils from Nicaea to Constantinople translated creeds into the Latin terminology and modified the meanings of "God," "Jesus," and "Holy Spirit" once again as trinitarianism and Jesus' dual nature, among other issues, were decided. During the Enlightenment, deism suggested that after nature's creation by god, nature has operated solely by its own power and laws. Many scientists and other scholars appreciated deism's outlook, since science could independently study nature's physical operations without worrying about miracles or other theological interferences. Christian theology quickly rejected deism by arguing that god must continuously sustain nature's existence and energies. Nevertheless, the notion that god has done nothing (or almost nothing) since creation has proven durable among many intellectual and lay Christians. Many Christians today are experimenting with fresh understandings of god, god's involvement with nature, and god's role with an afterlife as a result of their exposure to new ideas from science, other religions, and their own extraordinary experiences.

Christian theology can appear quite foundational if this moving picture of constant doctrinal change is suddenly frozen at some moment of time.

Select some year, say 1850, and some Christian community, say American Methodists in the Southern United States. To hear their doctrines, their Christian beliefs sound quite foundational, meeting the criteria of a closed CSE. Yet if you transported their versions of their basic creeds back to the medieval Papacy they would immediately be denounced as mostly heretical, and they would be almost incomprehensible to the early Christians of Jerusalem in 150. Contemporary Christians would be embarrassed by a couple other doctrinal views the Southern Methodists held back then. All the same, a closed CSE at any moment in time feels certain about its fundamental creeds.

Furthermore, a closed CSE may feel unable to provide any further justification for its foundationalism beyond the reasons (in scripture/revelation) that it already has for grounding its knowledge on some basic beliefs. Closed epistemic communities in general can't comprehend the choice made by open epistemic communities, and certainly don't regard that choice as justifiable. Open epistemic communities simply have made their choice. In other words, from the "closed" perspective, a preference for openness is just one more basic principle of an open community's body of knowledge. An open community presumes coherentism, while a closed community presumes foundationalism. At this higher level of choosing basic epistemic stances, coherentism simply looks like just another kind of foundationalism. Lacking any further justification, coherentism functions foundationally for open epistemic communities. Open epistemic communities may claim to have good (coherentist) justifications for preferring coherentism, but they don't seem to be good justifications from foundationalism's standpoint. Such attempted justification is viciously circular in any case, again suggesting the ultimate foundationalism really at work for open epistemic communities. A closed CSE would therefore conclude that all other epistemic communities are really as closed as it tries to be. We have ascertained a fourth principle of Theology In The Know:

ITK4 All epistemic communities ground their bodies of knowledge on special basic beliefs that they regard as reasonable and unchallengeable by any other kind of knowledge.

ITK4 regards foundationalism as the only legitimate epistemology: all knowledge must be ultimately justified by a set of special known beliefs that do not require any further justification and cannot be challenged by any other kind of knowledge. By imposing universal foundationalism on all other epistemic communities, a closed CSE can imagine that there is nothing epistemically special about its foundationalism, besides the fact that it selects different basic beliefs. The basic beliefs of a closed CSE may not coincide with those of any other epistemic community, and of course this may be the case for all epistemic communities as well.

6.5 The Arguments from Pseudo-theology

The limitations of theological epistemology set by reason need not destroy the religious value of epistemic communities. Liberal modernism, discussed in Chapter 8, endorse an open CSE model of religious knowledge in order to encourage opportunities for learning far richer than any guaranteed certainties.

However, if Theology In The Know would continue to gather enough resources to achieve domination over the Greek tradition, it can appeal to these four principles.

ITK1 Nothing could ever make belief in god unreasonable, so belief in god is reasonable.

ITK2 The Christian god created an intelligible universe and intelligent humans to understand creation and know Jesus.

ITK3 A closed CSE regards its religious knowledge as reasonable truths that cannot be challenged or contradicted by any other kind of knowledge.

ITK4 All epistemic communities ground their bodies of knowledge on special basic beliefs that they regard as reasonable and unchallengeable by any other kind of knowledge.

If Theology In The Know would guarantee that the Greek tradition could never challenge these principles, it must be careful not to claim that its principles can together demonstrate that the Greek tradition is incorrect or false. After all, if the Greek tradition fosters only more closed epistemic communities, as ITK4 imagines, the debate cannot be so simple. Of course, a closed CSE regards the Greek preferences for reason, logic, and science as quite inadequate for Christians. But that is hardly the same thing as regarding them as invalid and untrue. After all, reason, logic, and science can be quite useful as resources for the sorts of arguments advantageous for scriptural apologetics, evidentialism, presuppositionalism, and creationism. The real target of any debate at this stage could not be reason, logic, or science; these things are just intellectual tools, not entire worldviews competing with Christianity.

Debating with anti-Christian worldviews, such as atheism or naturalism, should take advantage of reason and logic. While anti-Christian worldviews, by ITK4, rely on their own basic beliefs and epistemic principles, that doesn't mean that they can't be criticized at all. There are two primary ways that Theology In The Know can argue for its emancipation and legitimacy. The first way argues that Theology In The Know is entirely reasonable and no rival can show otherwise. The second way responds to anti-supernaturalism by trying to expose its own unreasonableness. After examining these two arguments and exposing their problems, the collapse of Theology In The Know into mere pseudo-theology will be apparent.

The first argument, the "Christianity is securely reasonable" argument, proceeds as follows.

1. Nothing could ever make belief in god unreasonable, so belief in god is reasonable. (ITK1)
2. A closed CSE regards its religious knowledge as reasonable truths that cannot be challenged or contradicted by any other kind of knowledge. (ITK3)
3. All epistemic communities ground their bodies of knowledge on special basic beliefs that they regard as reasonable and unchallengeable by any other kind of knowledge. (ITK4)
4. Challenges to one epistemic community's rationality can only arise from another rival epistemic community that holds some contradictory basic beliefs.
5. The mere fact that two epistemic communities disagree over some basic beliefs is insufficient to show that either community is unreasonable.
6. No rival epistemic community could ever show that Christianity is unreasonable. (From 1–4)

Conclusion. A closed CSE's religious knowledge can never be shown to be unreasonable, so it remains securely reasonable. (From 1 and 5)

Arguments for premises 1, 2, and 3 were constructed in earlier sections, and now is the time to raise objections. We have seen how Theology In The Know culminates in closed CSEs. Closed CSEs have obvious limitations, as they simply regard their religious beliefs as securely reasonable, they do not persuade their own members through anything like reasoning, and they cannot persuade non-members by reasoning either. Neither the "No disproof is as good as proof" argument nor this "Christianity is securely reasonable" argument can ever really function to persuade anyone of anything. A closed CSE regards its known truths as reasonable anyway, and non-members will remain unable to appreciate a closed CSE's set of basic beliefs. Non-members will still be skeptical towards a closed CSE, not because a closed CSE holds irrational beliefs or uses an irrational method, but for the ultimate reason that a closed CSE offers no theological way to rationally persuade anyone.

This "Christianity is securely rational" argument only appears to be a theologically reasoned way to justify Christianity. It superficially looks like it is built on justifiable premises and logical arguments. But it really isn't. ITK1 is pretty irrational, even for Christians. ITK3 is simply a statement of fact about what a group of Christians happen to think that they know, and not an epistemic principle. ITK4 is similarly a statement of fact about what closed CSEs are capable of understanding about other epistemic communities, and it happens to be false. Furthermore, the vast majority of Christian communities that have ever existed have been partially open or fully open epistemic communities over time. Theology In The Know would want to appear as if it was a defense of Christianity, but it really only is relevant to a small subset of Christians at best. The "Christianity is securely reasonable" argument is just a piece of pseudo-theology. It encourages irrationalism, it cannot persuade anyone of anything, it cannot understand anything except fundamentalism, and it fails to apply to most people who have ever called themselves Christians.

Premise 4 is probably correct. The two primary ways of exposing irrationality are to complain that someone is using an irrational method of reaching beliefs or to complain that someone is holding beliefs that cannot be justified by a rational method. Either way, someone has to raise a challenge by offering a belief about what counts as a rational method. We might imagine a lone knower holding some basic beliefs, but how could a lone know ever acquire facility with rational methods of justifying knowledge? Surely at the level of rational methodology and epistemology, we must be dealing with a member of an epistemic community, and so an entire epistemic community is really involved.

Premise 5 might seem true on first reading. After all, mere contrasting contradictory beliefs cannot in themselves reveal where unreasonableness might lie. However, at this high epistemic level, some basic beliefs about epistemic methodology might do the needed work. For example, consider this principle about how to discriminate basic beliefs:

BB An epistemic community must be able to offer a reasonable criterion for distinguishing those beliefs which members ought to regard as basic from those which are not.

An epistemic community lacking this needed reasonable criterion could be immediately judged to be irrational. That judgment of irrationality could even be passed by members of a closed CSE if they realized that BB is a valid requirement. Recall what was just noted when considering premise 3: members of epistemic communities usually acquire and apply standards about rational methods. Why would Christians need such things? It is easy to imagine Christians growing curious why some parts of scripture are interpreted as basic, while others aren't. This is a notoriously common difficulty among Christians, especially those favorable towards foundationalism. If one's destiny as a Christian is entirely bound up with getting one's basic beliefs from scripture just right, ascertaining which beliefs are basic might be more complicated than simply being told, "This community regards these beliefs as basic, and that's that." The trouble begins immediately, especially when members can directly appeal to whatever scripture they want to and where the foundationalism of a closed CSE by definition has no helpful resources for satisfying BB even if it wanted to. A closed CSE can internally modify its set of basic beliefs, as we have already covered, by returning to its method(s) of revelation. We can imagine some Christians coming to agree that some new basic belief should be added, for example. But that possibility is not the same as the community of Christians knowing in advance what the criterion for "basicality" should be. What if only half of a closed CSE agrees on a new basic belief? Can this subgroup appeal to a criterion of basicality to persuade the rest, a criterion more impressive than "when a bunch of us are really impressed by some item of revelation"? Nothing in the definition or operation of a closed CSE provides any help with this problem.

We are again confronting the situation that, by the definition of a closed CSE, there is nothing to prevent the reasonable disintegration of a closed CSE into smaller and smaller parts (down to individuals, even). That means that Theology In The Know has no rational way to show that it truly offers a theology for a Christian community in the long run. We are dealing only with a pseudo-theology once again. Theology In The Know would appear to be a rational justification for a Christian community of believers, but it cannot fulfill this role.

The second argument of Theology In The Know, the "anti-Christianity proves Christianity" argument, tries to force the anti-Christian naturalist into an admission that god exists. This argument forces naturalism into a self-contradiction that can only be resolved by confessing its falsity. Even by Greek standards, self-contradiction remains a severe intellectual sin. A closed CSE respects its own version of this principle:

SKEP You should be skeptical about someone else's claim to know two things when one contradicts the validity of the other.

The "anti-Christianity proves Christianity" argument proceeds as follows:

1. Naturalism is a worldview that rejects Christianity's supernaturalism.
2. Naturalism's foundations all necessarily require that god exists. (PC7)
3. Naturalism contradicts itself, so naturalists should instead admit god's existence. (From 1 and 2)
4. The Christian god created an intelligible universe and intelligent humans to understand creation and know Jesus. (ITK1)

Conclusion. The only reasonable worldview is Christianity.

This argument executes three admirable Greek strategies in succession: exposing a self-contradiction, then identifying an alternative, and finally applying a dichotomy to arrive at the desired conclusion. First, naturalism's dependence on god is sharply contrasted with naturalism's declared opposition to god, convicting naturalism of self-contradiction. Since the god that naturalism must affirm has not yet been identified as the Christian god, premise 4 is required next. Then Christianity offers itself as the only other alternative worldview to naturalism, driving every reasonable person towards affirming Christianity as uniquely true worldview. Has Theology In The Know finally established its independent reasonableness over the Greek tradition? Let's examine this argument.

Premise 1 is accurate. Premise 2 is not. None of the PC principles supporting PC7 should be accepted, since they depend on the argument from nature and the fine-tuning argument, which don't work. Naturalism does not contradict itself, and no admission that god exists will be coming from naturalists. ITK1 similarly rests on the flawed arguments behind pseudo-history, pseudo-science, and pseudo-cosmology. Furthermore, Christianity is hardly the only alternative worldview besides naturalism. Even if naturalism were somehow compelled to admit its inadequacies (which it is not), no single supernatural religion (or pantheistic religion) could claim victory, since there are so many alternatives. By taking flawed arguments to be successful when they are not, Theology In The Know is again exposed as pseudo-theology.

One last tactic of Theology In The Know is heard in the most ardent forms of presuppositionalism. If god is entirely responsible for some people knowing god, then these two principles are mutually self-supporting:

ITK2 The Christian god created an intelligible universe and intelligent humans to understand creation and know Jesus.

ITK3 A closed CSE regards its religious knowledge as reasonable truths that cannot be challenged or contradicted by any other kind of knowledge.

ITK2 supports ITK3 because those Christians who correctly know god automatically compose a community that would rightly regard such knowledge as supremely certain and unchallengeable. ITK3 supports ITK2 because a closed CSE would defend ITK2 as a supremely valid basic belief at the center of its strong network of religious knowledge. Of course, this mutual defense only works on the presupposition that god is entirely responsible for some people knowing god. A presupposition, you say? Well, then let's add that presupposition to the short list of basic beliefs too! Theology In The Know is absolutely unchallengeable now. Never mind that this theology has simply assumed what it was supposed to prove: god's existence. This Theology In The Know abandons that aim, for the different aim of endlessly reconfirming belief in god to those who already believe in god. This entire plan is just an exercise in the fallacy of begging the question, a severe fallacy according to the Greek tradition. Assuming your desired conclusion should never be a persuasive move for anyone. Theology In The Know yet again is exposed as mere pseudo-theology.

There is another alternative for Christian theology after pseudo-theology. Theology In The Know is a fundamentalist project for Christians trying to know truths about god. What if this sort of knowledge is not essential to being a Christian?

7

Theology Into The Myst

Theology Into The Myst collect together theologies having a few important things in common: they do not prioritize knowledge, logic, or rationality, because these are less helpful for religion than the experience of faith. Reasoning is a tool designed to work with conceptual connections between literal propositions, propositions that are candidates for justified knowledge. Theologies expressing and justifying religious beliefs as knowable propositions have already been covered in earlier chapters. Theology Into The Myst offers the primacy of faith inspired by non-intellectual dimensions of human experience. Theology goes "Into The Myst" in more than one sense: into the "myst" of veiled obscurity where god cannot be clearly seen; into the "myst" of mysterious experiences which reveal something of god; and into the "myst" of mythical traditions with inspirational narratives about god.

If religious beliefs are not knowledge claims, what might they be? There are numerous options for theologies that seek some other way of understanding religious beliefs. What they all have in common is their view that a belief like "God sent his only-begotten Son Jesus" is actually not at all like a mundane belief such as "Aunt Martha sent her only recipe for oatmeal cookies." Superficially, these two beliefs are expressed in a similarly grammatical manner, but this may be misleading. Are religious beliefs about arranging, expressing, and conveying information just like mundane beliefs? Perhaps not. For Theology Into The Myst, religious beliefs are not trying to be true statements correctly describing the supernatural. Religious beliefs are not trying to be hypotheses explaining evidence. They aren't conclusions about god based on reasoning. They aren't about knowable information at all.

If religious beliefs are not for knowable information, what are they for? What other functions might they serve, if they don't serve the intellect? Christianity has traditionally used "faith" as a label for proper religious belief. From the standpoint of the intellect, faithful belief must either try to be reasonable knowledge or it must serve irrationality. Does Theology Into The Myst endorse irrationality? The other theologies overconfidently exhibit invalid arguments for proclaiming faith as religious knowledge, lapsing into irrationality. Misusing the tool of reason is irrationality; selecting a different tool for the job of religion is not necessarily irrationalism.

7.1 Believing in God without Knowledge of God

We shall continue to speak of religious beliefs as something that all theologies, including those gathered under Theology Into The Myst, continue to be concerned with. Occasionally, a theologian going beyond knowledge can be understood as claiming that human religion really isn't about anything like belief at all. There are, after all, many other sorts of things going on in a person's broad experience or consciousness or conduct beside belief. Mystical religious experiences or profound meditative states can be seriously misrepresented as religious beliefs or as routes to religious beliefs, for example. Some theologians might therefore claim that what religion is really all about cannot be characterized as holding the "right" beliefs, but rather more about having these special experiences. However, even as soon as they make this claim, they are expressing a religious belief: that some identifiable experiences are repeatable and desirable as religious experiences for people. Other theologians might claim that what religion is really all about is more the specific religious practices that a religion promotes than any state of belief. However, once again, any theologians who make this claim are expressing a religious belief: that some identifiable practices are repeatable and desirable as religious practices for people.

It is exceedingly difficult to disentangle a religion from religious beliefs. They seem inseparable, even if a religion recommends that a person seek a religious state of mind or state of grace or state of bliss or state of no-belief (etc., etc.) that is itself not a belief. It is in the very act of identification and recommendation, from one person to another, that some religious state is achievable and desirable that beliefs automatically get involved. Religions are nothing if not social, which means they use human communication about beliefs, even if the beliefs may not be the ultimate religious objective. If this is the case for religions, it is even more true for theologies, which communicate and theorize about religions. Theologies have to be fundamentally concerned with religious beliefs, even as religions themselves may be pointing towards matters that are not beliefs. Christian theology is a paradigm example. As long is there anything like Christian theology there will be Christians vitally interested in Christian beliefs, but they don't have to all be vitally interested in Christian knowledge. Theology Into The Myst suggests that Christianity is not really about gaining knowledge, in any mundane sense, about god or god's activities.

We can organize varieties of Theology Into The Myst by reverse engineering: we can break apart the essential components of a justifiably known proposition about god. A propositional belief has at minimum three aspects: the proposition attributes (a) a conceived quality or property or relation to (b) some existing thing in (c) an accurate manner. For example, the believed proposition "Frank is Mary's father" has these three aspects, since the person believing this proposition attributes the relational concept "father" to Frank (who is believed to exist) as the genuine father of Mary. Put another way, a propositional belief concerns something objective in reality and conceives of it in a certain manner, as having some quality (like size or color) or property (like well-dressed or expensive) or relation (like being two miles away or being employed). That is why propositional beliefs are good candidates for being either (mostly) true or (mostly) false (so long as they aren't too vague, confused, or self-contradictory). Such propositions are trying to describe something in reality which can make that proposition true or false (or approximately true or approximately false), namely the way that that the real objective object actually is. If the really existing Frank is not a father, or not Mary's father, then our example of a propositional belief is false. On the other hand, if no Frank actually exists (unbeknownst to the believer), then the proposition is simply false, or outright nonsensical.

Propositional beliefs start from something in experience (or recalled from experience), conceptualize it as a quality or property or relation, and attribute it to a really existing thing. What happens if we reverse this intellectual process behind all propositional belief?

A propositional belief proposes to make some accurate characterization of an objectively thing, so that this belief can be either true or false. Some "Into The Myst" theologies begin by denying that beliefs about god are appropriate candidates for being true or false, because the notion that a human being should even try to accurately characterize god is wrong. God can't be propositionally known.

ITM1 A religious belief about god should not attempt to accurately describe the way god objectively is, so it can't be true or false.

Theologies which appeal to ITM1 emphasize the way that beliefs about god are all mediated by all-too-human thinking, so that religion is thoroughly infused by special religious symbolism and/or mythology. Perhaps metaphorical or poetic or mythological or philosophical symbolism is involved with most, or all, of language. As long as language is essential to religion, we have to take this human contribution into account. Religious symbolism and mythology are really about god, ITM1 theologians hasten to assure believers, but it is inappropriate to expect accurate descriptions of god from religious beliefs. The mundane judgments of 'true' and 'false' simply can't apply to religious beliefs about god. ITM1 theologians are just as suspicious of fundamentalism as skeptics. Their rejection of literalism is characteristic of nineteenth- and twentieth-century liberal theology. This keeps liberal theologians busy with all of the business of interpretation required to extract the genuine religious meaning from so much scripture. But this enterprise is hardly new. From the times of the early Christian church, theologians have been picking and choosing among biblical passages, deciding which parts are just misleading symbolism, inspirational poetry, or outdated mythology.

Without theologians to guide the interpretation of scripture, readers can take the Bible too literally (did god make the world in six days?), or take the mythological language too seriously (did Jesus heal by casting out demons?). Not surprisingly, ITM1 theologians sharply disagree amongst themselves about which mode of interpretation is best. At this point, theological accounts of religious symbolism and mythological language diverge wildly. We needn't follow them or choose among them. What is fascinating is how each sect accuses the others of overlooking or eliminating the 'true' message or intent of the Bible. ITM1 theologians still seek correct interpretations, after all, even if they warn away the scientific-minded or skeptical-minded nonbelievers from trying to understand the Bible by themselves. ITM1 theologies even may speak of "religious truth" or "religious knowledge" – whatever remains to still be believed after proper theological interpretation – so believers have a reliable rival to scientific knowledge. This posturing locates ITM1 theology at a transitional stage not too distant from scriptural apologetics and fundamentalism. In any case, ITM1 theologies are all anxious to reassure believers that they believe in a really existing god, even if nothing in scripture or doctrine or creed should be taken literally. Christian ITM1 theologies also reassure believers that, despite internal dissention and splitting denominations, the Christian religion holds every advantage over other religions.

Other "Into The Mist" theologies reject ITM1 as inadequate, going farther to deny that god ought to be treated as just another entity having an existence in any ordinary sense. Theologians may sense how ITM1 theology remains too analogous to mundane notions of knowledge and truth. Perhaps they feel uncomfortable with a simplistic dichotomy between scientific knowledge and religious interpretation, or feel embarrassed by the way that theological interpretation is so fragmented into competing sects. Rather than contesting with science over what counts as truth, and competing amongst rival interpretations over correct religious belief, could god be isolated away from these dramas? If truth needs an object to be true about, what if there is no religious object? Perhaps god cannot be propositionally known in any sense, because god can't be even objectified.

ITM2 A religious belief about god should not consider god as an objectively existing thing.

The impact of twentieth-century thinkers like William James, Martin Heidegger, Martin Buber, Karl Rahner, Karl Barth, Paul Tillich, and Hans Küng inspired theology to probe deeper into the human–divine relationship. Without a specifiable divine object to relate to, what does religion do? Stating core Christian beliefs and interpreting scripture or creed only becomes more difficult. Language, with all of its symbolic modes of expression from metaphor and poetry to exhortation and description, works best when dealing with objects of some sort. If we cannot regard god as an identifiable object capturable by language, how can we deal with god? We would have to first decide what alternative kinds of existence are available besides existing as an object. Well, what does it mean to be an object? There are two primary alternatives: the 'object' may be contrasted with other objects, or the object may be contrasted with the 'subject'. Metaphysics is required to deal with notions of being/existence that are left after eliminating all modes of contrast between objects: stripping away the finitude of the object, or the qualities of the object, or the relations of the object. Existentialism is required to deal with notions of being/existence that are left after eliminating all modes of contrast between the object and the subject: stripping away any dichotomy between internal experience and external reality, or any alienation or estrangement between one's experience and what is being experienced.

Shifting theology away from objects, focus may therefore widen out to general universal existence (metaphysics), or it may narrow to particular experiential existence (existentialism). This yields three major theological alternatives. First, god can be identified with the ultimate mode of being, the supreme fundamental reality, which is unlimited, contains all qualities (or none), and includes all relations (or none). A lone metaphysical god is transcendently supreme, but we may next ask how it relates to finite persons, which now becomes a problem. Second, god can be identified with the special mode of personal religious experience, which is cohesively unifying and intimately familiarizing. An existential god is personally experienceable, but we may next ask how peoples' diverse experiences of god compare, which now becomes a problem. Metaphysics claims reason on its side, against outdated mythology. Existentialism claims emotion on its side, against transcendent infinity. Metaphysical and existential theologies have been competing since Christianity's origins, contrasting the cold god of philosophical argumentation (god is Prime Mover, etc.) with the warm god of immediate experience (god is Love, etc.). Pietism and romanticism make their perennial rebellions against intellectualist theologies. In the mid-twentieth century, religious existentialism mounted another rival theological challenge (there was even an atheist version in Sartre's humanist existentialism). There is no neutral way to decide this contest between reason and emotion. However, perhaps the reason/emotion dichotomy should be questioned, too.

The third alternative is that god could be located in some sort of metaphysical-existential overlap or relationship. There must be a way to identify genuine religious experiences for all people (so religion can't become an "anything goes" affair), and a way to identify the one god's presence to personal experience (so religion can't fail to become a relationship). Interestingly, if god is the supreme reality fundamental to everything else's existence, everything else (including personal experience) must already have some relationship with god. It would only be possible for a person to lack a relationship with god in some psychological sense, like being in a state of ignorance about god or a state of willful rebellion against god. Martin Buber describes religious experience as the participation in an "I–Thou" personal relationship with god, far different from any knowing relationship between people and ordinary objects. Paul Tillich describes religious experience as the ultimate concern for god, the "ground of being." In these kinds of theologies, a (potentially) universal mode of human experience is intimately related to the (actually) unique mode of universal being. These comprehensive ITM2 theologies have the additional advantages of explaining why some people are religious and others are not, how someone can become religious, and where religions may have common views (there are intriguing similarities with varieties of Hinduism, Buddhism, Taoism, and pantheism).

Comprehensive ITM2 theologies have a serious decision to make about Jesus. Noticing that the Jesus in the New Testament is as much human as transcendent, and hardly much like a "ground of being," Christian theologians can still treat Jesus like an object, as a particular entity having its own qualities and relations in space and time. Indeed, if Christians must believe that a real historical Jesus lived, preached, and died in a particular region of earth for some duration of time, then Jesus is an object again. One option is to revert back to ITM1 or outright fundamentalism for just Jesus, but not for transcendent god. Rudolf Bultmann exempted the gospel message and meaning of Jesus, the *kerygma*, as common Christian knowledge through revelation. Karl Barth stressed how Jesus is still a subject, still a person, while treating the revelatory knowledge of Jesus as objective for all Christians. These theologies all recommend a faithful relationship with god, either directly or through Jesus, which is not like a mundane knowledge relationship with some inanimate object.

Many possible combinations of fundamentalism, ITM1 and ITM2 theology can be constructed, but only a few significant combinations can be considered in this chapter. Creative combinations have almost irresistible advantages. Against naturalism's complaints about insufficient evidence, the ITM2 component helps a theologian isolate the transcendent god away from any factual evidence. Against fundamentalists too attached to their mythologies, the ITM1 component helps a theologian supply modernizing interpretations to make Christianity more palatable for contemporary believers. Against rival ITM1 interpretations, the fundamentalist component helps a theologian prove orthodox fidelity to core Christian dogmas. Such amazing flexibility would astonish even Christians, except that they are used to hearing it without comprehension.

Just a single recent case, supplied by the theologian John Haught (Haught 2008), amply illustrates how a popular book reassuring the Christian masses can go deeply into Theology Into The Myst. Against the application of naturalism, Haught appeals to ITM2 by saying that theology "rightly objects to the atheists' device of collapsing the mystery of god into a set of propositions" (p. 52). Haught constantly talks about the mysterious infinity and perfection of god when beating back atheist objections. However, Haught also tells us several propositions that Christians know about god, such as: "Ultimate reality . . . cannot be less than personal" (p. 91); "God as 'the ultimate ground of all being'" (p. 91); "Christianity's vulnerable God is not detached from the chaos of natural and historical processes" (p. 96); and "God is absolute self-giving love" (p. 97). Does Haught notice the hypocrisy in allowing Christians to describe god using propositions, but atheists are forbidden? Haught wields ITM2 against atheists, but he needs ITM1 in order to still have something to say about god to Christians. Haught is quite aware that diverse interpretations of scripture compete for theological supremacy, so he explains that we can talk about god "only in the imprecise yet luxuriant language of culturally conditioned symbols, analogies, and metaphors" (p. 98). ITM1 also helps Haught to declare that some interpretations of scripture are better than others: "early biblical symbolism of God is not to our tastes" (p. 98). Haught is no literalist: "The Bible includes frankly barbaric texts that no one finds edifying." Alas, some Christian sects (including many Protestant denominations and the Catholic church) regard every single line of the Bible as error-free. But Haught is also quick to point to his own fundamental orthodoxy, proclaiming his dogmatic creed that "God is fully present in Jesus the Christ" (p. 97). Is god extremely mysterious, or just somewhat knowable, or quite clearly recognizable? It apparently depends on which of Haught's audiences he needs to address.

The problem intrinsic to ITM2 theologies is that they are forced to balance the metaphysical and existential aspects of religious belief, but this effort renders them inherently unstable. A ITM2 theology makes any direct knowledge of god quite difficult or impossible, and actual symbolic forms to structure religious belief have to come from somewhere. Of course, each religion supplies its own needed symbolic forms, but ITM2 by itself can't help us decide what religion we should select. As a practical matter, we are all raised in religious cultures, so this problem is automatically solved for most people, as they simply drift into the local cultural religion. This is a ITM1 solution: by affirming a familiar religion, people use a satisfactory symbolic interpretation of the real god without worrying that it is the "true" one. On the other hand, the more familiar religion may not be entirely satisfactory for those having existential encounters with god. The existential dimension can expose where one's familiar religion needs supplementation, and it can also reveal where other religions offer satisfactory symbols as well. The realization may arrive that all the world's religions have richly existential dimensions, and that no religion should presume any greater accuracy about god. ITM1 and ITM2 theologies may not go far enough.

7.2 Believing in God without Concepts of God

Most theologians, in the end, are just people using human concepts of qualities, properties, or relations to attribute them to god. "Into The Myst" theologies can go even further by rejecting ITM2 as inadequate, preferring to deny that human concepts can be satisfactorily attributed to the divine. God is very mysterious.

ITM3 A religious belief about god should not presume to adequately conceive of god.

ITM3 is a natural match with ITM2, and completes its message. The transcendence of god explains the inadequacy of all religious concepts. Nevertheless, religious concepts are attempts by the human mind to deal with god. Because religious concepts result from existential encounters with the divine, this explains the potency of human symbolic interpretations of the divine. ITM3 is the pathway to religious pluralism in its deepest sense. ITM3 can offer explanations for the humanity-wide distribution of the varieties of religious experience, the spontaneous generation of religious beliefs, and the organization of religious beliefs into doctrinal religions (see Hick 1973, Smith 1976, Kaplan 2002, Griffin 2005). People encountering the divine tend to form religious beliefs about that encounter and its meaning, and people having a common language and culture tend to express their religious beliefs in a common manner. An ITM3 theology will view religions as originating in particular cultures, although it would be a mistake to suppose that religions are arbitrary inventions of cultures. Religions comes from human experiences of god through some sort of encounter, although the symbolic form those experiences take are controlled more by culture. People have to be taught some symbolic tools for shaping the extraordinary experiences that people call religious.

ITM3 can serve as a way to justify why religions exist, and as a way to justify any particular religion as a genuine effort to respond to god. Like ITM2, ITM3 can conveniently reassure the believers of any religion, such as Christianity, that symbolic expressions of god's presence or mythological stories about god's actions are legitimate and valid in their own way. A theologian from one religion might even speak of another religion's "genuine mysticism" or "true mythology." The measure of mysticism and mythology is not informational accuracy but rather sincere inspiration: is the believer's life transformed in the intended way by belief? Liberated from the cramped limits of propositional knowledge, mysticism and myth can do their proper work. A religion can point to the lives of believers, rather than the truth of its stories, as its justification. This reorientation of religion's aim is especially helpful when a religion seems highly dependent on historical events for its validity. Why should the one true religion originate from Palestine, or Persia, or India, or wherever, at that particular time so long ago? A liberal understanding of a religion's myths grasps their transformational function for believers, such as guiding them in mental discipline or social ethics. For Christianity, as an example, the belief that Jesus was divine or that Jesus died for our sins only means that Christians take Jesus' intimate connection with god and Jesus' morality as their own ideal for their lives. Christians don't have to actually think that Jesus was raised from the dead. When a religion wants to rapidly expand among uneducated peoples, preaching extraordinary miracles can work. In modern times, theology must have a different strategy for converting educated peoples. ITM3 is quite useful for theologies of expanding religions when human conceptions of god seem too narrowly parochial.

ITM3 is also highly convenient when human conceptions of god get too paradoxical. The clearest example is when a conception of god generates a logical contradiction, or when two conceptions of god contradict each other, and we cannot understand how god could be like that. Some definitions of god appear to contain such contradictions, as when a perfection or two or three are attributed to god but we can't understand how that is really possible. Omnipotence is often cited, especially by skeptics, as a perfection that entails contradictions. For example, if god can do anything, then god could make a rock so heavy that god could not lift it. If god can do anything, can god make $2 + 2 = 5$? Could god paint a Picasso? Even righteousness and mercy might appear to be contradictory if both are attributed to god in their most extreme measures. Certain Christian creeds seem paradoxical, such as the doctrine that Jesus has one eternal nature that is both divine and human, or the doctrine that Jesus (the whole Jesus) died on the Cross. Three main theological strategies for dealing with such conceptual paradoxes are available. First, ITM1, ITM2, and ITM3 could be ignored, leaving god as an objectively existing thing to obtain truths about, but requiring adjustment of the problematic concepts to evaporate the paradox. Second, ITM1 or ITM2 could be invoked, leaving the paradox as a merely conceptual paradox that cannot affect whatever unknown kind of existence god does have. Third, ITM3 could be invoked, implying that any conceptual paradox is no serious problem since god can't be adequately captured by human conceptions anyways. This third alternative regards paradoxes as rather inevitable when dealing with god, and recommends that paradoxes leave religious belief in god quite unaffected.

As a practical matter, it cannot be easy to sustain religious belief in the face of paradox. In the wake of Kierkegaard and other religious existentialists who recognize the challenge of paradoxical belief, the phrase "leap of faith" is sometimes applied to this situation. When dealing with ITM3, however, it is wrong to say that faith "makes" a leap where reason cannot go. Rather, faith in god requires a person to deliberately transcend mere rational understanding, so that paradox (the recognition of human inadequacy) points to way to faith in god (the transcendent). This paradoxical act of faith is not opposed to reason, but the completion of reason. Placing god beyond adequate human concepts is demanded by religion, so mere reason cannot challenge god or voluntary faith. According to ITM3, human concepts can still serve a helpful service for orientation towards god.

ITM3 theologians immediately appreciate how all theological interpretation are forbidden from claiming greater accuracy about god. And this is not only the case for competing Christian theologies, but for all theologies of any religion. All religious beliefs are human responses to a mysterious transcendent reality that cannot be known in any way. Unlike ITM2, accepting ITM3 forbids a Christian from regarding any Christian creed as a truth about god or Jesus, unless "truth" is watered down to mean something relative like "true for me" or "true in my religion" or "true in my culture," etc. Objective knowledge of god is impossible, but a person can possess a highly satisfactory kind of truth, or faith, since no other religion (or any worldview like naturalism) has a right to judge a person's religious beliefs. An example of the tension between ITM2 and ITM3 is supplied by Unitarian Universalism, which proclaims its Christian heritage while embracing many religions (see Grigg 2004, Church 2009). ITM3 regards all religions as symbolic interpretations of a supreme reality. Can one's faith in god be strengthened by regarding all religions as pointing towards the same divine reality? Can one's faith be encouraged by perceiving all believers as oriented towards the one mysterious god? Religion in general can seem more secure, more reasonable, if all religions agree on one transcendent divinity. Of course, religions will always agree to disagree on specifics about that divinity, and disagree about the best relationship to have with that divinity. Yet the fact that people encounter the divine in many similar ways seems to itself point beyond human religion towards the transcendent. Although the transcendent may be accessed as ITM3 says, people lose the ability to affirm that the same transcendent reality is accessed in everyone's mystical experiences. As descriptions begin to entirely fail the experience, there is no way to verify that such ineffable and inarticulate experiences really feel the same to different people, or whether such experiences are even of the same reality. Just because people are similarly unable to describe such deeply mystical experiences, that cannot imply that people are all having similar experiences. There many be many kinds of inexpressible experiences and many kinds of transcendent realities to access. You can't clearly express what a trumpet sounds like or what a pepper tastes like, but that can't mean that experiences of trumpets must be similar to experiences of peppers.

Finally, we might wonder if any human concepts attributed to god can really focus, guide, or direct people in the direction of god. ITM3 might be inadequate if no human conceptions should ever be applied to god. Perhaps people should not be trying to conceive of god at all. God is utterly mysterious.

ITM4 A religious belief about god should not apply any conceptions at all to god.

At this point, we have stripped away everything propositional and conceptual from a religious belief. This eliminates scripture and mythology, and all theology.

Why doesn't ITM4 eliminate god, too? It would, except for belief's remaining resources. Some peoples' conviction that there is "something more" besides everything that concepts can handle is not restrained by skepticism. Even concepts might be twisted around to point beyond them. Many religions comfortable with transcendence use negative propositions: God is not this, not that. Sophisticated theologies use dialectical categories: God is beyond this category, and that category. God is neither male nor female. God is neither personal nor impersonal. No miraculous mythologies or divine perfections can help believers appreciate god, but their paradoxes might orient believers towards god. Orientation is not enough, though; facing the right direction doesn't change anything. All religions agree that receptivity, an expectation of something completely unexpected, is involved with religious orientation. Receptivity is still not enough; only reception makes a real difference. But what is received? Religions cannot exactly say, of course; only personal experience can tell. ITM4 regards religions as effects, not causes, of religious belief – and religious beliefs are the effects, not causes, of something beyond belief. Everything about religions, all that talk of god, is not what religion is really about. One cannot become religious by mouthing creeds invented and taught by others, or by imitating the religious attitudes and conduct of others. What is the real cause of religious belief, a cause that has little to do with other people and has little to do with the intellect's use of concepts?

The ultimate cause of all religious belief according to ITM4 is personal mystical experiences of a divine transformation. Something divine deserves the credit as the cause. Religions do not regard genuine mystical experiences as originating entirely within a person. It cannot be merely personal, for two main reasons. First, the mystical experience is so incredibly unlike any ordinary experience, that it could not be self-generated in the creative imagination. The creative imagination excels at conceptual play, but the ITM4 type of mystical experience bursts all concepts. Second, the mystical experience itself includes the feeling of lack of personal control. Receptivity becomes reception, of something "other" and "beyond". But these two concepts of transcendence, and categories like "personal" and "impersonal", can't prove anything. People who have mystical experiences are just as likely to report that their experience cannot be captured by "self" or "other," or by "personal" or "impersonal," or even by "human" or "divine." Such are the paradoxes of mysticism. Nevertheless, the mystical experience is not consciously generated, it is not a normal conscious process (this does not rule out the subconscious brain, of course), and it seems to involve the transcendently divine (this does not rule out the empty nothingness, of course).

This is why the mystical experience can be so transformative, as one feels so different from anything ordinary. The transformation may not linger long or have lasting effects for everyone, and repeated mystical experiences can become deeper and more familiar by reacquaintance. Religious beliefs have the primary function of sustaining conscious attention to the mystical experience and any lingering effects, so that they may more reliably enhance the desired transformation. Mystical theology holds that mystical experiences serve as the ultimate origin of, and the ultimate justification for, all religious belief. Few people have full-blown mystical experiences, though. Here we must distinguish between mystical and religious experiences. A mystical experience cannot be adequately captured by any religious concepts or symbolism, while a religious experience is infused with religious concepts and symbolism. A person's mystical experience of the transcendent infinite while on a nature walk is quite different from her religious experience of participating in the Catholic Mass in a cathedral. Most people have religious experiences before they have mystical experiences, and many people only have religious experiences. By acquiring religious beliefs from others (usually while young), people can then have their own religious experiences if they participate in a religion's rituals and appreciate its sacraments.

If a person does have a mystical experience, other people's religious beliefs are again necessary for dealing with them. No Hindus report experiences of Jesus unless some acquaintance with the concept of Jesus had been first acquired; similarly, no Christians report experiencing Brahman unless they had some acquaintance with Hinduism. Presumably, people were having mystical experiences before anything like religious systems had formed; for all we know, animals may have mystical experiences, but they have no religious beliefs. In this sense language and culture is necessary to convert mystical experiences into religious beliefs, and the appreciated value of religious transformations accelerated the involvement of culture. The linguistic machinery of conceptualization and symbolism and metaphor and poetry and mythology, used by various cultures in diverse ways, eventually produced the vast variety of religions. Enculturalization can be reversed with great effort – the world's mystics can recognize and respect each other's mystical experiences after religious beliefs are set aside. Such harmony among so many mystics lends additional credibility to the notion of ITM3 theology and ITM4 mysticism that the same transcendent divinity is involved. Confident in their unity with divinity, mystics sometimes apply the categories of truth and knowledge and reality to this divinity, trying to emphasize a conviction that what is mystically experienced is supremely real and supremely important. Mystics are said to "know" god, to be "one with god" and to possess the "highest truth." Let fundamentalism or ITM1 take these claims too seriously. As for ITM4 itself, we can only say that mystics have extraordinary experiences and leave it at that. There could never be a ITM4 theology. As soon as a theologian tries to describe what mystical experiences share, or explain how mystical experiences arouse the symbolic interpretations of religions, mysticism collapses back into ITM3 theology. If a theologian adds that some religious symbols are better than others, this theologian is only doing ITM1 theology.

Each religion struggles mightily with mysticism, tempted on one side to use its own mystics to confirm its "true" mythology, yet forced on the other side to admit that mystics around the world encounter the divine. Theologians of many religions have even hoped for one world religion based on mysticism. This is probably an excessively optimistic hope, however. Harmony among mystics is partial at best, since religious belief soon divides the mystics again. The categories of the emotions have their immediate influence. Which emotion dominated the experience – love, or bliss, or peace, or awe, or some combination of these? The categories of space and time have their say, too. What dimensions did the experience have – total nothingness, infinite fullness, timelessness, insignificance next to the infinite, interconnectedness with everything, or some combination? The moral categories can get involved. How should you react – reverence towards the divine, love towards all, utter detachment from everything, or some combination? Each religion emphasizes some of these options over the rest.

Religions prepare the ground for the growth of religious belief from the seeds of mystical experience. The newly transformed person is easily inducted into the religion of the culture around them. We cannot have any idea what the "true" religion could be, since no one has ever been completely insulated from all cultural influence and then asked about mystical experiences. Anyone completely shielded from all notions of religion, were that even possible, would not understand the question and have no useful answer. Even mystics trained to minimize influence of local cultural religion would have little to teach the rest of us. Too many theologians impressed by ITM4 go so far as to recommend that we all become mystics. This suggestion is unrealistic, as the needed discipline, character, and receptivity is hardly evenly distributed across humanity. One substantive religion is unlikely to emerge from a worldwide league of sincere mystics or interpreting theologians. The moral of the "Into The Myst" story is religious pluralism, after all.

7.3 Belief, Faith, and Pseudo-faith

By adopting one or more of the four ITM principles, a theology makes it impossible for the Greek tradition, or any other tradition concerning propositional reasoning, to challenge religious belief. Theology Into The Myst might succeed where Theology In The Know failed: to finally gain immunity from all skeptical challenge. Reason works best with religious beliefs expressed in declarative propositions that can be known. If the beliefs central to Christianity cannot be adequately expressed in this way, reason is far less relevant and can't pose much of a threat to faith.

The intellect still complains that faith has gone too far into the darkness of ignorance and irrationality. Yet the entire point of Theology Into The Myst is to encounter and relate to god without depending too much on the intellect. Is this theology heading into the dark, or the light? But matters are no longer so simple, as we have seen. Seeing the "light" of god is not as easy as it once seemed. Even fundamentalism, so confident that knowledge of god is immediately available, requires that knowledge of god conform to the beliefs of a religious community. The other ITM principles similarly qualify the reception of god's light. Pursuing this analogy of encountering god as "seeing the light," we can distinguish the five options and their stance on the relationship between religious belief and faith.

> Fundamentalism: You directly see the pure light – with nothing between you and the light, direct knowledge is revealed. Your religious beliefs must conform to the community's religious beliefs.
>
> ITM1 theology: You see the light by reflection – distortions in the mirror change the image of the pure light. Your religious beliefs track the symbolism of your culture's religion.
>
> ITM2 theology: You see the light by refraction – you can't see the original light though the prism, only the colors coming out. Your religious beliefs use symbolism of your culture's religion.
>
> ITM3 theology: You see the light by filter – you can't see the original light through the filters, only the colors of the filters. Your religious beliefs can apply symbolism from any religion.
>
> Mysticism: You directly see the pure light – you are unified with the blinding light, mystically becoming the light. Your religious beliefs are not involved during the mystical experience.

There is an inverse relationship between the direction of ITM theology and the amount of faith in one's particular religion. The more direct contact one has with god, the less any religion seems to adequately describe god.

Fundamentalism can produce maximum faith in one's religion, while mysticism can produce much skepticism towards one's religion, leaving a middle range for more options about faith.

Fundamentalism is convinced that specific religious beliefs are revealed by god, while the mystic realizes that god does not authorize any religious beliefs. The fundamentalist has faith in god's revelation of knowledge, while the mystic has faith in god's revelation of presence. The fundamentalist is appalled by the mystic's broad dismissal of god's true religious creed, while the mystic is dismayed by the fundamentalist's narrow fixation on just one reaction to god. And both the fundamentalist and the mystic are confused by ITM ways of faithfully preferring one religion based on highly ambiguous experiences.

ITM1 offers a faith that can be called a "faith through reflection" of god. This kind of religious faith takes one's own religious symbolism as the preferred way, but not the perfect way, to conceive god. This faith avoids the dogmatism of fundamentalism and the presuppositionalism of a "closed" Christian community by loosening the grip of symbolism on god. Symbolic interpretations are unavoidable, but not regrettable. An "open" Christian social epistemology – an open CSE – can embrace the opportunity of perpetual improvement to its religious symbolism. This brings the spiritual and intellectual freedom of pluralism to Christian theology. Denominational disagreement can sharpen everyone's attention to the power and impact of religious symbolism on the faithful, and the ITM1 attitude restrains any denomination from exclusive correctness. For a ITM1 open CSE, the lessons learned from appreciating denominational diversity should also be applied to the challenge of philosophy and modern science. Regarding its mythological traditions as traditions and not blinders, an open CSE can reflectively revise its symbolism to avoid conflict with science at the very least, and potentially incorporate scientific knowledge at best. The most conservative option is retreat from conflict. Theology From The World and Theology Beyond The World pull god back from scientific knowledge and keep god useful in the narrowing gaps and outer margins. A ITM1 theology can avoid such timid irrationalism and be much bolder, selectively integrating science and philosophy with theology for improved religious symbolism. ITM1 theology encourages "faith through reflection" in a double sense: faith reflects god's light, and faith benefits from reflection about god. Another conservative option for an open CSE is to accelerate ahead into ITM2 or ITM3 theology, which safely shields god and faith from any scientific knowledge.

ITM2 offers what we can call "faith though refraction" of god. This kind of religious faith takes one's own religious symbolism as an optional response, one among many, to the reality of god. ITM2 is a powerful temptation for ITM1 theologies which choose not to integrate scientific method and scientific knowledge. By locating god beyond all ordinary knowledge, and leaving science and reason with no way to criticize any religious symbolism, tight security for religion is built up. ITM2 suggests a stable compromise between religion and science. An ITM2 theology can depict this compromise as either a neat division between two realities (supernatural v. natural) or as taking two perspectives on the one pantheistic reality (reality viewed religiously or scientifically). ITM2 by itself, as we discussed in the previous section, is unstable on its own. Any theology attempting to construct a purely ITM2 alternative for religious belief can only offer a pseudo-faith to Christians. Christian theology, as we have seen, can fruitfully combine ITM1 and ITM2, selecting supernaturalism and a Jesus mythology. The other option for ITM2 is to emphasize the existentialist dimension and convert into ITM3.

ITM3 offers what we can call "faith through filtering" of god. This kind of religious faith takes religious symbolism to be a necessary yet hopelessly inadequate response to a completely mysterious god. Like ITM2, ITM3 is also a powerful temptation for theologies wanting to avoid any entanglement or confrontation with reason and science. By locating god beyond all human conception, religion is supremely unchallengeable in its own realm. While prizing mystical experiences, an ITM3 theology is mysterianism but not outright mysticism (ITM4). Mysticism by itself is no theology since it makes no claims at all. Mysticism alone has no religious beliefs and only offers pseudo-faith. When people who are already in a religion have mystical experiences, they usually regard them as encounters with that religion's god, so this "local" spiritualism supports a ITM1/ITM2 theology. On the other hand, ITM3 is for people who think that all religions are just optional filters and mystical experiences cannot support any one of them, so this "universal" and "ecumenical" spiritualism supports ITM3 theology. Since ITM3 theology cannot prioritize supernaturalism (frequently opting for perspectivalism or pantheism like ITM2) and does not prioritize Jesus either, we may wonder whether this theology is still primarily about Christianity. We may safely leave that issue to Christians, who may rightly wonder about this pseudo-faith in Christianity.

If a religion's theology opts for the mysterianism of ITM2, ITM3, or mysticism, faith in that single religion can diminish, but direct faith in god can dramatically increase. Those people feeling "in between" and ready to leave Christianity behind for a much freer spiritual journal may well find a genuine faith in a god down that path.

7.4 The Argument from Pseudo-faith

We have classified ITM2, ITM3, and mysticism as "pseudo-faiths" for Christians. These mysterian kinds of Theology Into The Myst are pseudo-faiths only in the limited sense that none are genuine Christian faiths and no *Christian* Theology Into The Myst should embrace them. The limitations of mystical theology set by reason do not destroy the religious value of mystical experience, however. Liberal modernism, discussed in Chapter 8, accepts these rational limitations and considers an ITM1 Christian faith to be far richer than more mysterious faiths.

Outright mysticism cannot be used to defend Christianity in any way, since nothing particularly Christian could be authorized by such experiences alone. As far as pure mysticism is concerned, all religions have equal opportunities for accessing supreme reality. Some Christian theologians do try to explain and defend Christianity on the basis of ITM2 or ITM3. These defenses are not properly arguments at all; this is the realm of Theology Into The Myst, where propositions and logic are utterly inadequate. Still, theologians being theologians, their efforts at instruction and persuasion through exhortation, preaching, and rhetoric do somewhat resemble reasoned arguments. If brought together for one master "argument," these theological efforts based on the mysterianism of ITM2 and ITM3 have the following form.

1. Spiritual experiences are human encounters or absorptions with the supreme divine reality or a supremely divine aspect of reality.
2. Spiritual experiences are not information to be compared or contrasted against any other sort of human experience, belief, or thought.
3. Christian religious beliefs are faithfully grounded in spiritual experiences.
4. Non-Christian experience, belief, and thought, such as other religions or pantheisms or naturalisms, never have any relevance for comparison with, or criticism of, Christianity faith. (From 2 and 3)

Conclusion. Christianity's faith is absolutely secure.

If construed as a logical argument, this chain of reasoning is sound. Premise 1 is a definition for the sake of getting started. Premises 2 and 3 are agreed upon by ITM2 and ITM3 theologies, and their weaknesses have been discussed. Premise 4 does follow from 2 and 3, and the conclusion easily follows from 4. Yet this argument does not accomplish anything for Christian theology.

This "argument" only demonstrates how nothing but Christian pseudo-faith comes from ITM2 and ITM3. This argument proves too much. Suppose premise 3 is true – but is Christianity the only religion faithfully grounded in religious experiences? No doubt many Christians would like to believe "*only* Christian religious beliefs are faithfully grounded in spiritual experiences." But that different premise is precisely what neither ITM2 nor ITM3 can deliver. Believers desiring exclusively Christian beliefs return to ITM1 or fundamentalism. Unable to elevate Christianity to any special spiritual status, ITM2 and ITM3 cannot prevent any other religion's ITM2/ITM3 theology from appealing to its own identical version of this argument. Just substitute "Buddhism" for Christianity in this argument, for example. Any ITM2/ITM3 religion is equally certain and secure. This argument fails to advance or defend the Christian faith – it only offers pseudo-faith to Christians.

From the perspective of both reason and Christianity, the mysterianism of ITM2 and ITM3 heads into a "myst" where all religions begin to look pretty much the same. Skeptical atheists reject all religions for their mystical aspects, while many believing Christians are similarly suspicious of mysticism's tendency to bypass scripture and creed. However, Theology Into The Myst can be path into the light for people feeling "in between," rather than just for Christians.

8

Reason and Faith

The god debates have reached a level far from where we started. How does the contest between reason and faith stand now? Christian theology is well matched by atheology at every stage, which is not surprising for two well-designed intellectual systems. The evidentialism of Theology From The Scripture, Theology From The World, and Theology Beyond The World cannot prove its arguments. Evidentialism's difficulties first arouse fundamentalism and then the fideism of mysterianism. Fundamentalism, mysterianism, and skeptical atheism all converge on one point of agreement about religious belief. When fundamentalism and mysterianism both declare that human belief in god is ultimately based on a commitment of faith, skeptical atheism can only agree.

Christian theology can still offer a different kind of compromise between faith and reason. We have seen how a genuinely Christian theology cannot stray beyond the boundaries of ITM1. At most it can mix a ITM1-ITM2 blend to respect the existentialist dimension of spiritual faith through encountering god. This variety of Theology Into The Myst and its open CSE treatment of messianic scripture, mythical symbolism, and mystical spiritualism has been powerfully influential. In the nineteenth and twentieth centuries, the movements within Christianity advancing this theology had various labels, many involving "liberal" or "modernism" or their synonyms. For convenience, let us refer to this kind of Christianity theology as "Liberal Modernism."

8.1 Liberal Modernism and Its Rivals

Liberal Modernism is a serious candidate for a Christian theology that avoids degenerating into pseudo-history, pseudo-science, pseudo-cosmology, pseudo-theology, or pseudo-faith. Liberal Modernism's use of the open CSE model for religious belief attempts to respect philosophy's legacy of reason and science without capitulating entirely to anti-religious naturalism. Since Liberal Modernism is neither irrationalism nor rationalism, it offers a tempting compromise between faith and reason. This should not be surprising, because its proponents designed it to accomplish precisely these aims (see Cauthen 1962, Van Dusen 1963, Neville 2002, Rasor 2005).

Liberal Modernism received criticism and pressure from the more radical movements that it had made possible. The liberal method of appreciating Jesus' message of God's kingdom in its own historical context encouraged historians to question everything about Jesus' life and death. Even while liberal theologians interpreted the risen Lord symbolically as the hope for a new spiritual life, atheists dismissed the foundations of Christianity as only absurd legend. The liberal mode of applying Jesus' message of love in the present historical context encouraged philosophers to question everything about Jesus' moral example. Even while liberal theologians interpreted the sacrificed Lamb symbolically as the ideal for a new moral life, humanists dismissed the supernaturalism of Christianity and only retained ethics. The liberal manner of modifying Christian mythology to respect the scientific worldview encouraged naturalists to apply science to religion, understanding Christianity and all religion as just a natural manifestation of human frailties, fallibilities, and follies. In the face of skeptical atheism, ethical humanism, and scientific naturalism, the idea of Christian faith seemed unnecessary at best and dangerous at worst.

Even the liberal mission of preaching a Christianity more comprehensible to modern and global audiences was criticized for timidity and half-heartedness. Fundamentalists (with presuppositionalists), evidentialists (including creationists), and existentialists (along with mystics) tried to tear apart what Liberal Modernism had tried to keep together. Fundamentalists complained that the unique mission of Christianity is forgotten in liberal interpretations of Jesus. Evidentialists complained that the intellectual integrity of Christianity is diluted in liberal flexibility over mythology. Existentialists complained that the spiritual dimension of Christianity is lost in liberal exercises of intellectualism. Each of these challengers protected something from modernism that they took to be essential to Christianity. Fundamentalists insisted that Christian faith revolves around knowable dogmas, and if audiences aren't receptive that's because god has to bestow grace anyway. Evidentialists insisted that Christianity faith depends on successful arguments from scripture and nature, and if audiences aren't receptive that's because god is obvious only to rigorous intellects. Local existentialists insisted that Christianity faith depends on spiritual encounters with mystery, and if audiences aren't receptive that's because god decides to reveal itself only to some people and not others. Universal existentialists embracing ITM2 or ITM3 went further to insist that the supreme infinite reality is potentially accessible to all, so that all religions can find the same mysterious god.

In the face of fundamentalism, evidentialism, local existentialism, and universal existentialism, Liberal Modernism seemed quaint at best and stultifying at worst. Greater competition arose when its competitors began to forge combinations and alliances to form five worldviews challenging Liberal Modernism.

Skeptical atheists and scientific naturalists quickly merged in the early twentieth century as soon as science seemed capable of (eventually) explaining the features of natural world. At the start of the twenty-first century most atheists are naturalists in the broad sense; few atheists can sustain an agnostic suspension between naturalism and supernaturalism. Atheism rejects all forms of spiritualism and religious thinking, and atheism denies that the universe supplies any meaning of life or suggests any moral direction. In its most straightforward form, this atheism endorses the traditional sort of naturalism known as materialism. Materialism asserts that the supreme reality is the energy and matter studied by the physical sciences (e.g. physics, chemistry, cosmology), and the other sciences (life sciences, social sciences, cognitive sciences) study the living systems of organized matter. The only meanings and values that we can know about exist because individual organisms like us have them. We know humans best, and humans have values because they are trying to survive. Materialism is unable to find any meaning or value greater than personal desires and unwilling to endorse any ethical system that does more than aggregate private interests. People must bravely confront an uncaring and deadly universe, and they must admit that everything they care about (including themselves) will soon be irrevocably destroyed. One's attitude towards life and the universe must be stoic: we must control our emotions to avoid imaginative fantasies about pleasant afterlives or helpful gods. A stoic prioritizes reason over faith. The only sort of faith approved by stoicism is a faith that life is worth living if one boldly pursues every enjoyment that life can offer. This Stoic Materialism looks to philosophy for a rational and scientific ethics which is independent from any spiritual transformation, church sanction, or wisdom tradition. This rational ethics can justify the stoic approval of communal morality with a utilitarian demand of co-operative harmony from everyone. Stoic Materialism stays grounded on strict scientific naturalism. The sciences must be able to account for our capacity for responsible morality and to explain why morality has the forms it takes among the human species. The sciences must also explain people's richly aesthetic and emotional lives and their spiritual/religious experiences.

The strict naturalism endorsed by scientific rationality most directly leads to Stoic Materialism. However, the rationalism behind naturalism instead leads toward Nihilistic Rationalism. Pure reason simultaneously demands that everything happens for a reason and deprives all reality (including life) of any values or ideals. Nihilistic Rationalism is the unification of existentialism and rationalism. Existentialism and rationalism are typically taken to be opposites, as if the only existential mood is supposed to be effusively emotional, but there are many existentialist moods. When pure reason is the only mode of existential encounter with reality, logical determinism and existential predeterminism fuse together: the supreme reality necessarily does everything without choice or deviation. Faith is completely irrelevant, and the only attitude towards life should be resignation. There is simply no point in any human striving; there is nothing that anyone could do that the supreme reality does not do automatically. Although nihilists are atheists, very few atheists are nihilists. A courageous stoicism embracing the joys of life should not be confused with a Nihilistic Rationalism resigned to an uncaring universe.

Existentialists who are comfortable with naturalism but find Stoic Materialism and Nihilistic Rationalism unsatisfactory can opt for Religious Humanism instead. Humanism locates the foundations for all meaning and value in our human lives, not in any supreme reality and especially not in some dictatorial god. Discovering the inspiration and motivation for the ethical life in existential encounters with what they take to be the sacred or divine, these existential humanists are not worried about either scientific criticism or fundamentalist disapproval. Religious Humanism accepts naturalism, but it worries about materialism's disdain for spiritual dimensions of human life. For Religious Humanism, the spiritual dimension of life shows how science is only a partial perspective on supreme reality, while the human capacity for wise ethical reflection shows how morality should be liberated from any god's authority. This Religious Humanism is sustainable so long as its spiritualism fits a broadly flexible naturalism, or else it gets absorbed into a suitably hospitable supernaturalism. Unlike the older Christian humanism (see Franklin and Shaw 1991), Religious Humanism does not appeal to god's relationship to humans to justify our inherent dignity and liberty. Religious Humanism puts humanism first and religion second. Humanism in general emphasizes our moral responsibilities in this life and finds human intelligence up to the challenge of figuring out how to live ethical lives. Christians believe that we can be good humanists only because god helps us learn morality and guides ethical thinking. Religious humanists turn this dependence on god around – it is only because humans have the responsibility and capacity for figuring out ethics that we deserve to judge what is good in society, politics, and religion. We aren't worthy because of *god* – if we should be religious, it is because religion is worthy of *us*. Religious humanists gain inspiration and wisdom from religious traditions, spiritual leaders, communal rituals, nature's wonders, and extraordinary personal experiences. Ultimately, however, religious humanists take responsibility for judging what is worthy to adopt and adapt from these sources. Religious Humanism uses faith to help relate to supreme reality but sets boundaries to faith using standards of reason.

Religious Humanism's dependence on naturalism is sometimes judged as a fatal weakness, but this verdict wrongly assumes that naturalism strictly entails a denial of the reality of meaning, values, and ideals. Naturalism is too frequently equated with reductive and deterministic materialism, but other varieties of naturalism were formulated in the twentieth century, inspired by such thinkers as John Dewey, George Santayana, and A. N. Whitehead. Pluralistic and process naturalisms, only insisting that there is one natural reality coordinating diverse perspectives of human experiences and the sciences, can embrace the existence of human values and meaningful ideals, and make room for spiritual experiences of nature. Meanings, purposes, and values are quite natural, and science explains why. Naturalism replaces spiritualistic final causality with intelligently purposive causality. With rising complexity, species gradually become intelligent as they undertake more difficult survival strategies. The intelligent pursuit of purposes is an organism's pursuit of kinds of results it considers to be valuable. Material nature by itself may be amoral, but portions of the natural world containing life and especially sentient life do host natural values. Coming to our cultured species, some nature–human transactions have the potential to be aesthetically, morally, and spiritually valuable.

Uniting under the label of "religious naturalism," a spiritualized naturalism forges a powerful naturalism–existentialism alloy (see Stone 2009). Religious naturalism cannot stand on its own as a complete worldview, since its existentialist component gravitates towards mysticism or evangelicalism (abandoning naturalism), or towards humanism. Religious naturalism can supply the structural frame for religious humanism, which has long been enriched by the legacy of such pluralistic naturalists as Santayana (a most Catholic atheist, see Santayana 1905) and Dewey (an atheist speaking of a natural god in Dewey 1934). An integration of religious naturalism and religious humanism offers many mutual advantages. Religious naturalism's accommodation of transformative moral/spiritual experience holds off supernaturalism, while its dynamic pluralism makes a friendly overture to panentheistic, pantheistic, and nature religions and the world's wisdom traditions. Religious naturalism's enriched natural basis for the ethical life similarly removes any need for god's commands or atheistic stoicism. Religious naturalists may refer to themselves as atheists to indicate their denial of supernaturalism. However, religious naturalism's enthusiasm for spiritual experience, tendency towards pantheism, and willingness to learn from wisdom traditions repels strict atheism and secular humanism. Additionally, religious naturalism's piety and reverence for matters of cosmic or at least global scale can reorient religious humanism away from an outdated prioritization of merely human values, so that an ecological and environmental ethics gains due respect. Religious Humanism can enjoy the best combination of pluralistic naturalism, idealistic humanism, and religious evidentialism (see Olds 1996, Murray 2007). The "evidence" of religions is not any narrow special revelation gifted by god in heaven, but rather the broad common wisdom gleaned by humanity on earth.

Evidentialism by itself cannot establish a complete Christian worldview. Its reasoned arguments for god are unsuccessful and it tends to support naturalism instead. Even where evidentialism might begin to infer a supernatural creator, it is hard to recognize a Christian god or Jesus in the abstract divinity designed for reason's approval. When evidentialism confesses how scripture only lends itself to symbolic faith it helps invigorate Liberal Modernism, or else evidentialism just abandons sound evidence to relapse into fundamentalism. If evidentialism does admit that science can handle all of the evidence anyway, it mutates into naturalism. Liberal Modernism, Religious Humanism, and Stoic Materialism are therefore the primary alternatives for evidentialists. Evidentialists more impressed by scripture than science join Liberal Modernism. Evidentialists most impressed by science become strict naturalists, while those impressed by both science and spiritualism head towards Religious Humanism.

Existentialists enjoy the most opportunities for forming worldviews and making alliances. Existentialist reasoning about the fragile human condition overwhelmed by an all-powerful supreme reality can lead directly to Nihilistic Rationalism. If existentialism entirely sets asides reason instead, a purely faithful encounter with supreme reality will be mysteriously mystical. Ecumenical Mysticism is a more optimistic option for those impressed by universal accessibility to a supreme reality which positively infuses all life. Humanism offers an exclusive alliance with existentialism, but a combined alliance with both naturalism and humanism results in a stronger religious humanism. Existentialists who condemn a humanist ethical life without god as blind folly will either invigorate Liberal Modernism or head towards fundamentalism. The fundamentalism–existentialism alliance (evident in "born-again evangelicalism" and other Protestant variations) is exemplified by theologians who hold that Christian dogmas about Jesus, salvation, and the ethical life are valid revelations of genuine existential encounters with god. For this "local" existentialism, any "spiritual" experiences contrary to Christian dogma simply aren't encounters with god, and so they must be delusional or satanic. Fundamentalist existentialism is a sustainable worldview only so long as it can persuasively perpetuate its closed CSE model of knowledge from generation to generation. That's why this worldview is notorious for its dogmatic evangelicalism and hostility to different worldviews, such as another religion or naturalism, or even any new scientific theory (such as evolution). Since the prominent contemporary form of fundamentalist existentialism is Evangelical Fundamentalism, we will use that term here. Reason does not need to be abandoned on this worldview, but reason cannot dictate to religion. Evangelic Fundamentalism uses reason to help explain supreme reality but sets boundaries to rationality using the standards of faith.

Let's list the six worldviews discussed so far. These six worldviews offer six possible combinations of reason and faith, and offer three naturalisms and three supernaturalisms. The first two worldviews take the extreme options of either exclusive faith, or exclusive reason. The next two worldviews rely on faith, either a faith that dominates reason or a faith that relies on reason.

The last two worldviews rely on reason, either a reason that relies on faith or a reason that dominates faith.

Ecumenical Mysticism: faith for encountering god without any reason involved.
Nihilistic Rationalism: reason for knowing reality without any faith involved.
Evangelical Fundamentalism: faith about god and ethics by true revelation unchallengeable by reason.
Liberal Modernism: faith in god's transformations through symbolism adaptable with reason.
Religious Humanism: reason about nature and ethics with assistance from transformative faith.
Stoic Materialism: reason for understanding nature and ethics unchallengeable by faith.

8.2 Twelve Worldviews

These six worldviews do not exhaust the religious and nonreligious options. The six additional worldviews fit in between the primary worldviews: Ascetic Tanscendentalism between Ecumenical Mysticism and Nihilistic Rationalism; Theocratic Covenantalism between Nihilistic Rationalism and Evangelical Fundamentalism; Conservative Catholicism between Evangelical Fundamentalism and Liberal Modernism; Organic Personalism between Liberal Modernism and Religious Humanism; Secular Humanism between Religious Humanism and Stoic Materialism; and Radical Romanticism between Stoic Materialism and Ecumenical Mysticism. These twelve worldviews are distributed across the range of combinations of faith and reason. They offer stably coherent foundations capable of justifying a comprehensive understanding of reality, humanity, and morality. Some of these worldviews have far more adherents than others in the West at present; this categorization is not about popularity, but intellectual integrity.

To see how six additional worldviews fit in between the primary six, let's start with Evangelical Fundamentalism and Nihilistic Rationalism. The worldview that fits in between them shares their common view that supreme reality dictates everything that does happen and should happen. Is this supreme reality alive, or not? Nihilistic Rationalism is not a religious worldview because its supreme reality is just simple blind force and not anything to which humans could profitably relate. Evangelical Fundamentalism is a religious worldview because the supreme reality is a loving god who freely offers personal salvation. The bridging worldview, Theocratic Covenantalism, finds that humans must relate to a supreme god who strictly controls everything. A supernatural god demands covenants with a selected group of people who must fulfill the terms of the covenant as a group or else suffer a tragic life and (perhaps an even worse afterlife). Unlike fundamentalism's hope for each person's willing acceptance of god's free grace, covenantalism urges the group's dutiful subservience to god's binding contract. For this worldview, people need such fearful leadership by god because humans are deeply flawed by nature. Subservience to god is no personal matter; the entire group must strongly enforce the covenant's terms using all means available, including political power. Covenantalism implies theocracy: the political rule by an elite devoted to controlling society according to the terms of god's covenant. Theocratic Covenantalism credits the supreme deity for completely dictating the terms and fate of human life. A prominent example of theocratic covenantalism in the West is John Calvin's theology, which has inspired many contemporary varieties.

Once the only Christian theology, Conservative Catholicism now stands between Liberal Modernism and Evangelical Fundamentalism. Conservative Catholicism is the surviving remnant of the medieval synthesis of revelation, evidentialism, and natural law theory. Here "catholic" means "universal," the originally intended meaning used by Church Fathers to indicate the unified true church. Not to be identified only with the Roman or Eastern Catholicisms, which serve as paradigm examples, Conservative Catholicism also includes the more conservative Protestant denominations also claiming to be the true Christian church. Ethical and political conservativism closely tracks theological conservatism; their shared motivation is the quest for absolute certainties. Evidentialism's failures have been catalogued, yet the idea that the world's divine design dictates one absolute ethics still lingers for some faithful. Conservative denominations, each confident that they deserve the title of god's one true church, claim to best know the world's design and humanity's morality. Christians who admire the liberality of evangelical enthusiasm while also admiring the conformity of churchly orthodoxy energize the diverse groups of Conservative Catholicism. Their appeal to religious conversion and evangelical fervor unifies a principled moral front, yet that same fervor suffices to congregationally divide conservatives as much as the fundamentalists. Any conservative conclusions about an ethical matter are not necessarily based on the same premises; natural law theorizing only superficially resembles reading the direct Word of God. Conservative Catholicism demeans the separation of church and state, yet tearing down that wall could trigger renewed religious warfare among the conservative denominations struggling to be the next universal church. There is a heavy price to be paid for trying to supply the one true church on earth as it is in heaven. The struggles of Conservative Catholicism typically result in an aristocratic political rule by those few who best know god's law. Although Conservative Catholicism would have the same broad appeal as fundamentalism, it could not match fundamentalism's tendency to encourage the democratic freedom to find god for one's self. Evangelicalism by itself only seeks a universal body of spiritual believers; governing the secular world is not the essential aim. Evangelicals who come to a conclusion that god wants them to rule the world opt for the neighboring Conservative Catholicism or Theocratic Covenantalism.

On the other side of Liberal Modernism, discontent with an aloof supernatural God can lead to nature worship or to Religious Humanism. Christians who want to retain some theological connection with Christian tradition seek a compromise, unwilling to reduce Jesus to just a man, God to just a metaphor, and Holy Spirit to just an experience. Currently, panentheist personalism bridges Liberal Modernism and Religious Humanism by prioritizing the personal soul and legitimizing the trinity of three divine persons. Panentheism in general finds some sort of intertwining overlap and interaction between God and nature, so that nature is included within the divine but God retains some divine characters beyond nature as well (see Cooper 2006, Clayton 2008, Schroeder 2009). Akin to panpsychism's view that everything is conscious or mental (Skrbina 2005), personalism asserts that persons are the fundamental mode of reality, and Christian personalism adds cosmically important roles for God, Jesus, and the Holy Spirit. Panentheist personalism is a modern version of a worldview older than Christianity; speculations that god and nature are closely intertwined are found in ancient Greek, Indian, and Chinese thought. For this worldview, what god and nature must share together is life itself, so ultimate reality is organic and personal. God's personality and human personalities are intertwined, yet human persons are not reducible to the divine person. We can label this worldview generally as Organic Personalism. Organic Personalism is a useful haven for the most liberal of Christians advocating liberation theology, black theology, feminist theology, ecological theology, and the like. Branded as heresy by Catholicism and dismissed as religious by scientific cosmology, Organic Personalism remains small and nearby worldviews can offer tempting options. Panpsychism is difficult to reconcile with scientific physicalism. Contemporary panentheists who demand close adherence to trinitarian creeds from past centuries, especially formulations engaging anthropic personalities or entailing ethical consequences, can migrate into Liberal Modernism. Panentheists and personalists more interested in actual naturalistic knowledge and grounding ethics on naturalized culture can instead opt for pantheism and religious naturalism, joining Religious Humanism.

Secular Humanism has recently emerged as the most visible and politically potent kind of atheism, standing between Stoic Materialism and Religious Humanism. Stoic Materialism encourages people to exuberantly pursue their individual goals of happily fulfilled lives, restrained only by principles maximizing utilitarian happiness and rules preventing destructive cruelty. This is an ethical humanism in a minimal sense, but it emphasizes private tranquillity over civic activism. The long tradition of humanism has far more to offer. Atheists who want more from philosophical ethics freely borrow from the humanist tradition, impressed by humanistic social ideals of progressive civil liberty, the just moral community, and the peaceful global society. A synthesis of Stoic Materialism and the humanist tradition is represented by the Secular Humanism offered by Paul Kurtz (see Kurtz 1983, 2008; Radest 1990). Secular humanism stays very close to its scientific foundations, selecting from the humanist tradition only what a naturalistic ethics can approve. This severe restraint generates puzzles over justifying some ideals of twenty-first-century ethical humanism, such as prioritizing social welfare over private interests, advancing humble pacifism before starting "just" wars, extending humane treatment to animals, and protecting the environment from capitalist predation. Where naturalism can at most justify humans having values, humanism justifies values worthy of humans. This is why Secular Humanism can be convulsed by disagreements over whether its politics should be more personally libertarian (looking to John Locke) or more communally progressive (looking to John Dewey). Secular humanists can agree on naturalism, human rights, liberal democracy, and separation of church and state. After that, any Secular Humanist consideration of government regulation and welfare, equalizing economic prosperity, saving the planet, etc. tends to generate schisms.

Secular Humanism's naturalistic dismissal of all religions and religious wisdom hobbles its humanistic agenda right from the start, since rational ethics is left with little empirical information to evaluate, and few religious allies could be impressed by any accommodation of militant atheism. Furthermore, Secular Humanism must figure out how to independently justify, motivate, and practically apply its high ethical and political principles. Although Secular Humanism can echo selected principles from older humanisms, those humanisms are religious in inspiration and motivation. Credit for the practical impact of humanistic principles (such as the fights for abolition of slavery, women's suffrage, and civil rights) belongs to religious humanists, not secular atheists. And the very principles of secularism and separation of church and state were designed and implemented by religious believers to save religious faith from itself, not to make the world safe for atheism. This situation for secularism leads many humanists towards religious humanism. It is mistake to equate or subsume Religious Humanism together with Secular Humanism. Both humanisms are naturalistic, but they can diverge on many other issues. Secular Humanism prioritizes rational knowledge over a religious focus on the emotional/spiritual life, trying to finally break humanism's reliance on historical religions, religious symbolism, emotional aesthetics, and communal exercises. Many religious humanists still have churches, sing hymns, read scriptures, celebrate religious holidays, etc. This is a matter of relative emphasis, of course – secular humanists hold meetings and enjoy richly emotional lives – but secular humanism has clearly distinguished itself from all residual forms of religious conduct and experience. What remains to be seen is whether secular humanism's distancing from religious community and tradition will ultimately only amount to an echo of Stoic Materialism's prioritization of private tranquillity.

Both faith and reason claim to be able to understand supreme reality. However, neither the pure faith of Ecumenical Mysticism nor the pure reason of Nihilistic Rationalism seem to be much help for understanding the human world. For Nihilistic Rationalism, responsibility and morality are simply arbitrary, so people can fall into resignation or rebellion, making social cooperation impossible. For Ecumenical Mysticism, responsibility and morality are simply inspired, so people can rise up to compassion or congeniality, making social cooperation automatic. Contrary to these two worldviews, a social life really is possible, yet hardly automatic. That is why two nearby bridging stances offer more livable alternatives: Radical Romanticism is between Stoic Materialism and Ecumenical Mysticism, and Ascetic Transcendentalism is between Ecumenical Mysticism and Nihilistic Rationalism. Neither Radical Romanticism nor Ascetic Transcendentalism have had many followers in the West, though their impact has been all out of proportion to their numbers. They agree, along with the Ecumenical Mysticism that stands between them, that humans are deeply connected to ultimate reality, but they disagree about how to access that reality and what that access means in people's lives.

When compared to Ecumenical Mysticism's reliance on pure emotional faith, its two neighbors hold that some degree of knowledge of supreme reality is possible. Radical Romanticism leans towards naturalism (while prioritizing emotion over science), while Ascetic Transcendentalism leans towards transcendentalism (while prioritizing emotion over rationality). Furthermore, Ecumenical Mysticism encourages the loss of self within both spirit and society, because its deep mysticism erodes all real differences between people. Its two neighbors, by contrast, restore some importance to individuality but in quite difference ways. Radical Romanticism claims that you must keep your sense of individuality in the ordinary experience of community with one's greater society. Ascetic Transcendentalism claims that you must lose all sense of individuality in the mystical experience of unity with the one great spirit. For Radical Romanticism, individuality is ultimately real, but people should naturally have the same way of being good; only corrupt culture imposes moral differences between people. For Ascetic Transcendentalism, individuality is ultimately unreal, but people should spiritually have different ways of being good; only corrupt culture imposes moral conformity among people.

Romanticism is "radical" because people must deny the demands of cultural tradition in order to know how to stay naturally good. Transcendentalism is "ascetic" because people must deny the temptations of natural pleasures in order to know how to stay spiritually pure. Radical Romanticism holds that nature is best and that humans know that they are good by simply being born naturally, so life is best in a separate society in which everyone shares that natural goodness. On the other hand, Ascetic Transcendentalism holds that nature is illusion and that humans know how to become good by being re-born spiritually, so life is best in solitary self-reliance in which each person keeps a spiritual uniqueness. Like neighboring Stoic Materialism, Radical Romanticism holds that the social life is quite natural (so long as good people are isolated from corrupted cultures). Like neighboring Nihilistic Rationalism, Ascetic Transcendentalism holds that the social life is quite unnatural (so good people should isolate themselves from everyone else). An example of Radical Romanticism in the West is Jean-Jacques Rousseau's philosophy,

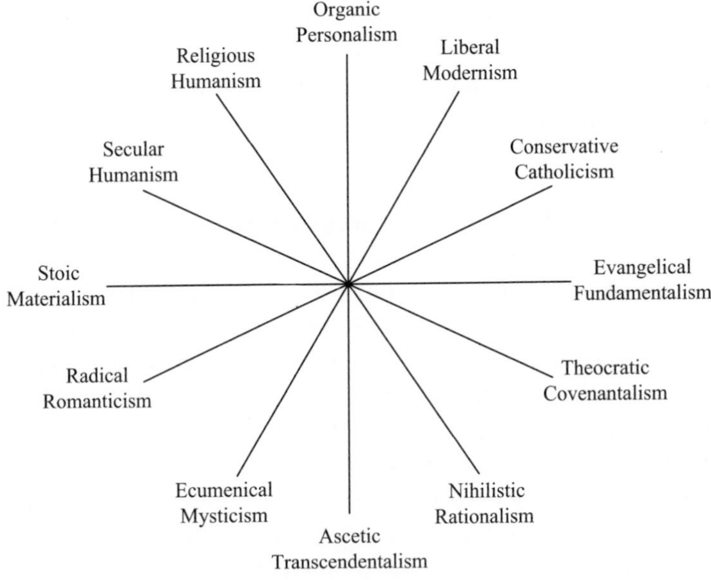

FIGURE 8.1

while an example of Ascetic Transcendentalism is Ralph Waldo Emerson's philosophy.

The twelve worldviews could be arranged in a linear fashion, but a circular diagram better captures their interrelationships (Figure 8.1). This circular diagram indicates how each worldview closely shares something with its neighbors, and sharply disagrees with worldviews on the opposite side. For example, Secular Humanism's disdain for Evangelical Fundamentalism's reliance on scripture is only exceeded by its dispute against Theocratic Covenantalism, which returns the antipathy. Religious Humanism is motivated by the potent human values that Nihilistic Rationalism is unable to even recognize. Organic Personalism and Ascetic Transcendentalism completely disagree over whether persons are fundamentally real and whether society fulfills personal development. Ecumenical Mysticism doesn't need the scientific knowledge that Liberal Modernism credits with upgrading religion. Radical Romanticism can't understand why Traditional Catholicism clings to stale conservative principles when fresh nature clears the best way. Stoic Materialism harmonizes each person's rational interests, while Evangelical Fundamentalism disrupts conformity with faith's gospel.

We have surveyed and catalogued the major possible worldviews and their varying stances towards the relationship between faith and reason. Let us descend from such atmospheric heights to the plane of contemporary Western civilization.

8.3 Faith and Reason Realigned

The medieval compromise between reason and faith of the fourteenth century assigned to reason the job of reaching the creator god through natural evidence and assigned to faith the job of discerning this redeemer god in the revelation of scripture. By the seventeenth century this medieval compromise was cracking under stress from science's increased capacity to explain nature. The Enlightenment compromise of the eighteenth century was then forged to assign to reason the job of explaining nature and to assign to faith the job of motivating ethics. Mysticism and fundamentalism lurked on the fringes, of course, and quickly revived once more as the Enlightenment compromise broke down in the face of existentialism and naturalism by the early twentieth century.

Liberal Modernism and Religious Humanism have been the most creative responses to the Enlightenment breakdown over the past century. Liberal Modernism sought imaginative ways to convey the mythological symbolism of transformative faith in response to the scientific knowledge of naturalism. No longer could Christianity expect technological peoples to picture god using Bronze Age notions. No longer could Christianity expect civilized peoples to limit morality to a Divine Dictator's commands. Liberal Modernism respects the way that people expect transforming faith to integrate and enhance everything they understand about reality and their lives. Spiritual faith should encompass rational nature. Religious Humanism similarly sought creative ways to faithfully reconstruct the scientific worldview of pluralistic naturalism in response to the transformations of spiritualism. No longer could naturalism expect self-motivated peoples to view themselves as mechanically robotic puppets dancing in rigidly predetermined ways to the tune of ghostly mathematical forces. No longer could naturalism expect generous peoples to selfishly surrender responsibility for their conduct to tiny uncaring genes or multiplying cultural memes. Religious Humanism respects the way that people expect constructive reason to supply a comprehensive system for everything that they need for inspired and ethical lives. Rational nature should encompass spiritual faith.

The Enlightenment breakdown continues. The rhythm of history suggests that at least another century is required to see how things will turn out. We cannot accurately predict which of the alternatives will eventually develop into the next dominant Western worldview. What will be the fate of reason, of philosophy, of the Greek heritage of Western civilization? Mysticism ignores reason while fundamentalism fears reason. History suggests that neither are fated for supremacy in the West. Christianity will remain dominant for another century, though, and an alliance of evangelicals and catholics would remain powerful over narrow moral issues. That narrow agenda cannot handle all the global problems of modernity, however. Some fruitful combination of Liberal Modernism with Religious Humanism may consolidate leadership to offer comprehensive solutions. If Religious Humanism instead moderates entirely into rationalistic ethics and Secular Humanism disintegrates into its separable agendas, then a struggle between Liberal Modernism and Stoic Materialism could also characterize the twenty-first century.

The future of the West rests mostly on the destiny of humanism. Ethical humanism has not stood on its own as an independent worldview, but its potency has only grown. The twentieth century witnessed ethical humanism's dramatic advancement of the idealistic project it began in the eighteenth century: the struggle for the equal dignity and rights of all people. By bringing along much of Christianity into a temporary alliance with religious naturalism and secularism to advance its moral ideals, ethical humanism has displayed impressive moral and political leadership. How did ethical humanism accomplish its successes? Ethical humanism does not rest on any faith divorced from reason; its moral knowledge does not come from any divine directives. Ethical humanism, inspired by its philosophical roots, grounds its moral knowledge in human reason and experience alone. Surpassing its forgivable twentieth-century emphasis on the importance of all humans, a twenty-first-century humanism is now demanding ecological responsibility towards other species and the whole planet. If Liberal Modernism has nothing more to contribute to the advancement of Western civilization than its fostering of ethical humanism, then Religious Humanism and Secular Humanism will compete as the proper home for ethical humanism. Could Religious Humanism and Secular Humanism reach any sort of satisfactory compromise? Since their competition rests mostly on disputes over the existential transformations of spiritualism and the ethical wisdom within religions, ethical humanism must decide whether the spiritual life and religious wisdom is essential to planetary ethics.

Does reason and nature exclude spiritual transformation? Medieval Christianity thought so, crediting god for the spirit, but civilization has moved on. The existential spirit of humanity may not need any god; but can it survive on reason and nature? Ethical humanism can incorporate spiritual transformation, so long as we consistently focus on knowing and doing what is right, and not on knowing god and doing what god wants. We must therefore be self-motivated to live ethical lives. Reoriented towards this world and this life, the humanistic spirit can faithfully pursue ethical ideals without having to be told how to live. For humanism, fidelity to ethical principles lends dignity and nobility to this mortal life. All ethics depends on aiming moral responsibilities correctly towards whatever deserves faithful devotion and ultimate concern. Ethics is not a matter of mere moral knowledge, as if the ethical life consisted solely of acknowledging the truth of some set of supreme moral rules. The moral rules are moral because they command respect towards what has moral value. Self-motivated people follow moral rules because they respect what has moral value, and not because they merely respect the moral rules themselves. Would people worship false gods all over again? Lists of moral principles do not create the ethical life – where does moral self-motivation come from? Ethical humanism promises an ethical life, which therefore must be a life faithfully devoted to our responsibilities towards whatever has moral value. The essence of wisdom should be reason's orientation to genuine value, and this humanist wisdom could be a complete philosophy (recent efforts include Kurtz 2008, Aronson 2008, Epstein 2009, and Maisel 2009). Reason and nature alone may suffice to indicate what has moral value, and where that knowledge takes root in the human spirit, fidelity to the ethical life can grow and flower. This ethical growth of the human spirit is described by ethical humanists as spiritual transformation.

If a naturalized spiritualism makes ethical humanism far more effective, then Religious Humanism prepares to announce its superiority. Secular Humanism therefore holds up its last objection, that ethical humanism really needs no "spiritual transformations" to energize full devotion to its ethical principles. Talk of "spiritual" experiences and "faithful" devotion to ethical "principles" alarms many secularists anxious to distinguish their atheist stance in the West's marketplace of ideas. Yet Secular Humanism's principles do demand respect for matters of ultimate concern and summon high fidelity to their advancement. Living faithfully according to reasonable ethical principles is quite different from merely believing in something on faith. By abandoning "faith" as a noun which points to another noun of "god" as its object, Secular Humanism can complete its humanist turn towards embracing fidelity in right conduct. Ethical fidelity with sound intelligence is the essence of the humanism in Secular Humanism, if secularism would remain humanistic. On the other hand, secularism could reject an alliance with ethical humanism instead, fulfilling religion's prediction that a stoic or nihilistic atheism is the only fate of strict naturalism.

For its part, Religious Humanism needs a safely naturalistic restraint on its transformative experiences and ethical principles in order to avoid inflating into just another supernaturalistic or mysterian theology. To these ends, many religious humanists and religious naturalists have been proposing a reunion with Secular Humanism for decades, and some secular humanists favor a sensible alliance too (recent proposals are Goodenough 2000, Griffin 2001, Solomon 2002, and Kitcher 2007). Scientists impressed by the vast wonders of nature, far more impressive than dim Bronze Age notions, have expressed their hope for a reverential religious humanism. But a careful balance must be struck here: do we need a humanistic religion, or just a religious humanism? Carl Sagan (2006) tells us of his hopes for a new religion: it would inspire us to follow our highest ideals while heeding science's knowledge of the cosmos. But the objection could be raised that, if we already know what ideals we ought to follow, and where to get information about the cosmos, then what does the religious aspect of the new creed contribute? Sagan charts a complicated route: he wants the scientific experience of contemplating the cosmos to arouse the religious experience of enthusiasm for just the right moral ideals we now need to survive. This sounds more like a religious humanism under science than any humanistic religion under god.

A staunchly naturalistic yet faithfully ethical humanism might, in theory, supply the most powerful atheological counterbalance to mysticism and fundamentalism in the West. This broad humanism could also supply the best dialogue partner with the East, especially with its pantheistic or naturalistic religions such as Hinduism, Theravada Buddhism, Taoism, and Confucianism. Theory only goes so far, however. Speculation about the wisest combinations of reason and faith can go on forever. We may not have that long. Pragmatic thinking is now required. The global challenges confronting all humanity are summoning the best efforts of the West's worldviews. Global challenges demand global cooperation, engaging all the world's civilizations. Engagements and alliances between West and East may prove decisive for practical solutions. We should be thinking about a planetary ethics to grapple with our planetary dilemmas.

At this final stage of our deliberations in this book, we leave Western theology and atheology where we found it at our start: at the inauguration of a truly global dialogue. Have our god debates prepared us for this next, grander conversation?

References

Alper, Matthew. (2008) *The "God" Part of the Brain: A Scientific Interpretation of Human Spirituality and God.* Naperville, Ill.: Sourcebooks.

Alson, William P. (1991) *Perceiving God: The Epistemology of Religious Experience.* Ithaca, N.Y.: Cornell University Press.

Antinoff, Steve. (2010) *Spiritual Atheism.* Berkeley, Calif.: Counterpoint Press.

Armstrong, Karen. (2009) *The Case for God.* New York: Alfred A. Knopf.

Aronson, Ronald. (2008) *Living without God: New Directions for Atheists, Agnostics, Secularists, and the Undecided.* Berkeley, Calif.: Counterpoint.

Barker, Dan. (2008) *Godless: How an Evangelical Preacher Became One of America's Leading Atheists.* Berkeley, Calif.: Ulysses Press.

Behe, Michael J. (2006) *Darwin's Black Box*, 2nd edn. New York: Free Press.

Behe, Michael J. (2007) *The Edge of Evolution: The Search for the Limits of Darwinism.* New York: Free Press.

Berger, Peter, and Anton Zijderveld. (2009) *In Praise of Doubt: How to Have Convictions without Becoming a Fanatic.* New York: HarperCollins.

Berlinerblau, Jacques. (2005) *The Secular Bible: Why Nonbelievers Must Take Religion Seriously.* New York: Cambridge University Press.

Berlinski, David (2009) *The Devil's Delusion: Atheism and Its Scientific Pretensions.* New York: Basic Books.

Blackford, Russell, and Udo Schüklenk. (2009) *50 Voices of Disbelief: Why We Are Atheists.* Malden, Mass.: Wiley-Blackwell.

Bruce, Steve. (2002) *God is Dead: Secularization in the West.* Malden, Mass.: Blackwell.

Calle, Carlos I. (2009) *The Universe: Order without Design.* Amherst, N.Y.: Prometheus Books.

Carr, Bernard, ed. (2007) *Universe or Multiverse?* Cambridge, UK: Cambridge University Press.

Carse, James P. (2008) *The Religious Case against Belief.* New York: Penguin Press.

Cauthen, Kenneth. (1962) *The Impact of American Religious Liberalism.* New York: Harper and Row.

Chalmers, David J. (1996) *The Conscious Mind: In Search of a Fundamental Theory.* New York and Oxford: Oxford University Press.

Church, Forrest. (2009) *The Cathedral of the World: A Universalist Theology.* Boston: Beacon Press.

Clayton, Philip. (2000) *The Problem of God in Modern Thought.* Grand Rapids, Mich.: William B. Eerdmans.

Clayton, Philip. (2008) *Adventures in the Spirit: God, World, Divine Action.* Minneapolis: Augsburg Fortress Press.

Clegg, Brian. (2006) *Quantum Entanglement, Science's Strangest Phenomenon.* New York: St Martin's Press.

Collins, Francis S. (2006) *The Language of God: A Scientist Presents Evidence for Belief.* New York: Free Press.

Comte-Sponville, André. (2009) *The Little Book of Atheist Spirituality.* New York: Viking.

Cooper, John W. (2006) *Panentheism: The Other God of the Philosophers, From Plato to the Present.* Grand Rapids, Mich.: Baker Publishing Group.

Corlett, J. Angelo. (2010) *The Errors of Atheism.* New York: Continuum.

Crossan, John Dominic. (1998) *The Birth of Christianity: Discovering What Happened in the Years Immediately after the Execution of Jesus.* San Francisco: Harper SanFrancisco.

Davidson, Donald. (1980) *Actions and Events.* Oxford: Oxford University Press.

Dawkins, Richard. (2006) *The God Delusion.* Boston: Houghton Mifflin.

Dawkins, Richard. (2009) *The Greatest Show on Earth: The Evidence for Evolution.* New York: Free Press.

Dembski, William A. (1999) *Intelligent Design: The Bridge between Science and Theology.* Downer's Grove, Ill.: InterVarsity Press.

Dembski, William A. (2004) *The Design Revolution: Answering the Toughest Questions about Intelligent Design.* Downer's Grove, Ill.: InterVarsity Press.

Dembski, William A. and Jonathan Wells. (2007) *The Design of Life: Discovering Signs of Intelligence in Biological Systems.* Dallas: Foundation for Thought and Ethics.

Dennett, Daniel. (1984) *Elbow Room: The Varieties of Free Will Worth Wanting.* Cambridge, Mass.: MIT Press.

Dennett, Daniel. (1989) *The Intentional Stance.* Cambridge, Mass.: MIT Press.

Dennett, Daniel. (2003) *Freedom Evolves.* New York: Penguin.

Dennett, Daniel. (2006) *Breaking the Spell: Religion as a Natural Phenomenon.* New York: Viking.

Dewey, John. (1934) *A Common Faith.* New Haven, Conn.: Yale University Press.

Drees, Willem B. (1996) *Religion, Science, and Naturalism.* Cambridge, UK: Cambridge University Press.

Drees, Willem B. (2010) *Religion and Science in Context: A Guide to the Debates.* London and New York: Routledge.

D'Souza, Dinesh. (2007) *What's So Great about Christianity?* Washington, D.C.: Regnery.

Eagleton, Terry. (2009) *Reason, Faith, and Revolution: Reflection on the God Debate.* New Haven, Conn.: Yale University Press.

Epstein, Greg. (2009) *Good without God: What a Billion Nonreligious People Do Believe.* New York: HarperCollins.

Everitt, Nicholas. (2004) *The Non-existence of God.* London and New York: Routledge.

Firth, Raymond. (1996) *Religion: A Humanist Interpretation.* London and New York: Routledge.

Flint, Robert. (1903) *Agnosticism.* Edinburgh and London: William Blackwood and Sons.

Ford, David, and Rachel Muers, eds (2005) *The Modern Theologians: An Introduction to Christian Theology since 1918.* Malden, Mass.: Blackwell.

Forrest, Barbara, and Paul R. Gross. (2004) *Creationism's Trojan Horse: The Wedge of Intelligent Design.* Oxford: Oxford University Press.

Frank, Adam. (2009) *The Constant Fire: Beyond the Science vs. Religion Debate.* Berkeley: University of California Press.

Franklin, R. William, and Joseph M. Shaw. (1991) *The Case for Christian Humanism.* Grand Rapids, Mich.: William B. Eerdmans.

Friedman, Richard E. (1995) *The Disappearance of God: A Divine Mystery.* Boston: Little, Brown.

Fuller, Robert C. (2001) *Spiritual, but Not Religious: Understanding Unchurched America.* Oxford: Oxford University Press.

Giere, Ronald N., John Bickle, and Robert Mauldin. (2006) *Understanding Scientific Reasoning*, 5th edn. Belmont, Calif.: Thomson Wadsworth.

Goodenough, Ursula. (2000) *The Sacred Depths of Nature.* Oxford: Oxford University Press.

Griffin, David Ray. (2001) *Reenchantment without Supernaturalism: A Process Philosophy of Religion.* Ithaca, N.Y.: Cornell University Press.

Griffin, David Ray, ed. (2005) *Deep Religious Pluralism.* Louisville, Ky.: Westminster John Knox Press.

Grigg, Richard. (2004) *To Re-Enchant the World: A Philosophy of Unitarian Universalism.* Bloomington, Ind.: Xlibris.

Hagerty, Barbara Bradley. (2009) *Fingerprints of God: The Search for the Science of Spirituality.* New York: Penguin.

Haisch, (2006) *The God Theory: Universes, Zero-point Fields, and What's Behind It All.* San Francisco, Calif.: Weiser Books.

Harris, Sam. (2004) *The End of Faith: Religion, Terror, and the End of Reason.* New York: W. W. Norton.

Harrison, Guy P. (2008) *50 Reasons People Give for Believing in a God.* Amherst, N.Y.: Prometheus Books.

Hart, David Bentley. (2009) *Atheist Delusions: The Christian Revolution and Its Fashionable Enemies.* New Haven, Conn.: Yale University Press.

Haught, John F. (2008) *God and the New Atheism: A Critical Response to Dawkins, Harris, and Hitchens.* Louisville, Ky.: Westminster John Knox Press.

Hauser, Marc D. (2006) *Moral Minds: How Nature Designed Our Universal Sense of Right and Wrong.* New York: HarperCollins.

Hecht, Jennifer Michael. (2004) *Doubt: A History.* New York: HarperCollins.

Hedges, Christopher. (2008) *I Don't Believe in Atheists.* New York: Free Press. Reprinted as *When Atheism Becomes Religion: America's New Fundamentalism* (2009).

Hick, John. (1973) *God and the Universe of Faiths: Essays in the Philosophy of Religion.* London: Macmillan.

Hitchens, Chrisopher. (2007) *God Is Not Great: How Religion Poisons Everything.* New York: Hachette Book Group.

Joas, Hans, and Klaus Wiegandt. (2009) *Secularization and the World Religions.* Liverpool, UK: Liverpool University Press.

Joyce, Richard. (2006) *The Evolution of Morality.* Cambridge, Mass.: MIT Press.

Kaplan, Stephen. (2002) *Different Paths, Different Summits: A Model for Religious Pluralism.* Lanham, Md.: Rowman and Littlefield.

Kauffman, Stuart A. (2008) *Reinventing the Sacred: A New View of Science, Reason, and Religion.* New York: Basic Books.

Kitcher, Philip. (2007) *Living with Darwin: Evolution, Design, and the Future of Faith.* Oxford: Oxford University Press.

Kosmin, Barry, and Ariela Keysar. (2008) *American Religious Identification Survey (ARIS).* Hartford, Conn.: Institute for the Study of Secularism in Society and Culture, Trinity College.

Kuhn, Thomas. (1962) *The Structure of Scientific Revolutions.* Chicago: University of Chicago Press.

Kurtz, Paul. (1983) *In Defense of Secular Humanism.* Amherst, N.Y.: Prometheus Books.

Kurtz, Paul. (2008) *Forbidden Fruit: The Ethics of Secularism.* Amherst, N.Y.: Prometheus Books.

Lesperance, Diana. (2009) *The Narrow Way: A Defense against Atheism and Religion.* Camp Sherman, Ore.: VMI Publishing.

Levine, Michael P. (1994) *Pantheism: A Non-Theistic Concept of Deity.* London and New York: Routledge.

Loftus, John W. (2008) *Why I Became an Atheist: A Former Preacher Rejects Christianity.* Amherst, N.Y.: Prometheus Books.

London, Herbert. (2009) *America's Secular Challenge: The Rise of a New National Religion.* New York: Encounter Books.

Maisel, Eric. (2009) *The Atheist's Way: Living Well without Gods.* Novato, Calif.: New World Library.

Martin, Michael, ed. (2007) *The Cambridge Companion to Atheism.* Cambridge, UK: Cambridge University Press.

Martin, Michael, and Ricki Monnier, eds (2003) *The Impossibility of God.* Amherst, N.Y.: Prometheus Books.

Martin, Michael, and Ricki Monnier, eds (2006) *The Improbability of God.* Amherst, N.Y.: Prometheus Books.

McDowell, Josh. (2006) *Evidence for Christianity.* Nashville, Tenn.: Nelson Reference and Electronic.

Menssen, Sandra, and Thomas D. Sullivan. (2007) *The Agnostic Inquirer: Revelation from a Philosophical Standpoint.* Grand Rapids, Mich.: Eerdmanns.

Micklethwait, John, and Adrian Wooldridge. (2009) *God Is Back: How the Global Revival of Faith is Changing the World.* New York: Penguin.

Miller, Kenneth R. (2008) *Only a Theory: Evolution and the Battle for America's Soul.* New York: Penguin.

Moser, Paul K. (2008) *The Elusive God: Reorienting Religious Epistemology.* Cambridge, UK: Cambridge University Press.

Murray, William R. (2007) *Reason and Reverence: Religious Humanism for the 21st Century.* Boston: Skinner House.

Neville, Robert C. (2006) *On the Scope and Truth of Theology: Theology as Symbolic Engagement.* London and New York: T&T Clark.

Newberg, Andrew and Mark Robert Waldman. (2009) *How God Changes Your Brain: Breakthrough Findings from a Leading Neuroscientist.* New York: Random House.

Novak, Michael. (2008) *No One Sees God: The Dark Night of Atheists and Believers.* New York: Doubleday.

Olds, Mason. (1996) *American Religious Humanism.* Minneapolis, Minn.: Fellowship of Religious Humanists.

Paloutzian, Raymond, and CrystalPark, eds (2005) *Handbook of the Psychology of Religion and Spirituality.* New York: Guilford Press.

Pasquini, John J. (2000) *Atheism and Salvation.* Lanham, Md.: University Press of America.

Paul, Gregory. (2009) The chronic dependence of popular religiosity upon dysfunctional psychosociological conditions. *Evolutionary Psychology* 7(3), 398–441.

Penelhum, Terence. (1983) *God and Skepticism: A Study in Skepticism and Fideism.* Dordrecht: D. Reidel.

Penrose, Roger. (1989) *The Emperor's New Mind: Concerning Computers, Minds and the Laws of Physics.* New York: Oxford University Press.

Phillips, D. Z. (1986) *Belief, Change and Forms of Life.* Atlantic Highlands, N.J.: Humanities Press.

Plantinga, Alvin. (1977) *God, Freedom, and Evil.* Grand Rapids, Mich.: Eerdmans.

Plantinga, Alvin, and Michael Tooley. (2008) *Knowledge of God.* Malden, Mass.: Blackwell.

Popper, Karl. (1959) *The Logic of Scientific Discovery.* New York: Basic Books.

Price, Robert M. (2004) *The Incredible Shrinking Son of Man.* Amherst, N.Y.: Prometheus Books.

Putnam, Hilary. (2000) *The Threefold Cord: Mind, Body and World.* New York: Columbia University Press.

Radest, Howard B. (1990) *The Devil and Secular Humanism: The Children of the Enlightenment.* New York: Praeger.

Rasor, Paul. (2005) *Faith without Certainty: Liberal Theology in the 21st Century.* Boston: Skinner House.

Reitan, Eric. (2009) *Is God a Delusion? A Reply to Religion's Cultured Despisers.* Malden, Mass.: Blackwell.

Rue, Loyal. (2005) *Religion Is Not about God: How Spiritual Traditions Nurture Our Biological Nature and What to Expect When They Fail.* New Brunswick, N.J.: Rutgers University Press.

Rummel, Rudolph J. (1998) *Statistics of Democide: Genocide and Mass Murder since 1900.* Munich, Germany: Lit Verlag.

Russell, Bertrand. (1957) *Why I Am Not a Christian.* London: George Allen and Unwin.

Ryder, John, ed. (1994) *American Philosophic Naturalism in the Twentieth Century.* Amherst, N.Y.: Prometheus Books.

Sagan, Carl. (2006) *The Varieties of Scientific Experience: A Personal View of the Search for God.* New York: Penguin.

Santayana, George. (1905) *Reason in Religion. The Life of Reason, Volume Three.* New York: Charles Scribner's Sons.

Schaeffer, Frank. (2009) *Patience with God: Faith for People Who Don't Like Religion (or Atheism).* Cambridge, Mass.: Da Capo Press.

Schlagel, Richard. (2009) *Seeking the Truth: How Science Has Prevailed over the Supernatural Worldview.* Amherst, N.Y.: Prometheus Books.

Schloss, Jeffrey, and Michael Murray, eds (2009) *The Believing Primate: Scientific, Philosophical, and Theological Reflections on the Origin of Religion.* Oxford: Oxford University Press.

Schroeder, Gerald. (2009) *God According to God: A Physicist Proves We've Been Wrong about God All Along.* New York: HarperCollins.

Schweitzer, Jeff, and Giuseppe Notarbartolo-di-Sciara. (2009) *Beyond Cosmic Dice: Moral Life in a Random World.* Santa Monica, Calif.: Jacquie Jordan Inc.

Searle, John. (1992) *The Rediscovery of the Mind.* Cambridge, Mass.: MIT Press.

Shermer, Michael. (2006) *Why Darwin Matters: The Case against Intelligent Design.* New York: Henry Holt and Co.

Skrbina, David. (2005) *Panpsychism in the West.* Cambridge, Mass.: MIT Press.

Smith, Houston. (1976) *Forgotten Truth: The Common Vision of the World's Religions.* San Francisco: HarperSanFrancisco.

Solomon, Robert C. (2002) *Spirituality for the Skeptic: The Thoughtful Love of Life.* Oxford: Oxford University Press.

Southgate, Christopher, *et al.* (2005) *God, Humanity, and the Cosmos,* 2nd edn. New York: T&T Clark.

Steigmann-Gall, Richard. (2003) *The Holy Reich: Nazi Conceptions of Christianity, 1919–1945.* Cambridge, UK: Cambridge University Press.

Stenger, Victor J. (2007) *God, the Failed Hypothesis: How Science Shows that God Does Not Exist.* Amherst, N.Y.: Prometheus Books.

Stenger, Victor J. (2009) *The New Atheism: Taking a Stand for Science and Reason.* Amherst, N.Y.: Prometheus Books.

Stone, Jerome A. (2009) *Religious Naturalism Today: The Rebirth of a Forgotten Alternative.* Albany, N.Y.: State University of New York Press.

Swinburne, Richard. (1998) *Providence and the Problem of Evil.* Oxford: Oxford University Press.

Taylor, Charles. (2007) *A Secular Age.* Cambridge, Mass: Harvard University Press.

Teehan, John. (2010) *In the Name of God: The Evolutionary Origins of Religious Ethics and Violence.* Malden, Mass.: Wiley-Blackwell.

Thrower, James. (2000) *Western Atheism: A Short History.* Amherst, N.Y.: Prometheus Books.

Van Dusen, Henry P. (1963) *The Vindication of Liberal Theology.* New York: Charles Scribner's Sons.

Van Til, Cornelius. (1969) *A Survey of Christian Epistemology.* Philadelphia: Presbyterian and Reformed Publishing Co.

Wade, Nicholas. (2009) *The Faith Instinct: How Religion Evolved and Why It Endures.* New York: Penguin.

Wells, G. A. (1988) *The Historical Evidence for Jesus.* Amherst, N.Y.: Prometheus Books.

Wells, G. A. (2009) *Cutting Jesus Down to Size: What Higher Criticism Has Achieved and Where It Leaves Christianity.* Chicago: Open Court.

Wright, Robert. (2009) *The Evolution of God.* New York: Little, Brown.

Zacharias, Ravi. (2008) *The End of Atheism: A Response to the New Atheists.* Grand Rapids, Mich.: Zondervan.

Zuckerman, Phil. (2007) Atheism: Contemporary numbers, in *The Cambridge Companion to Atheism,* ed. Michael Martin (Cambridge, UK: Cambridge University Press), pp. 47–65.

Zuckerman, Phil, ed. (2009) *Atheism and Secularity.* Westport, Conn.: Praeger.

Further Reading

Baggini, Julian. (2003) *Atheism: A Very Short Introduction.* Oxford: Oxford University Press. Reprinted as *Atheism* (2009) New York: Sterling Publishing.

Balabat, Janina. (2008) *Conversations with an Atheist: The Good News of God's Plan of Salvation for Mankind.* Lake Mary, Fla.: Creation House.

Barrow, J. D., and F. J. Tipler. (1986) *The Anthropic Cosmological Principle.* Oxford: Oxford University Press.

Berger, Peter L. (1999) *The Desecularization of the World: Resurgent Religion and World Politics.* Washington, D.C.: Ethics and Public Policy Center.

Broad, C. D. (1925) *Mind and Its Place in Nature.* London: Routledge and Kegan Paul.

Cave, Peter. (2009) *Humanism.* Oxford: Oneworld.

Churchland, Paul M. (1989) *A Neurocomputational Perspective: The Nature of Mind and the Structure of Science.* Cambridge, Mass.: MIT Press.

Craig, William Lane. (2001) God and the beginning of time. *International Philosophical Quarterly 41*, 17–31.

Craig, William Lane, and J. P. Moreland, eds (2000) *Naturalism: A Critical Analysis.* London and New York: Routledge.

Crossan, John Dominic. (1991) *The Historical Jesus: The Life of a Mediterranean Jewish Peasant.* San Francisco: HarperSanFrancisco.

David, Andrew, Christopher J. Keller, and Jon Stanley, eds. (2010) "*God Is Dead*" *and I Don't Feel So Good Myself.* Eugene, Oreg.: Wipf & Stock.

De Caro, Mario, and David Macarthur. (2004) Introduction: The nature of naturalism, in *Naturalism in Question* (Cambridge, Mass.: Harvard University Press), pp. 1–17.

Dilworth, David A. (1989) *Philosophy in World Perspective: A Comparative Hermeneutic of the Major Theories.* New Haven, Conn.: Yale University Press.

Dupré, John. (1993) *The Disorder of Things: Metaphysical Foundations of the Disunity of Science.* Cambridge, Mass.: Harvard University Press.

Edis, Taner. (2002) *The Ghost in the Universe: God in the Light of Modern Science.* Amherst, N.Y.: Prometheus Books.

Edis, Taner. (2007) *Science and Nonbelief.* Amherst, N.Y.: Prometheus Books.

Fergusson, David. (2009) *Faith and Its Critics: A Conversation.* Oxford: Oxford University Press.

Feyerabend, Paul. (1975) *Against Method: Outline of an Anarchistic Theory of Knowledge.* Atlantic Highlands, N.J.: Humanities Press.

Ganssle, Gregory E. (2009) *A Reasonable God: Engaging the New Face of Atheism.* Waco, Tex.: Baylor University Press.

Goldstein, Rebecca. (2010) *36 Arguments for the Existence of God: A Work of Fiction.* New York: Pantheon Books.

Goodman, Nelson. (1978) *Ways of Worldmaking.* Indianapolis: Hackett.

Haldane, J. J., and J. J. C. Smart. (2003) *Atheism and Theism*, 2nd edn. Malden, Mass.: Blackwell.

Harding, Nick. (2007) *How to Be a Good Atheist.* Harpenden, UK: Oldcastle Books.

Harré, Rom. (1987) *Varieties of Realism: A Rationale for the Natural Sciences.* Oxford: Blackwell.

Hasker, William. (1999) *The Emergent Self.* Ithaca, N.Y.: Cornell University Press.

Haught, John F. (2006) *Is Nature Enough? Meaning and Truth in an Age of Science.* Cambridge, UK: Cambridge University Press.

Holley, David M. (2010) *Meaning and Mystery: What It Means To Believe in God.* Malden, Mass.: Wiley-Blackwell.

Hunter, Cornelius G. (2007) *Science's Blind Spot: The Unseen Religion of Scientific Naturalism.* Grand Rapids, Mich.: Baker Publishing Group.

Johnston, Mark. (2009) *Saving God: Religion after Idolatry.* Princeton, N.J.: Princeton University Press.

Kearney, Richard. (2010) *Anatheism: Returning to God after God.* New York: Columbia University Press.

Kim, Jaegwon. (2007) *Physicalism, or Something Near Enough.* Princeton, N.J.: Princeton University Press.

Kornblith, Hilary. (2002) *Knowledge and Its Place in Nature.* Oxford: Oxford University Press.

Kurtz, Paul. (1992) *The New Skepticism: Inquiry and Reliable Knowledge.* Amherst, N.Y.: Prometheus Books.

Kurtz, Paul. (2000) *The Transcendental Temptation: A Critique of Religion and the Paranormal.* Amherst, N.Y.: Prometheus Books.

Lamont, Corliss. (1990) *The Philosophy of Humanism*, 7th edn. New York: Continuum Books.

Loftus, John W., ed. (2010) *The Christian Delusion: Why Faith Fails.* Amherst, N.Y.: Prometheus Books.

Markham, Ian S. (2010) *Against Atheism: Why Dawkins, Hitchens, and Harris Are Fundamentally Wrong.* Malden, Mass.: Wiley-Blackwell.

Martin, Michael. (2002) *Atheism, Morality, and Meaning.* Amherst, N.Y.: Prometheus Books.

McGrath, Alister E. (2009) *Science and Religion: A New Introduction*, 2nd edition. Malden, Mass.: Wiley-Blackwell.

McGrath, Alister E., and Joanna Collicutt McGrath. (2010) *The Dawkins Delusion? Atheist Fundamentalism and the Denial of the Divine.* Downders Grove, Ill.: InterVarsity Press.

Melnyk, Andrew. (2003) *A Physicalist Manifesto: Thoroughly Modern Materialism.* Cambridge, UK: Cambridge University Press.

Mills, David. (2006) *Atheist Universe: The Thinking Person's Answer to Christian Fundamentalism.* Berkeley, Calif.: Ulysses Press.

Moreland, J. P., and Kai Nielsen. (1993) *Does God Exist? The Debate Between Theists and Atheists.* Amherst, N.Y.: Prometheus Books.

Myers, David G. (2008) *A Friendly Letter to Skeptics and Atheists: Musings on Why God Is Good and Faith Isn't Evil.* Malden, Mass.: Wiley-Blackwell.

Neville, Robert C. (2002) *Religion in Late Modernity.* Albany: State University of New York Press.

Nielsen, Kai. (2001) *Naturalism and Religion.* Amherst, N.Y.: Prometheus Books.

Norman, Richard. (2004) *On Humanism.* London and New York: Routledge.

O'Connor, David. (2008) *God, Evil, and Design: An Introduction to the Philosophical Issues.* Malden, Mass.: Blackwell.

Oppy, Graham. (1995) *Ontological Arguments and Belief in God.* Cambridge: Cambridge University Press.

Papineau, David. (1993) *Philosophical Naturalism.* Oxford: Blackwell.

Pelikan, Jaroslav. (1995) *Christianity and Classical Culture: The Metamorphosis of Natural Theology in the Christian Encounter with Hellenism.* New Haven, Conn.: Yale University Press.

Rea, Michael C. (2002) *World without Design: The Ontological Consequences of Naturalism.* Oxford: Clarendon Press.

Robinson, Howard, ed. (1993) *Objections to Physicalism.* Oxford: Clarendon Press.

Rosenthal, Beth, ed. (2009) *Atheism.* Opposing Viewpoints series. Farmington Hills, Mich.: Greenhaven Press.

Schellenberg, J. L. (2007) *The Wisdom to Doubt: A Justification of Religious Skepticism.* Ithaca, N.Y.: Cornell University Press.

Schwartz, Gary E., and William L. Simon. (2006) *The G.O.D. Experiments: How Science Is Discovering God in Everything.* New York: Simon and Schuster.

Sinnott-Armstrong, Walter. (2009) *Morality without God?* Oxford: Oxford University Press.

Smith, George H. (1989) *Atheism: The Case against God.* Amherst, N.Y.: Prometheus Books.

Spong, John Shelby. (1998) *Why Christianity Must Change or Die: A Bishop Speaks to Believers in Exile.* New York: HarperCollins.

Steele, David Ramsey. (2007) *Atheism Explained: From Folly to Philosophy.* Chicago: Open Court.

Steinhardt, Paul J., and Neil Turok. (2007) *Endless Universe: Beyond the Big Bang.* New York: Doubleday.

Stenger, Victor J. (2009) *Quantum Gods: Creation, Chaos, and the Search for Cosmic Consciousness.* Amherst, N.Y.: Prometheus Books.

Vitzthum, Richard C. (1995) *Materialism: An Affirmative History and Definition.* Amherst, N.Y.: Prometheus Books.

Wagner, Steven J., and Richard Warner, eds (1993) *Naturalism: A Critical Appraisal.* Notre Dame, Ind.: University of Notre Dame Press.

Wallace, Stan W., ed. (2003) *Does God Exist? The Craig-Flew Debates.* Aldershot, UK and Burlington, Vt.: Ashgate.

Warraq, Ibn, ed. (2002) *What the Koran Really Says: Language, Text, and Commentary.* Amherst, N.Y.: Prometheus Books.

Wielenberg, Erik J. (2005) *Value and Virtue in a Godless Universe.* Cambridge, UK: Cambridge University Press.

Woodruff, Paul. (2001) *Reverence: Renewing a Forgotten Virtue.* Oxford: Oxford University Press.

Index